# HEMINGWAY
# IN LOVE AND WAR

# HEMINGWAY

# IN LOVE AND WAR

*The Lost Diary of Agnes Von Kurowsky*

## HENRY S. VILLARD
## AND
## JAMES NAGEL

HYPERION
NEW YORK

Library of Congress Cataloging-in-Publication Data

Von Kurowsky, Agnes.
    Hemingway in love and war : the lost diary of Agnes von Kurowsky / [edited] by Henry Serrano Villard, James Nagel—1st. ed.
      p. cm.
    Includes bibliographical references (p.    ) and index.
    ISBN 0-7868-8214-X
    1. Von Kurowsky, Agnes—Diaries. 2. Hemingway, Ernest. 1899–1961—Relations with women. 3. World War, 1914–1918—Personal narratives, American. 4. Novelists, American—20th century—Correspondence. 5. Hemingway, Ernest, 1899–1961—Correspondence. 6. Nurses—United States—Correspondence. 7. Von Kurowsky, Agnes—Correspondence. 8. Nurses—United States—Diaries. 9. Von Kurowsky, Agnes—Diaries. 10. World War, 1914–1918—Italy.
I. Hemingway, Ernest, 1899–1961. II. Villard, Henry Serrano, 1900–
    III. Nagel, James. IV. Title.
PS3515.E372915   1996
813'.52—dc20                      96-24830
  [B]                                   CIP

FIRST EDITION

10 9 8 7 6 5 4 3 2 1

*Take not from the Past its ashes but its fire.*
*—Anon.*

# CONTENTS

· · ·

# CONTENTS

# ACKNOWLEDGMENTS

. . .

This volume has been a collaboration in every sense. I am deeply grateful to Henry Villard for his trust and confidence in bringing me into the project, for his unfailing generosity, and for sharing his personal reminiscences of Ernest Hemingway and World War I. We are both grateful to Mr. William Stanfield for permission to publish Agnes's diary and letters along with photographs from her scrapbook. We are indebted to Jack Hemingway, Patrick Hemingway, Robert W. Lewis, and The Ernest Hemingway Foundation for permission to publish Hemingway's letters and photographs from the John F. Kennedy Library. Through the courtesy of Waring Jones we are able to present eight letters of Agnes von Kurowsky hitherto unknown. Maurice Neville made available to us the X-rays of Hemingway's legs and a photograph of Hemingway with Theodore Brumback. I am deeply grateful to Sondra Taylor and the Manuscripts Department of the Lilly Library, Indiana University, for assistance in verifying the text of Hemingway's letters. My contributions to this volume would not have been possible without the assistance of Mary Armato, Amanda Roberts, and Heather Stone, who work in the office of *Studies in American Fiction*. Megan Desnoyers, curator of the Hemingway Collection at the Kennedy Library, and her assistant, Lisa Middents, were consistently gracious and helpful throughout the research on this book. Alan Spector, M.D., was gracious in providing an orthopedic interpretation of the X-rays of Hemingway's legs. We especially appreciate the guidance and courtesy of William Frohlich, Director of Northeastern University Press, who was thoroughly professional throughout every phase of this project. Finally, I owe my deepest debt to Gwen L. Nagel for her scholarly judgment, her humane sensitivity, and the support in love and war that only she can give.

JAMES NAGEL

*April* 1989

# PREFACE

· · ·

When Henry Villard asked me to get involved in this book, I was delighted. I knew that Villard had known Ernest Hemingway in Milan in World War I because I had read his articles in *Yankee* and *Horizon*. I had seen a photograph of Henry and Agnes von Kurowsky in a carriage in Italy, so it was evident that he had known her as well. He had initially phoned to relate that Agnes had kept a diary throughout her relationship with Hemingway, and Henry had just finished reading it. He described it to me. The question was whether I thought anyone would be interested in it. I did.

At our first meeting Henry explained that he had kept in communication with Agnes over the years and had met with her and her husband, William Stanfield, in Florida. Later, in declining health, Agnes had asked for Villard's assistance in gaining permission for interment in the Soldiers' Home National Cemetery in Washington, D.C.. Henry, who had spent a lifetime in government service, quickly agreed, and with his assistance she obtained the necessary papers. In gratitude, after her death on November 25, 1984, her husband sent Villard the "lost" diary of Agnes von Kurowsky.

Henry asked for my collaboration on a book containing the new document. He could bring to the endeavor his personal experiences as an ambulance driver on the Italian front in World War I along with his own diary, letters home, and files from 1918. I was asked to work on the transcriptions, find what additional information I could, and write an essay placing all the material in a biographical and scholarly context. Henry agreed to expand rather substantially his earlier article "Red Cross Driver in Italy: A Memoir," following Agnes to the end of her life, and to share with me his memories of Italy. These reflections appear not only in his essay but in the notes as well. He also brought to our meetings a box of photographs from 1918, many of which appear in this volume.

We were able to add eight previously unknown letters from Agnes to Hemingway, including the "Dear John" letter that had been presumed lost. It is a key document for understanding the end of one of the most important relationships in Hemingway's life. Similarly, the X-rays of Hemingway's legs are valuable in lending credence to the report that he was hit by machine gun fire as well as shrapnel. The discovery of a bullet in Hemingway's coin purse from World War I is of related interest in that it matches the object in the X-rays, a matter of significance not so much for medical reasons as for assessing Hemingway's veracity and character. The simultaneous discovery of the medals also helps establish another facet of the true adventures of young Hemingway in Italy.

We added a number of photographs and reproductions to the collection, including the citations to go along with the medals. Our research also took us into official records of various kinds, reports from the American Red Cross in Italy, the *Red Cross Bulletin* (which Villard had saved from 1918), and background information on the ambulance service, the canteen unit Hemingway was operating when he was wounded, the hospital where he was treated, and a number of related matters. The final result is the most complete gathering of primary documents ever assembled about Hemingway's military service in World War I, his romance with Agnes von Kurowsky, and the biographical background for a number of short stories and his finest novel, *A Farewell to Arms*.

It has been difficult to sort out the truth from what has been written about Hemingway's experience. For some five decades his publisher ran a blurb on the covers of the paperback editions of his novels that said that in World War I he "served as an ambulance driver and infantryman with the Italian army," which is not true. The documents in this volume help establish what really happened in Italy. The diary of Agnes von Kurowsky, covering the most important period of her relationship with Hemingway, sheds new light on the character of the two people involved and on the nature of their romance. Since she records her thoughts and activities on a daily basis, the diary gives insight into her thinking at the same time it provides a chronological record of Hemingway's surgery, recovery, interaction with other patients in the hospital, and emotional involvement in his first romance.

The diary offers an immediate and private look at the behavior and thoughts of the woman who would capture the love of Ernest Hemingway, a relationship that would first captivate and then wound him deeply. Apart from his fiction, which must be approached as creative imaginings based in uncertain ways on autobiographical episodes, the diary provides the only inside look at the events and the romance that would inspire *A Farewell to Arms*. It has never before been published, nor has it been previously available in any form to Hemingway scholars.

Her letters to him, fifty-two in all, many of which have never been published before, add a great deal of information, particularly the "Dear John" letter. Here are not only Agnes's love letters but, by implication, suggestions of what he was writing to her, what concerned him about his recovery, his career as a journalist (he seems never to have mentioned fiction writing as an option), and his preparations for the responsibilities of marriage. Hemingway's letters to Agnes have not been found, if they still exist, but his correspondence to his parents reveals a great deal about his youthful enthusiasm, undimmed by his wounds, and the way he and other members of his generation viewed the Great War. Only four of these letters have been published previously. In addition, the memoir by Henry Villard, who occupied a room next to Hemingway's in the hospital in Milan, contributes irreplaceable insights into the life of a Red Cross ambulance driver on the Italian front, the routine of the hospital, the character of Agnes von Kurowsky, and the personality of the young man who would become one of the most celebrated writers of the twentieth century.

My essay, the last chapter in the volume, is not so much a conclusion as a reconsideration of this period in Hemingway's life based on the new documents and related materials. In it I attempt to establish what can now be said about Hemingway's Red Cross experience, his wounds and medals, whether he served with the Italian Army, what hospital he was in, and the true nature of his romance with Agnes. I have tried to base these comments not on speculations and psychological theories but on private diaries, letters, photographs, X-rays, and official records. I do not regard Hemingway's fiction as biographical "evidence," as is now a frequent practice, although I admire his work beyond measure, enough to attempt to discover the truth about the experience behind it.

Although I bear responsibility for any errors in the editing of this volume, I am grateful for the generous assistance of Henry Villard in sharing his personal diary, his letters to his parents, and his unpublished memoir. The quotations from Villard in the notes refer to this memoir, now on deposit at the John F. Kennedy Library in Boston and at the Hoover Institution for War, Revolution, and Peace at Stanford University. Henry also supplied many of the photographs here presented, although others came from Agnes's scrapbook, the extensive archives at the Kennedy Library, and from private collections. Villard's memories were especially crucial in writing the captions for the photographs, understanding the tenor of wartime Italy, and assessing the character of both Agnes and Ernest. Henry alone remains to share his personal knowledge of the people and events in the American Red Cross Hospital in Milan.

JAMES NAGEL

# HEMINGWAY
# IN LOVE AND WAR

# ONE

. . .

## Henry Serrano Villard
# Red Cross Driver in Italy

It was nearly midnight when I arrived at Milan's cavernous, murky railroad terminal, thick with coal smoke, after an exhausting journey from my base at Bassano, forty-five miles northwest of Venice at the foot of towering, fortified Monte Grappa.[1] Outside in the dimly lighted square, I asked a pair of carabinieri for directions. Four blocks away were the Giardino Pubblici, the public gardens. From there the Via Alessandro Manzoni, a main thoroughfare, led straight to the Piazza del Duomo. I couldn't miss it. They weren't sure about an Ospedale Americana but the Croce Rossa, where I had been instructed to report, was close to the famous cathedral. Tired, grimy, and sick as I was, I decided to walk after riding the rails all day.

Fired by patriotic fervor, bent on helping to make the world safe for democracy, I had left my freshman class at Harvard, over strong parental objections, to drive an ambulance for the American Red Cross, attached to the Italian Army with the "assimilated" rank of *sotto tenente* (second lieutenant). The United States had declared war on Germany on April 6, 1917, and throughout the land college students not yet eligible for the draft were deserting their teachers to serve the nation in any way they could. The undergraduate body as a whole was out to hang the Kaiser. Who could concentrate on such dull subjects as economics or math or ancient history when the world was in turmoil and history in the making was screaming from the headlines every day? Those concerned with the future of education sought in vain to stem the exodus. King Canute might just as effectively have tried to prevent the ocean tide from receding.

To banish forever the scourge of war didn't seem at all naïve to young collegians imbued with Wilsonian ideals; it was an attainable goal for mankind, worth any sacrifice, any risk or hardship. After all, this was a war to end all wars—there would never be another. Not to join the crusade, to be thought a "slacker," was impossible. As Ernest Hemingway put it in an interview with his hometown newspaper after the war, "I went because I wanted to go. . . . My country needed me, and I went and did whatever I was told."[2] It was as simple as that.

But along with Hemingway and others of our generation I had found a further reason to enlist. Not for anything would I have missed the opportunity for a ringside view of the greatest spectacle likely to unfold in our time. To many of us the war in Europe resembled a gigantic stage on which the most exciting drama ever produced was being played out; as the poet Archibald MacLeish described it, it was something you "went to" from a place called Paris, as if going to a current hit at the theater, and I knew for a certainty I would have to get over there and see the show for myself before the curtain fell. My chance came when the Red Cross began looking for recruits to replace some of its drivers in the Italian sector whose term of service had expired. It was a shortcut to the front, a passport to adventure in a romantic foreign land, the chance of a lifetime. I lost no time in seizing it.

American Red Cross headquarters, at number 10 on the Via Alessandro Manzoni, were shut for the night when I got there, and the hospital section, a short distance away at 4 Via Cesare Cantù, did not look in the least like what it purported to be. A moderate-sized stone and stucco structure with big rectangular windows, it had formerly been used as a *pensione*; except for the familiar emblem over the doorway, the old-fashioned mansion had nothing to indicate that it housed the first medical and surgical institution ever to be opened by Americans on Italian soil. In the half-light from a street lamp the building belonged to an era of horse carriages and opera lovers, of prosperous Lombardy bankers and businessmen, genteel folk who might have lived out their lives unaffected by the vicissitudes of war. No porter was in evidence, but near the grilled elevator cage a brass plate told me that the hospital was located on the fourth floor. I pressed the button and rose slowly to the top.

"Why, hello there! I guess we've been expecting you." The fetching night nurse who answered my ring at the landing smiled cheerfully. "Come right in. We have a room all ready for you."

I didn't have to be asked twice. It was the first feminine voice with an American accent I had heard since leaving the States and it belonged to a tall, slender, chestnut-haired girl with friendly bluegray eyes, who seemed to combine brisk competence with exceptional charm. Though hardly at my best, I couldn't help responding to her encouraging welcome. What luck, I thought, to encounter such an

*Agnes von Kurowsky in her Red Cross uniform.*

attractive person instead of some grim, sour-faced matron! Her loose-fitting, ankle-length uniform, open at the neck, with belt and Red Cross arm band, was crisp and white; a starched white cap perched like a butterfly on the back of her head.

I was ushered into a commodious hall with medicine chests on one side, a desk and chair and filing cabinet on the other. The green-shaded night lamp cast a square of light on her long, tapering fingers as they rustled among a stack of papers, while I took stock of my surroundings. Obviously, the place had been newly renovated. Above the typical odor of disinfectant, I could smell the fresh, white paint that glistened on the walls. The floor had a shiny varnish, and gaily colored curtains draped the windows. So different was it from the bleak impersonal reception room I had expected, so clean, so neat, so informal and homelike, that I felt as if I had never left the U.S.A.

"Yes, here we are. Villard, Henry S. Second lieutenant. Section 1, Ambulance Service. They telephoned you were coming. Nice, isn't it?" following my gaze. "We had an awful time with the painters and plumbers. But now everything's spic and span."

"It's pretty," I agreed.

Still smiling reassuringly, she picked up a chart and said lightly, "Come with me, please. Everyone's asleep. Let's be as quiet as possible."

We tiptoed down a corridor enclosed by glass doors and windows, something like a sun parlor, till we came to a pleasant, airy room, whitewashed in a soft tint, with a single bed and a French window opening onto a small balcony; curtains of bright cretonne, an armoire of oak, a washbasin with hot and cold running water, a night table, and a couple of chairs completed a picture of calm and privacy.

I caught sight of myself in the narrow, full-length mirror on the side of the armoire and was startled at what I saw. The fever danced in my eyes and the color of my face was a ghastly yellow-green. Suddenly, I realized how tired I was.

"All the rooms connect with one another. You can walk right through, like in a ward, and yet you can be all by yourself if you want to. Get undressed, please, while I draw you a hot bath. You can have an eggnog if you're hungry." Then, to my surprise, "What kind of a cocktail would you like?" She gave me an impish glance and stuck a thermometer in my mouth.

I wasn't sure whether I had heard right, but on the chance she meant it I ran over in my mind the agreeable possibilities, drinks I had begun to experiment with at college: an orange blossom, a Bronx, an Alexander, a stinger—finally settling for a very dry Martini. And that was what my ministering angel brought me, none of your insipid European vermouths with a whisper of gin, but a clear, cold, American-style cocktail, only there was a joker. At the bottom of the glass, instead of an olive, lurked a fat glob of castor oil. I managed to smile wryly and downed it all at a gulp. The bathroom was another surprise: modern plumbing, the tub a sensuous treat after the cold-water ablutions I had performed in the swirling eddies of the Brenta river at Bassano.

I had become ill in the overpowering heat of mid-July, perhaps as the result of questionable food (for one thing, we suspected that our "steaks" were mule meat), perhaps too much black coffee and choco-late bars, cigarettes and peanut butter, or perhaps it was unwashed fruit. Whatever the cause, I had developed a burning fever accom-panied by a queasy feeling in the pit of my stomach, and my stomach would accept nothing but watery soup or tea. When I would look into the pocket shaving mirror over the washstand where I splashed cold water over my torso every morning, I would notice that my eyes were turning yellow and that my face showed an unnatural tan. After hop-ing against hope that the distressing symptoms would subside, I top-pled to the floor one day in a dead faint; I knew I faced a sojourn in the hospital, however reluctant I might be to leave my post for the uncertainties of hospitalization in a strange and distant city.

By the time I departed for Milan, I had undergone most of the experiences that befell a driver in the area of Monte Grappa, linchpin of the line of trenches that ran along the Piave River and then swung into the mountainous regions of the Alps. Grappa was "the lock in a door that kept out intruders," according to Italy's General Cardona; "unlocked it would open the whole country to invasion." To bring down casualties on a hazardous road from the heights, the Red Cross used four-cylinder Fiat ambulances, big, gray vehicles that looked

*Section 1 of the American Red Cross ambulance service, Bassano, 1918. Henry S. Villard is in the back row, far left. Nearly all the drivers were Harvard students. Note the high collars of the official Red Cross uniforms.*

like elephants alongside the brown-beetle Model-T Fords that operated in the foothills and plains.

Behind me, in addition to the Italian counteroffensive that had stalled Austria's last desperate attempt at a breakthrough, were the forty-eight hours I had driven without stop and the anxious moments in a violent storm when I found myself cut off by the Austrians at a salient. I had witnessed my first and biggest air raid, a grandiose, theatrical demonstration of air power, at midnight. With my Ford I had run the gauntlet of low-flying enemy aircraft bombing the road on which I was traveling with a load of wounded. And I had had my share of close calls, as when I had fallen asleep at the wheel one dark, exhausting night and awakened in the nick of time as a freight train crossed my path at a junction. Blinding, choking dust or drenching rain (the cars had no windshields), running without lights on shell-pocked roads were an integral part of the experience. Whatever I would see later would offer no novelty; I had become a seasoned participant in the war.

No Roman noble could have enjoyed the baths of Caracalla more than I relished that sybaritic hospital setting, getting rid of the grime and the cooties, luxuriating in the warm suds as long as I dared. At length, I put on a freshly laundered pair of pajamas, crossed the hall, and announced myself ready for bed. When I crawled in between the cool, clean sheets on a real honest-to-God mattress, the guns at the front ceased echoing in my ears and I knew I would have my first decent sleep in months.

Just before she switched off the light, I asked the name of the angelic creature who had admitted me into this spot of heaven. "Agnes von Kurowsky," she said, "from Washington, D.C." As I drifted off, I kept thinking how sympathetic and lovely she was, doubly attractive so far from home. All right, she was a few years older than I, but then older girls are quite likely to appeal to young men who have lately turned eighteen.[3]

When I awoke next morning I found that another nurse had taken over where the lissome Agnes had left off. Elsie MacDonald, as Scottish as her name implied, was not so beautiful, not so young as Agnes, nor was her figure so tall and slim, but her kindliness and good humor were unmistakable. "You can call me Mac," she said in a motherly tone, fussing with my pillow. "There'll be a glass of milk for breakfast, and that's all until the doctor sees you." I felt at ease with her at once.

Dr. Sabatini, attached to Milan's Ospedale Maggiore with the rank of *capitano*, was a short, red-faced man, happy to be consulted by an establishment whose regular physician was off caring for the refugees in the north. He had no need of the inevitable black satchel to diagnose my case as jaundice. "Maybe touch of malaria, too," cocking his head judiciously; "that no dangerous. But for yellow disease— must rest, obey rules, take medicine. If not . . ." (his stern expression was belied by the twinkle in his dark-lashed eyes), "I wash my hands from you." And he suited the gesture to the words.

I felt dizzy and weak after the doctor left, but Mac thought I might as well become acquainted with the patient who was my next-door neighbor. I would be seeing a lot of him, she said, Second Lieutenant Hemingway. An ambulance driver, too. From Section 4. He was the first patient to be admitted after the hospital was opened, and he was badly wounded, as I would see for myself. She knocked, and without waiting for a reply opened the door to a room in every respect like mine, except that it was larger. "Ernie," she said, familiarly, "I'd like you to meet a new arrival. Lieutenant Villard came in last night from Section 1."

Hemingway was a good-looking son-of-a-gun, I thought, lying there fresh-faced and clean-shaven on the white-painted iron bedstead, and good-natured, too, considering that he appeared totally disabled. He had a strong jaw and a wide, boyish grin that revealed an even row of dazzling white teeth, and his jet-black hair and dark eyes contrasted starkly with the snowy pillows that propped up his broad shoulders as he reclined at full length, one leg in a plaster cast, the other swathed in bandages. I judged him to be about my age or a little older. Whatever the extent of his injuries, there was no question about his magnetism or his mental alertness. "You'll like it here," he said warmly, taking my hand in a vigorous clasp. "They treat you royally."

"They" had counted 227 shrapnel wounds in his legs, explained Mac. "But he's doing fine. He's the first of our boys to be wounded in Italy—and we're very proud of him." This was no ordinary patient, I surmised. By the worshipful look on Mac's face, she and, I assumed, the other nurses regarded him as their special pet, a prize specimen of wounded hero.

"Sure thing," I responded. "Great place, this hospital." And I meant it; it had far exceeded my expectations. "How long since you've been laid up?"

"Since July the eighth. That's when I was wounded." He grimaced. "Arrived here the seventeenth. Where's your home?"

"New York," I told him. "The big city. Where's yours?"

"Oak Park, Illinois — place you never heard of." He laughed a boyish laugh. "That's near Chicago. Out where the west begins. Maybe I should say Kansas City. I was working on a newspaper there." He had sailed on a ship of the French Line named, by coincidence, the *Chicago*. "When did you come over?"

"Middle of May," I said. "Had a week or so in Paris. Got to

*Ernest Hemingway at nineteen in Milan. Photograph courtesy of the Ernest Hemingway Foundation.*

Bassano on the thirtieth—Memorial Day. In time for the fireworks on June fifteenth."

"Me too. Got to Schio with a few days to spare. The 'Schio Country Club,' you know." I could see he was sizing me up with those lively, penetrating, black eyes, glad of a chance to talk shop with a fellow driver. "Left New York May twenty-third but didn't make Section 4 till the tenth of June. Paris and red tape, temporary duty here in Milano. Some show put on by the Austrians. But you guys at Grappa saw lots more action than we did around Monte Pasubio. That's why I had to get down to the Piave, to see what was happening—and that's where I got mine," glancing at his legs.

I didn't try to prolong that first encounter because my head was swimming.

"Come back when you feel like it, Villard. You don't have far to go." Hemingway's voice was strong and resonant, his grin cordial and infectious. I had the impression he was eager to receive visitors and would always be ready for a chat.

The Red Cross was fortunate in having found quarters within sight of the Duomo, that magnificent pinnacled and fretted showpiece of the Italian nation. Rooms and furnishings of the erstwhile *pensione* had been readily adapted for use in the hospital and a prodigious effort had been made to transform the two upper floors into a miniature America in time for its official opening on June 17, 1918. Calcimine had been applied in liberal quantities to the walls and ceilings of each room, existing pieces of furniture had been redone or covered with cretonne, piece goods brought from the United States had attractively embellished the whole. In gala dress for an afternoon reception, bright with flowers and flags of the Allies, it had won high praise from a hundred invited guests, including noted Italian doctors and the commanding officer of the French and British Forces in Italy, General Angelotti.

The hospital proper on the top floor, which I came to know so well, consisted of sixteen bedrooms for as many patients, a number which could be doubled in case of emergency. To have all the rooms communicating was considered a particular convenience by the nurses, and in the summer heat (nobody had heard of electric fans) the arrangement made for good ventilation as well. There were two toilets and several baths, each one as satisfyingly up-to-date as that placed at my disposal when I arrived; there was a small but well-equipped operating room with exceptional lighting advantages, a sterilizer, basins, and doctors' scrub facilities next door; there was a separate anesthetizing room and an elegant diet kitchen. The kitchen was a source of justifiable pride: the *Red Cross Bulletin* bragged about "a beautiful set of utensils containing enough copper to make the German High Command copper-green with envy," with one kettle that was "big enough to hold all the envy too." What came out of those spotless precincts three times a day never failed to remind American expatriates, at least those whose digestion allowed, of the meals that mother used to make.

On the floor immediately below was the Nurses' Home and Center. It comprised ten bedrooms, a bath, a small office, a salon, a snug and comfortable library, a dining room, a kitchen, and a porch. In the library, known also as the music room, were a piano, a large Victrola, and two singing canaries, Martha and George Washington; it had been designed for use by nurses and patients alike. On the regular staff of the Nursing Service were five registered American graduate nurses, including their supervisor. "We need to have them fairly young and strong, this climate is a little trying," maintained Sara Shaw, director of all American Red Cross (ARC) nurses coming to Italy. In addition, there were one or more Italian nurses, as might be required to act as aids under the direction of the Americans, and two orderlies. For the combined quarters of the establishment, upstairs and downstairs, seven people served as domestic help: a cook, two chambermaids, two cleaners, a kitchen maid, and a furnace man. From my contented viewpoint, the place seemed more like an exclusive rest home or country club than a war-begotten hospital for Americans serving in a foreign land. One thing was certain: no pampered patient ever complained about the accommodations, the food, or the service.

What made the small hospital premises an inordinately pleasant spot to spend an illness was the fact that half the rooms had balconies and the other half gave out on a capacious terrace. As the *Bulletin* pointed out, "convalescent cases requiring a great deal of sunlight and fresh air" (both in plentiful supply in Italy) could be brought to recuperate in the terrace area, which ran completely around two sides of the building. Under the striped awnings, which could be rolled up or down according to the temper of the sun, ambulatory or wheelchair patients were able to lounge at ease and have their meals brought to them: there were large wicker chairs, a chaise-lounge, green potted plants, and, on the balustrade, decorative flower boxes. Within easy reach on a low table lay a selection of magazines and a portable, hand-cranked phonograph with all the current hits: "Keep the Home Fires Burning," "Tipperary," "There's a Long, Long Trail," and so on.

Well above the hubbub of street noises, the top floor view em-

*Henry S. Villard on the terrace of the American Red Cross Hospital in Milan, August 1918.*

braced a sea of red-tiled roofs, topped by the Duomo's lofty spires. Aeroplanes flew constantly over the city from their nearby base at Taliedo, while an aluminum dirigible would float intermittently into sight, a silver fish in an ocean of blue. At night the aerial entertainment would take on a spectacular tinge: penciled rays of light would pick up the machines and turn them into gigantic, golden insects, whose red and green eyes blinked secret messages to one another in the dark.

As the *Bulletin* had noted in one of its early issues, "only a few patients were on hand at the start to care for," but with the expected arrival of American troops in Italy, the nurses were "prepared for vigorous activity in case of need." Meanwhile, when not lavishing attention on the first handful of cases, the young women were kept busy with a special Demonstration Room for the benefit of visiting Italian nurses, where model white beds and lifelike dolls showed the latest American methods of practical nursing, the use of surgical dressings, and the principles of child welfare and hygiene. Most of the hospital beds were empty, I soon discovered, waiting for casualties among the American soldiers yet to arrive. I didn't care. I would make the most of this comfortable wartime haven while it lasted.

And that was the real-life setting for the opening chapters of Ernest Hemingway's enormously successful novel of World War I, *A Farewell to Arms*. Against the background of the hospital's confines, which made for an intimacy that was unusual to say the least, he conceived the poignant love story of *Farewell*, basing it on his romance with the most glamorous of our nurses, Agnes von Kurowsky. As Lieutenant Frederic Henry, the protagonist of the story, tells it,

> There were three other patients in the hospital now, a thin boy in the Red Cross from Georgia with malaria, a nice boy, also thin, from New York, with malaria and jaundice, and a fine boy who had tried to unscrew the fuse-cap from a combination shrapnel shell for a souvenir.[4]

The boy from Georgia remains unidentified in my mind and may have been invented. The souvenir hunter was Coles van B. Seeley, a tall, strapping fellow with a bristling moustache from Newark, New Jersey, who had nearly blown his hands off and lost his eyesight in that ill-advised quest. I was the thin boy from New York with malaria and jaundice. It was ironical, as everyone agreed, to have come through the recent Italian counteroffensive against Austria-Hungary unscathed, only to fall victim to the distinctly unheroic maladies endemic at the time.

For the first few days I was too sick to do anything but doze or play an occasional game of solitaire on the bedspread with cards that Agnes brought me. To my regret, I didn't see as much of Agnes as I would have liked, for she didn't mind the night duty that the others were inclined to shun. Agnes was seldom around in the daytime; but the plump, warm-natured Elsie MacDonald looked in frequently to see how I was getting on. When Agnes did appear, the entire place seemed to brighten because of her presence. Besides having what the boys called "it," she was kind, quick, intelligent, and sensitive to the moods of a patient; what's more, she was blessed with a sense of humor that verged on the mischievous. She was firm without being too strict, light-hearted yet professionally serious. Altogether the perfect temperament for a nurse.

Every day through the half-open door I could see Hemingway holding court with her and whoever else happened to drop in, guffawing and joking about the multiple wounds that had incapacitated him. "Look, are they going to amputate just one leg, or two?"

Agnes or Mac would be laughing and kidding back. "Two, of course. What good's one leg?"

"All right, make it two. When do we start?"

"Maybe today, maybe tomorrow. Maybe next week. When the sawbones are good and ready."

"Jesus, I'm ready now."

I knew it was banter because I felt sure he would never let them cut off his limbs, no matter how long it might take to extract, piece by piece, that awesome collection of metal fragments from his flesh. From Agnes in one of her spare moments I learned the details of how he had been hit by the explosion of a trench mortar (what the soldiers referred to as an "ash can"), lobbed over from the Austrian lines, that burst on contact and scattered pieces of junk steel in every direction. In addition, he had been wounded in the right knee by machine-gun fire. The Red Cross had officially labeled all except ten of his injuries as superficial, but that didn't prevent me from admiring his intestinal fortitude in enduring pain, not to speak of the excrutiating tedium of lying immobilized for weeks on end. And in spite of his own strong-willed attitude, the possibility of amputation seemed to be always present if things should take a turn for the worse.

As soon as my temperature dropped and the dreadful yellow color began to fade under a milk-and-egg diet, I was allowed to take the few steps through the connecting door and sit at Hemingway's bed in my dressing gown. I looked forward to this ritual as much for the companionship as for taking a turn, like everyone else, in helping the wounded warrior, so much worse off than I, to while away the hours and forget his plight. He was generous with his time (he had plenty to spare), and he was insatiable in his desire to hear what was going on at the front. "You're the first guy I've met out of Section 1," he observed, as I took the chair next to his bed after the siesta hour one sweltering afternoon. What was it like at Bassano? How often were we being shelled? How many *feriti* was I carrying per week? How many *malati*? What kind of car was I driving? How was the chow? How were the Arditi, those shock troops he admired so much, doing up in the mountains? Nothing escaped his interest: names, places, dates. His own memory for detail seemed remarkable. It was almost as if I were being quizzed by a lawyer for the prosecution; years later it would occur to me that this probing was the instinct of the born storyteller. On the other hand, he paid you the compliment of listening intently when you spoke, soaking up everything you were saying like a sponge, only now and then interjecting a "why?" or "what for?" or a personal comment which, as likely as not, would be studded with blasphemy. Profane remarks often peppered the war-nurtured talk of American boys suddenly growing into manhood while serving the cause of democracy in Europe, but in that respect Hemingway's conversation displayed far more than the usual share.

We were quickly on a first-name basis; it wasn't hard to strike a friendship with Ernie. That was what most of us called him, though

I preferred the more masculine-sounding "Hem." I liked this big bear of a fellow from the start and I think he liked me. He had celebrated, if that's the word, his nineteenth birthday, confined to bed, on July 21, which made me the youngest inmate of the hospital by a good eight months. Actually, we had a lot in common. For one thing, we were both volunteers in the ambulance service, both hospitalized in a strange land far from home, neither of us old enough to have been in a hospital before, a bond unconsciously felt but not openly talked about. Another factor that brought us together was the fact that the Red Cross had become the chosen instrument of the United States government for keeping Italy in the war. The devastating defeat of that country in a German-led surprise attack at Caporetto on October 24, 1917, had resulted in wholesale desertions and an alarming loss of morale. Not yet able to send support in the form of troops, Washington had decided on a massive program of relief and rehabilitation to aid the stricken nation. Tangible evidence of official determination was the ambulance corps hastily put together by the Red Cross with orders to spread the message "Stand fast, the Yanks are coming!"

That had held a dramatic appeal for us: the entrance of these units on the scene, together with other Red Cross personnel, was

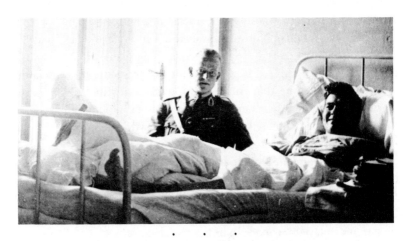

*Hemingway in his room in the American Red Cross Hospital, August 1918. With him is Captain Meade Detweiler. Photograph by Henry S. Villard.*

designed to make the man in the street and his brother in the trenches take heart and react accordingly. Ernie and I could testify that the policy had fully paid the expected dividends. Wherever our vehicles went they aroused hope and enthusiasm among the soldiers. As drivers we felt that, however small our contribution, we were playing a part in strengthening the resolve of the fighting men to keep the enemy at bay until help arrived from overseas. We shared also the unique experience of being attached to a foreign army while scrupulously preserving our allegiance to the American flag, for we looked at the war through American eyes and knew nothing could lessen our attachment to and pride in our own country. America, only America, could show the world what had to be done to rout the Teutonic hordes and bring the Kaiser to heel, and we shook our heads, groaning in unison, when we spoke of the spirit of defeat that pervaded Italy's army after the disastrous retreat at Caporetto the year before.

We were American to the core, too, in our preoccupation with the great game of baseball, quickly slipping into the idiom of the sport like the most avid fans. Hem was a stalwart supporter of the Chicago Cubs, who were destined to win the National League pennant that season, I of John J. McGraw's New York Giants. Baseball scores from the U.S. were hard to come by and we devoured eagerly what scraps of information that came our way about the rival teams' standings. One of us, I forget which, came up with a doggerel that provided us with no end of private amusement:

> Here lies the body of Mary Jones
> For her life held no terrors;
> She lived a maid and died a maid—
> No hits, no runs, no errors.

The last line we adopted as a form of riposte to any inquiries as to how we were faring, when one hot, hospital day was much like another: "no hits, no runs, no errors." And in amateur strategy sessions or arguments about the war we evaluated reports from the front in terms of box scores or innings, as if we were zealous rooters for the home team against opponents from out of town.

I was struck particularly by what Ernie had to say about journalism, for I had ambitions in that field myself. His brief career as a cub reporter on the *Kansas City Star*, the job wangled for him by an uncle, impressed me enormously. Six months of covering the police blotter, the morgue, the city hall, and the railway station spelled volumes of experience to me and I looked up to him as an authority on what I thought might one day be my own profession. Next to watching a war, he would say, newspaper work was the best way to learn to think for yourself, and the best way to learn to write was to write about what you yourself actually *saw* and *felt*. When I remarked that one of *my* uncles was editor and publisher of the liberal *New York Evening Post*, he promptly accepted me as a literary aspirant: "Christ, Harry, we talk the same language!" Maybe he would have been intrigued to learn, a year later, that he had not encouraged me in vain and that I had in fact become a reporter and an editor of my college daily, the *Harvard Crimson*.

I took it for granted that Ernie would continue writing after the war, though he was never specific as to the form his writing would take. A college education didn't seem to interest him; firsthand experience in a sphere like journalism was schooling enough. He had contributed a number of pieces to his high school newspaper and magazine (that, too, commanded my respect) and he hinted at the satisfaction of seeing his stories in print, but a novel was never mentioned as one of his goals. There was no intimation that he might use the war or the hospital as background for a book one day or that he intended to go in for fiction in preference to anything else. He was basically a reporter, and that was that.

My reverence for Hem's qualifications as a reporter was immeasurably increased when he showed me a copy of a newsletter called *Ciao*, published sporadically by a group of kindred spirits in Section 4. It featured a clever parody he had written of the popular Ring Lardner epistles "You know me, Al." *Ciao's* inspiration may have been a British Expeditionary Force sheet that began to circulate in France on August 15, 1917, selling for one franc per copy. The pages of the *B.E.F. Times* were filled with good, clean, morale-building humor: sketches, innocuous jokes, verse, satirical articles, and short serials such as "The Bound of the Baskervilles: Another Herlock Sholmes Episode." While *Ciao* didn't represent so ambitious an effort and boasted nowhere near as large a circulation, it had the same general aim: to afford an outlet for irrepressible Anglo-Saxon wit and, by gently tickling the funnybone, to relieve the monotony of life at the front.

"Well Al we are here in this old Italy," began the Hemingway gem entitled, "Al Receives Another Letter."[5]

> And now that I am here I am not going to leave it. Not at all if any. And that is no New Years resolution Al but the truth. Well Al I am now an officer and if you would meet me you would have to salute me. What I am is a provisional acting second lieutenant with a commission but the trouble is that all the other fellows are too. There aint no privates in our army Al and the Captain is called a *chef*. But he don't look to me as tho he could cook a damn bit. And the next highest officer is called a *sous chef*. And the reason they call him that is that he is *chef* of the jitneys and has to cook for the 4ds. But he has a soft job Al because there are no 4ds left.

Other passages, referring to Jenahvark (Joan of Arc), Garry Baldy (Garibaldi), and "making the world safe for the Democrats," were as laugh-provoking at the time as the original Lardner, whose style we both admired extravagantly. Ernie had captured that style in brilliant fashion, with all its hallmarks of misspellings, lack of punctuation, and sardonic humor, and I urged him to send in another contribution as soon as he could. But he shrugged off the suggestion: the hospital was no place for writing, he laughed, too many interruptions.

There was another point of contact that made us congenial, and that was an unbounded love of the outdoors, a love that was to survive for the rest of our lives. Hem never tired of talking about his family's summer place on a lake in Michigan with its multiple attractions for anyone our age: camping, fishing, hunting, swimming, canoeing, and hiking through the green fields and forests. "That's the life!" he would exult over and over again. He had owned a "peach" of a twelve-gauge shotgun, and he illustrated with his muscular, hairy arms how he had used it. In turn, I told him about the two boys' camps I had attended, one on a lake in hilly New Hampshire, the other in much wilder country in northern Maine, where I had reveled in the same kinds of sports.

We swapped tales, embroidered, of course, about the size of the trout we had caught, then cooked with bacon strips over an open fire; we reminisced about idle days under a tent when it rained; we recalled with satisfaction hours of paddling through placid waters far from "civilized" intrusion. Hem listened attentively when I described a ranch on the south fork of the Shoshone river in Wyoming, where I had spent the previous summer, a graduation present from my parents. Although not as wild and woolly as I had anticipated, the West had captivated me; I could think of nothing I would rather do right then than vault into a western saddle, fish a mountain stream, or pitch a tent "miles and miles from anywhere." Ernie had no experience at all as a horseman and cared little about horses, but he liked the picture I drew of galloping through sagebrush in the best movie manner, wearing chaps like a cowboy and firing at coyotes or prairie dogs with a .22 Winchester rifle. "I'm going to live out there, Hem," I declared, grandly, "Wyoming, Arizona, Montana, the great open spaces. Wherever they are, that's for me."

"Sure, I know how you feel," he agreed, "but it's a good way to feel. Hell, I'm going out there myself someday. Wish to Christ I had my hand on a flyrod or a gun right now. That'll have to wait, though, like everything else. *Dopo la guerra.*"

We discoursed about the world in general, about sports in particular, but mostly about the conduct of the war and the seeming ineptitude of Italy's soldiers. After all, the war was what we were there for and the progress of the Allied armies overshadowed all the rest. It wasn't easy to find out what was going on at the front, for in those days we didn't have the benefit of hourly radio bulletins or color telecasts, much less a flow of weekly commentary and analysis from the printed media. We had to depend on hearsay or rumor, on official communiqués appearing in Milan's *Corriere della Sera* or yesterday's newspapers from Rome, which invariably told of success for the Italian army, or on tidbits gleaned from between the lines in letters from friends. One treasure did come into our possession, a rudimentary map of the Austrian-Italian front clipped from a tattered copy of the *New York Times.* Every day we pored over the priceless document with its English legend, trying to relate the events we heard about to the names and places inscribed upon it.

Early in our relationship, I noticed that the Hemingway stamina was being bolstered by a bottle of cognac, or some other spiritous liquor, hidden under his pillow (strictly against the rules, naturally), from which I would share a surreptitious nip on occasion. My own illness, unpleasant though it was, seemed trivial compared to the physical discomfort Ernie had to put up with. Who could blame him for "fortifying the organic functions," as one Cuban rum company used to advertise the purpose of its product, in order to keep up his morale, to still the shock of that terrifying moment of injury, and to speed his recovery? "Here, have a swig!" he would say, wiping the neck of the bottle on a bedsheet, and I would let the unadulterated warmth trickle down my gullet like a medicinal prescription I was gradually learning to appreciate.

Hem didn't hesitate to point with pride at what he liked to call his army of "dead men," empty bottles of brandy, vermouth, Cointreau, or plain "red ink" stashed away in the big oak armoire against an opportunity to have them smuggled out by the porter, who had brought them in for a small bribe in the first place. If the nurses didn't exactly countenance his tippling, as visiting friends did, they tolerated the habit as long as he kept it under control and didn't exhibit signs of intoxication. Not so, however, with Miss Katherine C. DeLong, the establishment's small, dignified, gray-haired supervisor, with whom Ernie had more than one violent run-in on the subject of alcoholic beverages. He had an unlimited capacity to swallow the contents of a bottle without betraying the fact that he had been drinking, but he couldn't disguise his breath and Miss DeLong was adept at detecting this telltale sign.

Under the stimulus of one of those periodic libations, Hem would embark on a long-winded discourse about the conduct of the war, the sporting life, or the apparent shortcomings of Italy's soldiers, which would be interrupted only by an addition to his audience or the appearance of a nurse on some hospital chore. At such times, as likely as not, he would break out with a "Christ Almighty! what is it now?" or a "Come in, Goddamit, and listen to this." Despite his usual ebullient good humor, despite the disarming smile that won him so many friends, male and female, he could be imperious if not downright irascible. He was in fact far from being a cooperative patient. One of the nurses, Mrs. Charlotte M. Heilman, would observe years later in a letter to Red Cross headquarters that he was "impulsive, very rude, 'smarty,' and uncooperative," that he gave the impression of being badly spoiled, and that he "always seemed to have plenty of money which he spent freely for Italian wine and tips to the porter who brought it."[6] But he got away with such unruly behavior because of his spectacular wounds, the hospital's main conversation piece, and because of his unusual personal magnetism. Not only was he popular with men but, owing especially to his good looks, he was undeniably attractive to women; everyone melted before his youthful, seemingly unaffected, and spontaneous charm.

Contrary to many people's impression, Hemingway did not receive his injuries while serving as an ambulance driver. He had strayed into the role of warrior by accident. "Let's say I was bored with the routine," he grinned at me one day. "All right, I was restless." During the Austrian offensive in June things were relatively quiet in his sector, and he decided to get a look at the war somewhere else. The Piave was where the excitement was, and his chance came when they asked for volunteers to man some new field kitchens in the area. "On a temporary basis, you understand. I thought it would be a nice change from chauffeuring the *blessés* around." With several other drivers who could be spared, he made the transfer from Ambulance Section 4 and ended up at Fossalta, a small, broken-down, shot-up village at a bend in the meandering Piave River. Fossalta was near San Bernardo, a known danger spot, where Red Cross Lieutenant Edward Michael McKey (a talented New York portrait painter who had lived long in France and Italy and whose poor health had disqualified him for military service) had been instantly killed by an

Austrian shell while putting his Rolling Canteen No. 1 into operation on June 16.

It was no secret that, along with the ambulance corps, the Red Cross branch that ran the most risks in Italy was the rolling canteen, or field kitchen, service. Originally planned as a string of trailers to be towed along just back of the lines, dispensing hot coffee, cold drinks, cigarettes, and chocolate bars to the soldiers, most of them, because of impractical road conditions, soon developed into stationary units attached to a designated regiment. These *cucinas*, or "American bars," as they were called by the soldiers (the Red Cross maintained twenty-seven of them), were invariably located in the danger zone, close to the front-line trenches or at strategic crossroads frequented by the troops. In some cases, such as that of the *cucina* in the mountains near Bassano, first manned by a likable chap from New York named Beverly Myles, they developed into solid wooden structures that provided all the amenities of a rest house. There the fighting men could obtain refreshment, spread jam or sugar on their gray army bread, or write a letter home if they wished. Almost certainly the hut would be equipped with a phonograph and a collection of popular or classical records, or else would be graced by a guitar, a mandolin, or an accordion.

At its best, the *posto di ristoro*, decked out with patriotic posters, crossed flags, and bunting, was a focal point for the propagation of the faith, faith that the Yanks were coming, faith in the invincibility of the United States, faith in the unwavering friendship of Americans. As we were constantly reminded, the whole point of the Red Cross operation was to bolster Italian morale and keep our wavering ally in the war. Living in adjacent quarters, the Red Cross officer in charge of a *cucina* had to combine the attributes of a propagandist, a scoutmaster, a y.m.c.a. director, and a father-confessor; he had to be equally at home with the officers and infantrymen who rallied around him. He had to be tactful and versatile, too, and, like the ambulance drivers, cool and courageous under fire.

Lieutenant McKey, the first a.r.c. officer to fall in Italy, had played the role to perfection: perpetually cheerful, able to carry on his one-man show with a human touch and, if necessary, to circulate through the trenches on foot distributing supplies in person, he had spread encouragement to disheartened defenders of the line with a nod, a smile, or a carefully rehearsed jest in Italian. It was also a role well suited to the temperament of an Ernest Hemingway—genial, outgoing, gregarious—to whom it didn't matter that Fossalta was little more than a primitive outpost, bereft of the perquisites found at some of the other centers.

"Handing out smokes and chocolate bars was the best way to see the forward posts," Ernie smiled broadly, "only I didn't think the Austrians would oblige with a demonstration so soon." Actually, he had been on the ground only a few days when, during a night attack, he caught the contents of the trench mortar in his legs. An Italian near him was killed, another lost both his legs, a third was badly hurt. Hem managed to lift this man on his back, just how he never knew, and was carrying him to the rear when he was hit in the knee by machine-gun fire. He didn't have any idea how he made it to the first-aid station. "All I know is that's where I passed out. They took me by ambulance to Treviso; then by hospital train, complete with flies and gore, to Milano and the hospital here. Jesus H. Christ, they weren't even ready for business, this place was so new. But, oh, boy! Take it from me, they've made up for it ever since."

What was it like to be almost killed on the battlefield? "It was like the blast from a furnace. There was a deafening roar. . . . My knee felt warm and sticky. I was covered with blood, my blood and that of the Italian. I tried to breathe and I couldn't." That fearful sensation of having the wind knocked out, as if by a blow to the solar plexus, has been described many times in many ways, but if I had then known about the legendary Persian character named Hajji Baba I would have found a parallel in Hajji's graphic expression "my soul came into my mouth." But Hemingway made it clear enough: "I went out fast and thought I was dead. When you have no breath, you're dead. Then I was able to breathe again and I was back." He remembered seeing star shells and a search light, and then he heard someone crying "*Mamma mia! Mamma mia!*"

I would never forget my first encounter with the anguish that went with war. I had brought my ambulance, Number 13, from the hospital at Romano Alto, a few days after our unit had reached the front, to answer an urgent call from a small dressing station near the shattered village of Crespano. A soldier had his legs blown off by the explosion of a hand grenade. I was totally unprepared for the sight that awaited me, for never in my life had I come into contact with anything approaching such a pitiable semblance of a man, his legs conspicuously absent, his gray-green uniform in tatters, spattered with blood, his rugged, tanned peasant face contorted and his eyes tightly closed in pain, his handlebar moustache dripping blood. Groaning, moaning, he was placed on the stretcher from my car by two orderlies, quickly staining the canvas with his blood, and shoved inside like a package of raw meat, while I, too stunned to register emotion, mechanically started the engine and began to drive as carefully as I could to avoid the bumps and jolts of a rutted road. It was a hopeless effort. Every turn of the wheels brought more protests ("Mamma mia! Piano! Piano!"), and there was nothing I could do to ease his suffering. Torn between a desire to drive slowly and the need to reach the hospital as soon as possible, whatever I did seemed only to make matters worse. As in many subsequent cases, death won the race; the patient, mercifully released, was dead on arrival. It was just as well that the shock of my initiation came early; the sooner an ambulance driver becomes inured to horror, the better is he able to carry out his duties.

"Mamma mia!" That tortured cry summed up the whole melancholy business, the endless killing, the smashed bodies, the ruined homes, the waste of resources. It deeply affected most Americans as young as we were, and I know it had made a profound impression on Ernie. Our horizons were being altered by war, though we didn't speak about horizons in so many words. Instead, we compared notes and exchanged observations about what we had seen at the front with almost clinical detachment. Ambulance drivers still in their teens, living more intensively than ever before in their existence, didn't have much time to formulate a philosophy on the basis of day-to-day occurrences. That sort of thing would come later.

It wasn't necessary for Hem to add that his exploit was about to gain for him a formal commendation from the Red Cross and, more tangibly, a citation by the Italian government, along with its second highest decoration, the *medaglia d'argento al valore militare*. At least that was the drift of the conversation in the hospital corridor, as relayed by the nurses; everyone seemed to be talking about the imminence of the award, including the prospective recipient who, with pardonable pride, made no bones about his anticipation of the honor that was to come his way.

Nevertheless, Hemingway played down the episode when writing home. In comments to his parents, published by the Red Cross at the end of the war, he was practical and matter-of-fact about the whole affair: "The 227 wounds from the trench mortar didn't hurt a bit. . . . The machine gun bullet just felt like a sharp smack on my leg with an icy snow ball. I got up again and got my wounded into the dug out." He went on: "It does give you an awfully satisfactory feeling to be wounded. It's getting beaten up in a good cause." He then inscribed a few lines that would be widely quoted one day. "There are no heroes in this war. We all offer our bodies and only a few are chosen. . . . They are the lucky ones. I am very proud and happy that mine was chosen, but it shouldn't give me any extra credit."

"There are no heroes in this war." Maybe so, but I wasn't so sure that Hemingway didn't think of himself in heroic terms. No doubt it was "an awfully satisfactory feeling to be wounded," but for more reasons than "getting beaten up in a good cause." The fact was that Hem was besieged by admirers, idolized by visitors and by those around him, and, so far as I could tell, he never tried to discourage the attention he received during his long, enforced idleness.

To us the war against Austria was one thing, the ebb and flow of battle in France another. Though developments were beginning to favor the Allies, an end to hostilities didn't really appear to be in sight that summer, either to Hem or to me. After four years of carnage, with the armies still deadlocked, one didn't take anything for granted. When we talked about prospects for the future we assumed the conflict would go on and on over an unpredictable span of time. Hem was vague as to what he wanted to do when he got well, postponing decisions and not looking too far ahead. Plainly he didn't know whether he would be able to resume his duties as a driver or whether he would be invalided home; everything would depend on the extent of his recovery. But he knew as well as I that with the passage of time the draft would catch up with those of us then under the statutory age of twenty years and nine months, that the United States army was soon due to take over in Italy with its own ambulances and enlisted men, and that while the Italian government had signified its desire to have the Red Cross stay, we volunteers might suddenly find ourselves out of a job one day. Perhaps, I said, we ought to think about training for a regular military commission. Hem didn't respond to that. I could see that his independent spirit wouldn't let him be cast in any orthodox mold, not even to serve with the increasingly respected American Expeditionary Force in France led by General John Pershing.

I didn't realize it then, but there was something else that was contributing to his indecisive frame of mind. For the first time in his life, Ernie was falling in love, and the object of his affections was none other than our glamorous night nurse, Agnes Hannah von Kurowsky. There was a tacit acceptance, a subtle understanding, by nurses and patients alike, of the special relationship that was developing between them. But possibly because he would have brooked no potential rivals, Ernie did not confide to me his amorous inclinations. We did not talk about Agnes except in general, noncommittal terms, and there was nothing in his demeanor, so far as I could tell, to call attention to the true state of his feelings. Not until later would I hear that he and Agnes had engaged in a running underground correspondence, exchanging notes and letters at a prodigious rate, usually with Mac as the trusted intermediary. But I was not privy to this little game and, during the relatively short period I was in the hospital, I remained unaware of its existence.

Agnes herself was impartial in the way she encouraged her patients, making them feel individually that she really cared about their welfare. But one couldn't help noticing that Ernie received an extra share of her attention, partly because of the growing fondness between them, partly because Ernie had a compelling, not to say demanding, way about him that required her attendance on every conceivable occasion. Agnes would be the first to agree that he was not an easy patient to handle, that he could assert himself with no little authority if matters weren't exactly right or if he found the unrelenting discipline of Miss DeLong too irksome. At times, it would take all the sympathy and tact that Agnes possessed to calm him down and keep him from scolding. Yet, as Bill Horne, another hospital inmate, was to recall in later years, "her romance with Hem was a beautiful thing to watch," even if, as proved to be the case, the love light was burning a lot more brightly in his eyes than in hers.

It was easy to see why Hemingway should fall as he did for Agnes. If he was the invalid luminary, then she scintillated among the nurses. She had a sparkle the others didn't possess. Fresh and pert and lovely in her long-skirted white uniform, moving lithely as she went about her tasks, wasting no time yet never seeming to hurry, she radiated zest and energy. Obviously her work took precedence over everything else, and just as obviously she liked her work. I myself came to have a real crush on Aggie, or Ag, as she was called by those who got to know her best, but then all the boys fell for Aggie to some degree. No wonder. In the close quarters of our top-floor ward, we were always conscious of her comely presence when she was around. It gradually became clear, however, that Ernie had been smitten to a far greater extent than the rest of us, and I knew that he had the inside track to her affections when I caught him holding her hand one afternoon in a manner that did not suggest she was taking his pulse.

Agnes was born in Germantown, Pennsylvania, on January 5, 1892, the daughter of a naturalized citizen of Polish-German extraction and the granddaughter of a Polish general. On her mother's side she was the granddaughter of Brigadier General Samuel Beckley Holabird, Quartermaster General of the United States Army. When Agnes was thirteen, the family moved to Washington, where she spent two years at the Fairmount Seminary; after her father died in 1910, she found employment in the catalogue department of the Carnegie Library. "But that was too slow and uneventful," she told me one quiet evening. "My taste ran to something more exciting. So I went into training as a nurse." Agnes enrolled at Bellevue Hospital's School of Nursing in New York, graduating on July 17, 1917, and applied for a Red Cross assignment abroad as soon as possible. Because of the "von" in her name, enough to hold up anyone's passport at a time when dachshunds were regarded as enemy aliens, her departure was delayed until June 15, 1918, when she sailed for Europe on the S.S. *La Lorraine* of the Compagnie Générale Transatlantique. The other members of her contingent had already left, but she had plenty of company on the crossing; a group of Belgian officers who had served in Russia were returning from leave and she quickly made friends among them.

It was a wartime coincidence that, of eleven Red Cross nurses who at one time or another during 1918 served in the American Hospital at Milan, four were Bellevue classmates of Agnes. Besides the motherly, tender-hearted, and much-liked Mac, there was young and pretty Loretta Cavanagh, a kind, helpful type familiarly known as "Sis Cavie"; the somewhat flirtatious Ruth Brooks, who for some reason or other rubbed Ernie the wrong way; and the widowed Mrs. Charlotte Anne Miller Heilman, a tuberculosis specialist who also did field work for the Home Service department of the Red Cross. They had all arrived in Italy before Agnes.

The Bellevue contingent was linked by a common background, but its members got on well with the other nurses, too: Anna Scanlon, who had admitted Hemingway to the hospital, Ruth Harper Fisher, Veta Blanche Markley, Elena Crough, Valeria Rittenhouse from Canada, and Mrs. Katherine Rahn (later Mrs. Bresnam). Miss DeLong, the alert, capable supervisor, also of Canadian origin, was a graduate of Johns Hopkins and would become superintendent of nurses at Bellevue after her return from Italy; she was to appear in *A Farewell to Arms* as the acerbic and suspicious "gumshoe" Miss van Campen, having promptly incurred Hem's enmity because she wouldn't accept his violation of the rules about drinking or his generally contumacious behavior.

Life was especially bearable for the convalescents when one or more of the nurses, off duty or pausing in their rounds, would join the group lounging on the terrace "to chew the fat," as Ernie would loudly proclaim over a glass of milk or orange juice (both rarities at the front), to crack a few jokes, pose for an amateur snapshot, or listen to a favorite record or two. Somebody had introduced a parody of "Smiles," that immensely popular hit of the war years 1917 and 1918; the parody was called "Styles" and the words were considered delightfully risqué for mixed company. We hummed them with a glint in the eye when the nurses were present:

> There are styles—that show the an-kle,
> There are styles—that show the knee,
> There are styles—that show the vaccina-tion—
> There are styles—that hadn't ought to be,
> There are styles—that have a certain mean-ing—
> Which the eyes—of love alone may see,
> But the styles—that Eve wore in the gar-den—
> Are the styles that appeal to me.

As the summer progressed, our numbers were augmented. William D. (Bill) Horne, Jr., then of Bridgeport, Connecticut, an affable Princetonian of winning personality from the class of 1913 and a close associate of Ernie's in Section 4, arrived with a mysterious internal ailment, eventually diagnosed as "sub-acute enteritis," to join in the bedside chats with his buddy. Intestinal troubles of one kind or another were as numerous as the fleas or flies that helped to promote them; nobody escaped the prevalent diarrhea or dysentery. "June" Darling, Herbert H. Darling, Jr., of Brookline, Massachusetts (the "June" was an abbreviation of Junior) soon came in from Section 2 with jaundice, the same malady that had laid me low. George N. Carpenter of Castine, Maine, a member of the Harvard unit from Section 3, checked in with the typical Piave complaint, malaria, and there were more to come. We and a few other congenial souls formed a nucleus around the chief guest at the Ospedale Americana, visiting with him in turn or, if qualified as "patients requiring a great deal of sunlight and fresh air," lolling around the terrace like privileged brothers of a small fraternity. Hemingway, because of his wounds, couldn't be moved and instead looked out on the world through open French windows, while we were permitted to roam around our oasis in shirt sleeves or dressing gowns at will. Over pipe tobacco and endless packs of Macedonia cigarettes we debated the war through the hot afternoons, indulging in low-stake poker games to while away the evenings.

Gradually, I gained strength with the addition of oatmeal and boiled chicken to my diet, so that I began to think seriously of the day when I could aspire to asking Aggie out to dinner. The prospect of a tête-à-tête meal with her was a standing incentive to get well quickly, and the vision of a splendid restaurant where I could have her all to myself for an evening was enough to set my spine tingling. Here, I thought smugly, I had the advantage over poor handicapped Ernie, for it would be many more weeks before he could expect to get out of bed and hobble around on crutches.

"Kindly do not laugh when you read this," I wrote my parents, "but I am raising a moustache. That is, if I don't get disgusted and shave it off soon. Nearly everyone over here is trying to raise a moustache and I have the second niftiest one in our crowd right now."

I didn't dare date my letter Milan, for I worried constantly that my family would find out I had been hospitalized; realizing they would suspect the worst, I refrained from giving them a clue to my whereabouts, pretending I was still at the front, even though I was hard put for topics to write home about. Meanwhile, I hoped fervently that the incipient adornment to my upper lip would add years to my appearance when the time came to take Ag out on the town.

A milestone was reached in my recovery on August 10, when I was allowed to step into the street and take a short walk in the teeming city. On the same day I made note in my diary that "Hemingway was operated on early in the morning." The air was tense in the hospital; a lot depended on this, the second operation for its Very Important Patient. Would he be able to walk again, and if so, how soon? Everyone was concerned about the outcome. But much to our relief, Hem came through with flying colors, and the *Bulletin* reported that he was "progressing toward complete recovery." Captain Sammarelli, the attending surgeon, deftly removed the machine gun slugs from his knee and foot and presented them to him as a souvenir; they went into a basin at the side of his bed, which contained an impressive assortment of shrapnel he had picked out of his legs with a pen knife and saved for the edification of visitors.

In the days that followed, I explored Milan on foot and by horse cab, sometimes alone, sometimes in the company of June Darling, also an ambulatory patient, or a *permissionaire* from the front. We consumed quantities of *gelato* and sherry flips and sipped buckets of *café latte frappé* at such cozy spots as Cova's or Biffi's or at the lesser cafés in Milan's great shopping center, the cool, arched Gallerìa. My stomach was behaving well and my color had returned to normal. Once a group of us went to the races at the suburban track at San Siro, as Ernie would do when he was well enough. As Agnes would write to her mother in Washington, "It's great fun—there are so few amusements here." Another time I inspected the aerodrome at Taliedo, with its squadrons of fighter planes and bombers, courtesy of the volubly pro-American *commandante*. I was rapidly getting in form for my anticipated date with Agnes.

About this time a significant event took place for Americans and Italians alike. Because of the extreme need for troops on the Western front that spring and summer, American forces were disappointingly slow in reaching Italy; but on July 27–28, the 332nd U.S. Infantry Regiment, formed largely of Ohioans, many of them tall, bronzed sharpshooters, arrived in Milan from France to be deployed ultimately in the area around Treviso. It was only a token representation but the propaganda value was enormous: welcoming crowds lined the streets, vociferously cheering the star-spangled banner, while the *manifesti* rained down on the Austrian lines advertising the U.S. presence. The regiment's real mission (it was the only American fighting unit, aside from some aviators, to get to Italy before the war's end) was similar to that of the Red Cross: namely, to build up Italian morale and correspondingly dismay the Austrians. When its thin battalions finally did get to the battle area late in the summer they set out to give the impression of being more than one regiment, appearing each morning on different roads, wearing different uniforms and equipment, slipping back to their base as quietly as possible after nightfall. Coupled with brightening news from France (the Aisne-Marne offensive had been stopped cold and reduction of the Amiens salient by French, British, and U.S. troops under General Haig was in progress) were reports that Americans were turning into seasoned warriors, their morale relatively high, and that they were doing well because they were convinced their cause against German "frightfulness" was a righteous one. Yet hard fighting was still ahead; notwithstanding the lift to our spirits, no one in our hospital talk-fests ventured to predict that the end was anywhere in view.

When at last I found the courage to ask Aggie for a date, I was not aware that, in conformity with Italian custom, the Red Cross frowned on unchaperoned social contact between the sexes. After all, a precedent had been set by one of the habitual callers at the hospital, Captain Enrico Serena, of the hard-fighting, courageous Alpini troops, who with his blond hair and patch over one eye was to be the unwitting prototype of Captain Rinaldi, the surgeon in *A Farewell to Arms*. Agnes had accepted a dinner invitation from him for the evening of August 10, the same date as Hem's second operation, and nobody had mentioned a chaperone. As I discovered later (my imagination hadn't run that far), Serena had engaged a private dining room, complete with couch and piano; but, as the story went, Agnes had managed to squelch the Captain's ardor by insisting that she had to report back for duty by midnight. She did not try to go out alone with a man again.

My chance came sooner than expected. Shopping in the Gallerìa nearby, my uniform neatly pressed and my overseas cap cocked at a rakish angle, I ran across Agnes and her closest companion in tow, the good-natured Elsie MacDonald, whose counterpart was to be "Fergy" in *Farewell*. On the spur of the moment I proposed a carriage drive in the public gardens, followed by dinner. Ag made it plain that since her date with Serena "we have to travel in pairs, you know."

Not that I didn't enjoy Mac's company, but well, three is a crowd. I swallowed my disappointment and wedged myself between them for a leisurely ride in an open one-horse carriage, the driver up ahead with his varnished hat brandishing a whip; when it was over I took them to dinner at the Hotel Manin, a centrally located hostelry on the street of the same name, where the food and the Asti Spumante were better than average. It was more than a pleasant evening, away from the hospital atmosphere, though hardly what I had dreamed of. I tried to play the impartial host but caught myself listening chiefly to Aggie's musical voice, sensing the merriment in her eyes

*Agnes von Kurowsky and Henry S. Villard on their only date, Milan, 1918.*

at my discomfiture that we were not alone, and responding to her ready smile. It was an evening the memory of which I would treasure for the rest of the war.

Late in August, I was granted a short convalescent leave and spent it at the picture-postcard resort of Rapallo, on the coast south of Genoa, an ideal change of scene. From the terrace of the Kursaal Hotel there was nothing to remind one of war except a squadron of noisy flying boats that patrolled the adjacent waters. There was swimming off the rocks, there were English *permissionaires* to talk with, an English-speaking contessa to dance with to an unreal background of music, moonlight, and roses, the ancient harbor, the sea, and the mountains veiled in midnight mist. And always, after dinner with friends, there would be a cherry brandy and a crème-de-menthe to complement the miniature port and starboard lights of the vessels maneuvering offshore.

I stopped off in Genoa on the way back to inspect an assembly plant for U.S. Army ambulances, a reminder of what was to come. It made me wonder how much longer our volunteer Red Cross units would be needed. In my absence, the hospital on the Via Cesare Cantù had become engaged in the "vigorous activity" for which it had been intended with the advent of American troops. There wasn't a spare bed, and I found I would have to sleep under the stars on a mattress laid out on the terrace.

The first thing I did was to pay my respects to Ernie. He seemed to be in the same general state of incapacity as when I had left, but the broad grin and cheerful frame of mind were there as usual. It wouldn't be long before they would measure him for crutches. What was Rapallo like? What about it as a place to recuperate? Had I met any snappy-looking dames? Was there any interest in the war down there? I told him about the seaplane base, the ambulance camp near Genoa, the sociable evenings on the Kursaal terrace. "Maybe I should go there when I get out of here, Harry." I had the impression he was more enamored of Aggie than ever, but I couldn't tell how she felt; with the influx of new arrivals there was no time for her to talk with me.

On the morning of the second day Dr. Sabatini pronounced me cured, fit to resume my duties at the front. I went into Ernie's room again to say goodbye. It would be almost exactly a month later that I was to hear he had chosen for *his* convalescent leave not Rapallo but Stresa on Lake Maggiore, where the luxurious Grand Hotel would one day supply part of the background for the second half of *Farewell*. We exchanged a few jokes; our laughter was a bit forced, as it is with newfound friends uncertain whether fate will ever bring them together again. It was time to start back for Bassano and Section 1. We toasted each other with that vulgar Italian ode to man's pleasures in life, the words redolent of army slang:

> Acqua pura, vino fresco
> Bella fica, cazzo duro.[7]

Then we shook hands and wished each other luck, hoping we would meet *dopo la guerra*. That, however, was not in the cards. It was the last time I was to see Ernest Hemingway, and years would roll by before I saw Agnes again.

In spring of 1962 I was tracked down at my home in Switzerland by Carlos Baker, who was beginning his definitive biography of Hemingway. He had learned of my wartime association with the Red Cross and asked to be supplied with such details as I could remember. In turn I asked him if he knew whatever had become of Agnes, and he responded by sending me her address in Key West, where she was living with her husband, a retired hotel manager named William C. Stanfield, Jr. I decided then and there to try to bridge the formidable gap in time by writing her a letter, enclosing a few snapshots from those long-gone days, including one taken of us together on our carriage drive in the park before dinner.

"What a delightful surprise to hear from you after so many years," she replied warmly.

> My, Italy and the First World War seem so far away, and there have been so many changes since, that I can't understand how you even remembered me. And the pictures were a big help— there were so many nice boys in our Milan hospital. . . . We came here in 1951, and at first were just here for the winter, as my husband was operating a hotel in Virginia Beach at the time. At first we thought we were "retired," but, first Bill got busy helping a friend of his out, and I—in a reckless moment— volunteered to help at the new Public Library here 2 years and more ago, and found myself on the payroll ever since, as cataloger.

I had asked what happened to her after the war, whether she had stayed with the Red Cross or ever seen the now celebrated Hemingway again. Let her tell it in her own words:

> The year after my return from Italy, I joined up again in the Red Cross, and was sent to Roumania; spent nearly 2 years there, doing visiting nursing, and Junior Red Cross work. Then, after a few years in N.Y., I again asked for assignment, and the Red

Cross sent me to Haiti, where I spent 5 years, and was married
to an American in the Financial Adviser's Office.[8]

That marriage hadn't worked out. She offered no reason or details, no
explanation, merely that she had "gone to Reno" after the termination
of her Haitian assignment and return to America. Obviously, she preferred not to expand on that experience.

Much later, I found out that the name of her first husband was
Howard Preston Garner, familiarly known as "Pete." Born in Georgia, Garner had served as an American delegate on various claims
commissions in Europe. He had become acquainted with Agnes on a
Haiti-bound steamer while she was rejoining her post after a vacation
in the United States. They were married on November 24, 1928. The
following day an announcement in the *Washington Post* said the
ceremony had been performed by the Bishop of Haiti in the Episcopal
Church at Port-au-Prince, and on November 26 Agnes addressed an
"unofficial and personal" letter to Miss Clara B. Noyes, Director of
the Red Cross Nursing Service, "to relay my most recent news and
hope you will approve of it."

> With Dr. Melhorn's[9] full consent and approval I was married on
> the 24th to Mr. H. P. Garner who is now a civilian member of
> the American Occupation Force here attached to the financial
> adviser's office as auditor. We are both avoiders of publicity so it
> was not generally announced and the wedding was as quiet as
> could be done in Haiti, for it to be officially recognized there
> must be a civilian wedding, or a council present, and a religious
> wedding. Dr. Melhorn gave me away.

Miss Noyes replied on December 5, expressing great surprise: "While
some years ago I should probably have regarded it as not quite the
proper thing for a nurse to marry while holding a nursing job, times
have changed and our attitudes toward such matters have undergone
a complete adjustment, consequently I am sending you my blessings
and best wishes that you will be very happy."

Despite the failure of her marriage, Agnes won high marks for her work in Haiti from Dr. Lucius Johnson, administrator of the Haitian General Hospital, where from 1926 to 1931 she was director of nurses, in charge of all the nurses in the hospitals of the country's Public Health Service. This is what he had to say about her services, in a testimonial as much to her character as to her proficiency as a nurse:

> During that time there has been almost constant political and anti-American propaganda and efforts to break down the organization that she has built. In spite of this, she has held the Training School together and has consistently raised its standards. She has retained the liking and respect of all her associates, no matter what their race, color or political affiliations. She has displayed unusual diplomatic ability in harmonizing antagonistic personalities and getting them to work together. It is hard to imagine a more difficult position than hers has been. Her success in it has been conspicuous.
>
> We greatly regret her departure and take pleasure in recommending her for either administrative or nursing positions.

From all accounts, it could have been no easy post to fill. Agnes never talked about the difficulties, though in correspondence with the Red Cross late in 1927 she admitted to a "terrific depression" following a bout with that dangerous and debilitating tropical disease, dengue fever.

Agnes's letter continued, filling me in on what I wanted to know about her life after she left Pete Garner and Haiti:

> Then more institutional work around N.Y., and in 1934 I married a widower [William Stanfield] with 3 children. This has turned out very well. The children were all grown up and married and have children of their own.
>
> When the Second World War came along, my husband and stepson joined the Navy, and the two girls and I went to New York City, where I took a refresher course, and then worked at the Red Cross Blood Bank on Fifth Avenue. When Bill came back after the War, he wanted to live in Virginia, so we moved to

Virginia Beach, and then later to Key West. Here we feel we live in the ideal climate for old folks—never have any frost and it doesn't get as hot as it used to in parts of Virginia.

I never saw Ernest Hemingway after he left Italy. When we went over to Cuba a few times from here, I was told he drank so heavily, that I did not feel like looking him up. Since I have met his wife, Mary, I am rather sorry now, that I didn't see him again. . . . [She] came down to clear out a store of old papers, books, and souvenirs that Ernest had collected and stored in a saloon—Sloppy Joe's. She called me up, and we saw her several times, and I found her delightful and so friendly. She even sent our library a set of her husband's books. Among the photos I gave her was one of a group at the hospital in Milan, and that is the only one I regret not holding on to, as it showed many of that group of people that you and I knew. So many have gone—Elsie Macdonald, Ruth Brooks, Miss de Long, Loretta Cavanagh, and I suppose many more that I did not hear of after I left Italy. . . . By the way, Mary turned over 3 of my old letters to Ernest written from Italy, which she found when sorting out his collection. Imagine keeping them so long!

I had wondered if people were beating a path to her door, now that she had appeared in a book about Hemingway by his brother, Leicester. "Don't know about anybody else beating a path to my door," she commented, "as I've kept quiet about all our War experiences, and so far, nobody has recognized my picture in Les Hemingway's book. Of course, folks down here never heard my maiden name anyhow."

After Ernest's death, Leicester had come to see her several times, and she had given him "a few pictures." She had given all her "snapshots with Hemingway in them to a friend of his here before he died, thinking he would like to have them," and she "had heard he had lost all his photos of the war in Italy." "Well," she added, "it seems that brother Leicester is persona non grata with the rest of the family, so he was only allowed to use a few of them in his book. . . . Forgive my delay in replying," she concluded. "I seem to have a complex about letters. Funny, too, as I used to be quite a letter writer. I think it's because I haven't much to write about nowadays."

That satisfied my curiosity and brought me up to date. Still, a lot of questions remained. How did her relationship with Hemingway come to an end? What was her impression of *A Farewell to Arms*, published more than a decade after the events it described had taken place? I had read it, with an interest born of shared experience, while serving as vice-consul at Teheran, in what was then Persia. How did she feel about the common assumption that she was the model for Catherine Barkley of the novel? The answers would have to wait until we could talk over those days in person.

"Do you ever come back to the States?" she had inquired in the course of a sporadic correspondence over the ensuing years, implying that I would be welcome if I should call. Eventually, I was able to plan a trip to Florida for the winter of 1976. "Please forgive my slow reply to your nice letter," she wrote on September 21, 1975, from a new home at Gulfport, near St. Petersburg. "Truth is that I've slowed down lots since I last saw you. I did some digging and found a few old letters, but, it became too long for a letter. Would it be possible to give it all to you when you look us up this winter. . . . I certainly hope you go ahead . . . and look us up here. I am really looking forward to that."

Life seemed to have come full circle when she answered my ring at her apartment early one Florida afternoon the following March. More than half a century had elapsed since the night we had met at the hospital door in Milan, and it would be fatuous to pretend that we hadn't both changed. Alas, Agnes at eighty-four was no longer the blithe spirit her patients had known. Not in the best of health, she was nonetheless tall and straight as ever and the old charm came through as she ushered me into the parlor of the comfortable Stanfield home. Bill, her staunch, considerate husband, let us spend the rest of the day undisturbed and the years dissolved in a flood of reminiscences.

Of course, the talk turned quickly to Hemingway and the hospital, as it inevitably would between two veterans of that tight little world apart on the Via Cesare Cantù. Our discussion was frank and to the point. Ernest had been very serious about wanting to marry her, no doubt about that; he had done his best to persuade her. She, on the other hand, had "liked" him without being "in love" with him;

she had found him "interesting" but he was "impulsive, hasty, not to say impetuous." "He didn't really know what he wanted." He "hadn't thought out anything clearly." In short, he was just too young and immature for a girl seven years older, as she was, to fall truly in love with him. She had been afraid that he was going to turn into an aimless wanderer after the war, an expatriate, without roots, as he had shown signs of doing. She had put him off, advising him, perhaps in the manner of an older sister, to return to America after hostilities ended. He had departed in January 1919, and when she ultimately broke with him that spring she had simply "put him out of" her mind. Admittedly, they had had what she chose to call a "flirtation," but the relationship, she said firmly, had never gone beyond that. I had no reason to think otherwise, knowing her as I did.

But, Agnes confessed, there was another reason for her cooling off. She had become enamored of an irresistibly attractive Italian artillery officer, Domenico Caracciolo, scion of an old Neapolitan family, jealous to a fault. He had forced her to burn all of Hemingway's letters. "I was pretty fickle in those days," she said quizzically, and I remembered that she was reported to have been involved with a doctor in New York whom she had dropped abruptly after leaving for Italy. She was convinced that Domenico's intentions were "completely sincere," that if it hadn't been for his mother they would "most certainly" have been married. But the mother was strenuously opposed to letting the friendship of her son for an unknown American girl, probably an adventuress, turn into an engagement. The last time she had seen him they had passed her in a carriage in Naples: he had stood up and looked back and she would never forget the expression in his eyes. There was no such sentiment in her recollection of Hemingway.

As for her reaction to *Farewell*, one thing was clear: Agnes thoroughly resented being taken for "the alter ego of the complaisant Catherine Barkley" and thus indirectly the mistress of the man who wrote the book. I thought of a passage from the novel:

> "Is there anything I do you don't like? Can I do anything to please you? Would you like me to take down my hair? Do you want to play?"

"Yes and come to bed."
"All right. I'll go and see the patients first" [p. 121].

"Let's get it straight—please," she insisted. "I wasn't *that* kind of girl." So strongly did she object to the insinuation that she and Ernest were lovers in the fullest sense of the word, that she and her husband had decided to move away from Key West, where the tourist guide at Hemingway's former home, turned into a museum in 1962, persisted in referring to her as "Hemingway's girl." Catherine was "an arrant fantasy" created by the writer in the same way he had produced a "macho" image of himself as the virile, resourceful ambulance driver, Frederic Henry. "Ernest never conceived the story while he was in the hospital," she went on. "He was much too busy enjoying the attention of friends and well-wishers to think about the plot of a novel; he invented the myth years later—built out of his frustration in love. The liaison was all made up out of whole cloth," wishful thinking, if you will. Never, in all her experience, had she heard it suggested that an affair of this kind could run its course in a bedridden patient's quarters. "It was totally implausible," and in this I could well concur, given the restricted logistics of the Ospedale Americana. Surely, no more improbable environment could have been devised for a clandestine love affair that culminated in the woman's pregnancy than the two upper floors of a building converted into sanitized, vigilantly supervised hospital premises by the American Red Cross.

On the other hand, the borderline between fact and fiction can be a thin one and fleeting moments for a "flirtation" certainly were there, after hours, for example, when the other patients were asleep and Aggie could pay more visits to Ernie's room than were strictly necessary. By her own admission, she did not mind night duty:

> She looked toward the door, saw there was no one, then she sat on the side of the bed and leaned over and kissed me. I pulled her down and kissed her and felt her heart beating. . . .
> "You mustn't," she said. "You're not well enough."
> "Yes, I am. Come on."
> "No. You're not strong enough."

"Yes. I am. Yes. Please."

"You do love me?"

"I really love you. I'm crazy about you. Come on please.
. . ."

"All right but only for a minute" [pp. 95–96].

I asked Agnes whether any of the patients had tried to "get fresh" with her. No, they were all "nice boys." None of them gave her trouble, with a single exception: a naval aviator, who used to ring for her in the middle of the night and order her to come close to his bed. The remedy for that was to switch on the light and turn her back on his advances.

Rather to my surprise, Agnes indulged in some disparaging remarks about Ernie. The medal of valor awarded to him by the Italian government had been won at an outpost "where he had no business to be," a place "where he had been expressly told not to go." He was "completely spoiled" at the hospital. Contrary to his oft-quoted line "there are no heroes in this war," Hemingway thought of himself in heroic terms. He "thrived on adulation" and "learned to play on the sympathy he received." As time went on and he was able to get around on crutches, "all decked out with his wound stripes and medals," he became "vainglorious." With his cane and emblazoned uniform, he was the "laughing stock" of American soldiers when he paid her a visit at Torre di Mosta near Treviso, where she had been sent to help combat the influenza epidemic: "It was just too much for them to take."

The real cause of his problems in later life, she said with conviction, lay in the way he viewed himself. Everyone at the hospital overindulged him. This completely changed his fresh, boyish character and laid the foundation for a self-centeredness that saw himself in every action and led in turn to the paranoia from which he couldn't escape at the end. From my own observation of what went on at the hospital, I couldn't help feeling that Agnes had put her finger on the underlying reason for Hemingway's behaving as he did as an adult. "It was a messy way to die," she added, shaking her head, "but what he did was understandable, considering that his mind was impaired, that his powers as a man and a writer were failing. The whole world knew that he had been undergoing psychiatric treatment."

Notwithstanding her attempt to play down the affair, there is no question in my mind that Agnes was strongly drawn to Hemingway, as her numerous extant letters attest, and that he thought, in the inexperience of youth, he was going to marry her after the war. Anyone less in love might have been more conscious of the difference in their ages, but in light of the evidence the conclusion is inescapable that she led him on, whether or not she realized what she was doing.

Ernie took his dismissal very hard. Bill Horne, who became his bosom friend and confidant, wrote me years later that "it was a tremendous blow" and resulted in Ernie's writing him "the most heartbroken, heartrending letter" Bill had ever received. To Elsie MacDonald, Hemingway wrote bitterly that he had hoped Agnes would stumble and break all her front teeth when she stepped off the boat in New York. And when the first movie version of *Farewell* appeared in 1932, starring Helen Hayes and Gary Cooper in the saccharine Hollywood manner, an angered Hemingway was said to have told a reporter for the *Arkansas Democrat*: "I did not intend a happy ending." To an impressionable young man, who had never loved before, the shock of being rejected by the girl he believed was his must have been exceptionally severe and may well have conditioned his future attitude toward women.

There was one last point to discuss: just how much was Hemingway influenced by his remembrance of her in composing the imaginary person of Catherine? Agnes was reluctant to speak of herself in this connection. She had informed the Red Cross of her own belief that a tall, blond nurse named Elsie Jessup, who had been with her on duty in Florence and who subsequently went to Milan, was the pattern for much of the characterization of Catherine. But I had no doubt that the major contribution was that made by Agnes herself. Agnes might not have been her precise counterpart, but without Agnes there would have been no Catherine. In no other work did Hemingway describe his heroine in terms of such passionate tenderness; so many of his women appear tough or cynical in comparison. There is not one iota of cynicism in the story of Catherine; surely, the tale had its wellspring in something wholly unfeigned by the writer. And the fact that Ernie had in his possession three of her letters until the day of his death showed that he had not forgotten.

Agnes did not feel like going out in the evenings, but I took her to lunch at her favorite restaurant, the Sand Dollar, the next day. "You are a sentimental man," she said with a smile when I kissed her goodbye. Yet it could only have been for sentiment's sake that she presented me with her passport picture and some photographs of herself torn from a battered album. [10]

We kept in touch, regularly exchanging cards at Christmas. Nor was sentiment lacking in some of the greetings she chose: "When thoughts go wandering, / The best thing they can do, / Is take a sentimental journey, / Across the miles to you." "I am still around," she appended to her last message, "tho' very lazy and not able to be very active. Hope you are in good shape."

Then one day came a letter signed by both Agnes and Bill. Her advancing years had led Agnes to apply for eventual interment in the Soldiers' Home National Cemetery at Washington, D.C., in the same plot as her distinguished grandparent Quartermaster General Holabird, her grandmother, and her parents. The regulations were inflexible: permission would not be granted. A plea that exception be made was mired in a mass of bureaucratic red tape. Could I, as a retired ambassador of the United States, be of any possible assistance? I did not see how I could exert any influence, but I made as strong a case as I could in her behalf, stressing her wartime patriotism in volunteering for duty overseas. In January of 1983 I was rewarded by word from Lt. General George H. McKee, President of the Board of Commissioners of the United States Soldiers' and Airmens' Home, that after "careful, thorough and compassionate consideration," and in keeping with her "exemplary dedication to the nation," the Board had finally approved her request. What is more, it had extended the authority to her spouse as well. "Your efforts . . . paid off handsomely," wrote a delighted couple, and again in June of 1984, "we shall always be grateful."

Agnes's memory was fast failing, but she was "hanging on" without pain or medication. Bill had hopes she would make it to her ninety-third birthday. It was not to be. By September, she "was living in another world." She had forgotten everything about herself, her travels, and her surroundings. Her final two months were spent in the Gulfport Convalescent Home with a broken pelvis; in her husband's words, "she left this world easy and without . . . long suffering" on November 25, 1984. A six-man marine guard rendered honors at the funeral ceremony in accordance with what the Board of Commissioners called "her gallant and commendable services" with the American Red Cross in Italy during the First World War. I expect that Hemingway would have joined in the tribute.

# TWO

· · ·

# *The Diary of*
# *Agnes von Kurowsky*

INTRODUCTION BY HENRY S. VILLARD

The wartime diary of Agnes von Kurowsky, the existence of which was known to no one, perhaps not even to her husband, is a cloth-bound volume purchased in Italy labeled AGENDA 1918, with a calendar listing the saints as frontispiece and at the back a space (untouched) for monthly accounts. Frayed and stained, it shows the ravages of time; nevertheless, its pages retain to a remarkable degree the clarity of their finely handwritten contents. Two days to a page, the account now and then overlaps into a running narrative rather than a chronicle of events on the exact dates they occurred, giving the impression of a continuous story.

The picture that emerges is that of a young woman in quest of adventure, keenly interested in people and the world around her, with an unfailing sense of humor and a readiness to have fun; a woman who discovers that she is attractive to men and enjoys their company yet gives none of herself away until her attachment to Hemingway begins. She does not like being lonely; she is susceptible to the romance of Italy, to the "moon, soft music," and wine; she admits to being confused emotionally and she is conscience-stricken about her lack of feeling for the doctor she had been going with in New York. Against the details of hospital routine, including the harrowing loss of a patient, her devotion to duty stands in clear outline. Whatever the extent of her relationship with the wounded ambulance driver she fondly calls "The Kid," it never takes precedence over the work for which she volunteered to go overseas.[1] Interestingly, even while her affection for Ernie grows apace over the weeks, Agnes never confides the word "love" to the diary, candid though private journals of this nature are supposed to be.

The circumstances that led to the discovery of the diary begin with a letter R. J. Costanzo wrote to Agnes's husband, Bill Stanfield: "I regret to advise that current National Cemetery regulations will not permit your wife's interment at Soldiers Home National Cemetery with her parents and grandparents. I am sorry that my response to your request could not be favorable. The regulations for burial or inurnment in Army National Cemeteries are firm. I have no discretionary authority in the matter." Jurisdiction, it subsequently developed, lay elsewhere, with the Board of Commissioners, U.S. Soldiers' and Airmen's Home. When I added what weight I could to the Stanfields' appeal, nearly two years later, I had no idea what it would bring in return.

When the Board reversed the initial ruling, Bill and Agnes were effusive in their gratitude. "By this time you have received the good news," wrote Bill on January 24, 1983. "Very deeply we both thank you for your great deciding help"; and a few weeks later, on February 17, "due to you everything turned out so well." Agnes left no family or descendents, and after her death, well aware of the bond between us that had been forged in the Great War so long ago, Bill decided to forward all her letters and memorabilia to me. "Do whatever you like with this material," which included the 1918 diary, "as I do not want to destroy anything. Some you might send to the Kennedy Archives. Please do what you think best." Following his suggestion, I presented the lot to the John F. Kennedy Library in Boston, where it now forms part of the Hemingway Collection.

·    ·    ·

# GIUGNO [JUNE 1918]

12 MERCOLEDI                    [*Wednesday, June 12*][2]

Today Daddy[3] and Bonny had their commencement exercises, & I invited them to dinner with Betty. Owing to Bonny insisting on changing from his uniform into mufti, they were about an hour late in coming. Otherwise it was a very nice dinner—my farewell, too, as it turned out—Daddy stayed an hour after the others left, but, he left me with a bad impression of him for my last, I'm sorry to say.

· · ·

13 GIOVEDI                         [*Thursday, June 13*]

Daddy started for Watch Hill in the machine with his cousin & I threatened to sail while he was gone if he insisted on staying until Sun. He said he'd come back if there was any danger of my going while he was away.

I am dreadfully lonely, & restless. This waiting is certainly getting on my nerves.

· · ·

14 VENERDI                         [*Friday, June 14*]

At 11.30 A.M. just when I was getting up, the phone rang, & the man at the Red Cross told me I was to sail the next morning at 9— A.M. I spent a lively day, getting my steamer ticket, saying goodbye to Betty, Miss Brink, & all, & wound up by making a lemon meringue pie before I even began to pack. So, of course, I didn't finish until about 1 A.M. & then couldn't sleep from excitement.

· · ·

15 SABATO                          [*Saturday, June 15*]

Up with the dawn. Miss Lockhove gave me a wonderful breakfast for my last in the U.S. of bacon & eggs. After I got through having my baggage exam. I & the 8 other nurses & 1 aid went on board & settled in our cabins. All of the Red Cross party are travelling 2nd class, but what difference does that make? We had a farce of a line drill at 4 P.M. & sailed—or rather steamed away from N.Y. about 6—P.M.[4]

. . .

16 DOMENICA                    [*Sunday, June 16*]

It's very hard to believe I've gone at last—& that it's Sunday & Daddy will come back tonight & find me gone. I can't help saying "It serves him right"—& that is wrong of me. We are having lovely weather, except at night when we have to sleep with portholes closed. I'll never forget last night, & Miss Gallegher—a Chicago girl who has the bunk under me. It was so close to mine she couldn't breathe, & she kept us laughing at her antics until after 11.30 P.M.

. . .

17 LUNEDI                      [*Monday, June 17*]

We are beginning to get used to the meals. The bread, with butter— is dark & sour & served in large hunks. But, our appetites are equal to anything. All sorts of French & Italian classes started today. I began energetically in the A.M. but, alas, in the P.M. I got very drowsy & slept all afternoon. I am very much taken with a French girl in the cabin across from ours. She has been teaching French in Amer. for some years, & speaks very good English. Her corner of the deck is swarming with fascinating French officers & Belgians. These Belgians have been fighting in Russia for 4 years & are going home by way of Siberia & Amer. They are such wonderful men—covered with medals. After staying in M'mselle's corner all A.M. & talking to these French people, I decided I'd get on better with my French if I enjoyed myself & played with these people than if I went to classes all day.— so—an end to classes.

*Agnes von Kurowsky in Milan, 1918. Photograph from her scrapbook.*

19 MERCOLEDI                                   [*Wednesday, June 19*]

One Belgian, Adjutant Collins, has been very kind in teaching me French. His English is worse than my French, so I must talk in French to make any conversation at all. He is very musical & plays the piano beautifully—also composes. M'mselle Fallot says he is not like the others—that he is serious. He tells me he has never talked to a girl as much as he has to me. I'm afraid I'm forgetting Daddy already.

.    .    .

20 GIOVEDI                                       [*Thursday, June 20*]

These Belgians make me feel so sad. M'mselle Fallot & I listen to their tales, & it makes us both très triste. The other nurses are jealous of me for deserting their crowd which is very slow so I have induced Miss Bean & Miss Sleicher to join us when we play games with the French & Belgians. They play just like children—with all their hearts—& it is such fun. Especially M. Courcelle. He is married & told me had had no news from or of his wife for 4 yrs. & she was in Germany. He made me feel so sorry for him.

.    .    .

21 VENERDI                                        [*Friday, June 21*]

Today was the inevitable ship's concert but, we have notables on board. Walter Damrosch—the Princeton quartette, & M. Cloesen, the Belgian who sings, & M. Collins. Mr. Perrin, a French Canadian in the Y.M.C.A. wrote a song called 'Soldats de Lafayette' which M. Collins arranged for piano & they all sang with great gusto—especially M. Perrin, who simply yelled & marked time, until M'mselle & I almost cried with ecstasy. I gave an imitation after.

22 SABATO                                    [*Saturday, June 22*]

The end of our charming trip is very near, & everyone seems a little sad, though we played as heartily as ever. M'mselle Fallot lectures me all the time on the subject of M. Collins, telling me not to break his heart as he is too nice. I have no intention of doing so as these men are too near to death all the time, to make one feel like fooling them. M. Rigaud, a French interpreter with the American Army is certainly devoted to M'mselle & he and I are great friends. He is simply brimming over with spirits & life. & his gaiety is very contagious.

·   ·   ·

23 DOMENICA                                    [*Sunday, June 23*]

Mmselle is worrying for fear I'll forget her. I am fascinated by her so it is not likely. When I take to anyone as I have to her, I never forget them. M. Collins is giving me "souvenirs" every day, & looks very sad when he speaks of tomorrow. He got hurt because Mmselle & I walked about after dark without asking him—so I did not see him until 10.30. I was so sad & lonely *before*. At 12 I had to go to my cabin, but how I hated to!

·   ·   ·

24 LUNEDI                                    [*Monday, June 24*]

A horrible day for me! The Customs & Police officials came on board, & I went through the 3rd degree with my passport[5]—to the evident amusement of a terrible man—Spaniard, I think, who conducted the torture. Then at about 8 P.M. we landed at Bordeaux, & said goodbye to my dear French & Belgian friends. They all call me "Belle Ange." I hope I see them again—but war times are so uncertain. Then at 10—the night train to Paris! M. Carton & M. Collins dashed down to the train to see me off & promised to see me in Paris in 3 days.[6]

25 MARTEDI                                    [*Tuesday, June 25*]

Arrived in Paris about 9.30 A.M. & we were met by a R.C. representative & busses. Miss Brooks, our lovely chaperone, Miss Bean, Sleicher & I went to Hotel Internationale, & the others to the R.C. Nurses pension—Galilee. Both are near the Rue Champs Elysee & Arch of Triumph. Paris is simply beyond description. I adore it & hope we stay here. Alas, Miss Sparrow & I must leave tomorrow night with the Canteen workers who go to Rome. I am too disappointed for words. No more M. Collins, & must leave these girls I have grown to like so much. We had to go to the Provost Marshalls & the U.S. Passport Agency, & the Prefeture [Préfecture] of Police before our papers were O.K. to leave Paris, which was put in the war zone yesterday. They are expecting a bombardment anytime. Miss S. & I with 5 women & 3 men going to Rome left the Gare de Lyon at 8.45 P.M. for another lovely night sitting up on the train.

.    .    .

27 GIOVEDI                                   [*Thursday, June 27*]

The scenery on the way to Modane is simply enchanting. All waterfalls, lofty snow-capped peaks, & quantities of wild flowers. At Modane, Miss S. & I first left our party, for a separate compartment, & finally parted at Turin. At Milano, Miss De Long & Cavie, met us, to our great relief & delight, as we arrived at 11.20 P.M. & did not know whether we would be met or not. They left us at the Hotel Manin, & we dropped into real beds for a good rest. In the P.M. Miss MacDonald and Miss Fischer, 2 of the nurses, called & took us to the Amer. Red Cross Hospital which has just opened. It is charming, & I am simply crazy to get to work in it. They have 1 patient, an Amer. ambulance chap.[7] I wish they would make room for us, so that we could be with them as soon as possible. It seems just like a bit of home to with Miss De Long, Miss MacDonald & Cavie.

29 SABATO                          [*Saturday, June 29*]

I was so tired I slept until almost 10. Then after our chocolate, Miss S. & I went in search of the Police place where we were supposed to register. After waving our passports at several places, we were finally escorted to the proper place, where, thank goodness, the man spoke French.[8] In the afternoon I dropped asleep again until 4, when we went on a tour of discovery, spent an unknown sum of money on foolishness, & had a wonderful time.

·  ·  ·

30 DOMENICA                        [*Sunday, June 30*]

A most wonderful day! Miss Sparrow & I rode with Major Hereford, & Capts. Bywater & Moore to Luino on Lake Maggiore, where they had a banquet for us, and flowers were showered on us from all sides. We had to lead a parade with a band—all over the town. Then to a grandstand, where several fiery speeches were made. 1 by the nephew of Garibaldi, who gave me a carnation, & a tribute with his signature, and one by a remarkable young Italian Capt. Enrico Serena,[9] blind in one eye and walks with a limp, but simply full of personality, and attractive in spite of his disfigurement. Then we all visited the Hospital and met some sweet Italian nurses, whom we talked with in French. Then we started home—taking with us Mr. Garibaldi and Capt. Serena, both of whom dined with us at Lake Como. We had a delightful dinner out of doors right close to the lake shore. The Capt. fascinated me, and was so bright. He spoke English & French besides his own tongue. On the way home the Major & I sang "Smile, Smile, Smile" & "Long, long trail" & the 2 Italians cried "Bellissima."

·  ·  ·

LUGLIO [JULY]

1 LUNEDI                           [*Monday, July 1*]

Exhausted after such a strenuous Sunday. We got our expenditures reimbursed by R.C. also our salary. I rec'd 883 lire altogether, & my pockets were sagging. Then we registered with the police—(Questura) and went to the Porte Garibaldi and got meal tickets—tessere. Miss Shaw came back, & we saw her at the Hospital, & were invited to dinner at the Hotel Du Nord[10] at 8 P.M. with Miss Jessup. After which we all went to visit the R.C. Rest house for soldiers at the station.

.   .   .

2 MARTEDI                                    [*Tuesday, July 2*]

We ordered our dress white uniforms today & had such fun finding the stores & buying the goods. It is surprising how well we can get along without understanding the language. Brooksie arrived from Rome today, & she & I had a wonderful evening exchanging romances & experiences. Of course she has much more romance to tell than I have, as she always was inclined to draw romance to her, and I have only lately broken out.

.   .   .

3 MERCOLEDI                                  [*Wednesday, July 3*]

A busy day, but uneventful. I went shopping with Brooksie and we had great fun in our attempts. I got white shoes, a Panama hat, & 2 uniforms to prepare for the granda festa Americana tomorrow. Brooksie is a worse heart-smasher than ever, I believe, & I am becoming degenerate in that respect. This cutting loose from home ties may not be the best thing for one in some ways.

.   .   .

4 GIOVEDI                                    [*Thursday, July 4*]

8 of us—Misses De Long, MacDonald, Strickler, Fischer, Sparrow, Mrs. Heilman, Brooksie & I, all dolled up in white from head to feet, went to the Conseratoria [sic] dell Musica to see Maj. MacDonald get his medals. As soon as we entered the crowd broke into applause &

"Vive l'Americanos." It is certainly warranted to make one prouder than ever of being American. We all dined at the Du Nord, and then went to the Duomo square, where they had a huge demonstration, & such crowds & 5 bands all playing together. This was a great 4th, & the Italians made it so in our honor. I shall not soon forget.

.  .  .

5 VENERDI                                              [*Friday, July 5*]

Brooksie & I went to lunch with Lts. Warehouser & Robinson[,] U.S aviators whom we saw the night before at the Duomo. We were joined by another Lt. Lambert & had a very nice lunch. I also saw my Italian Capt. in the Galleria.[11] Then we went to movies, & drove about hunting for the Victrola store. After we went back to the Hospital & danced. Lt. Landon (whom I liked very much) & another came with the others & they seemed to enjoy it. Miss De Long was ill all day.

.  .  .

6 SABATO                                              [*Saturday, July 6*]

To Como today, so will have to write when I return.—Such a beginning to a wonderful trip! Miss Strickler & Mrs. Heilman went with us as far as Como, & we had a great argument there as to where we would go. Finally Brooks and I settled it, by taking rooms at the Hotel Metropole where we dined last Sun. for us 2 & Cavie. Then they went on up the lake with a man they met on the train. We had tea & then took the funiculare to Brumate, where we bought olive wood souvenirs, admired the view, & had a delicious dinner. Coming down, we enjoyed the sensation, & all were reminded of Coney Island. Near the hotel we found a very nice young boatman who offered to row us, & we went out on the lake for an hour. It was too lovely & romantic for words, & we forgot there was such a thing as war near us.

Then when we got back to the hotel, we certainly put down a piece of sleeping.

7 DOMENICA                                    [*Sunday, July* 7]

Cavie arose early & went to church, & Brooksie & I strolled by to see the beautifully carved old Duomo, & then fell prey to an antique jewelry shop. We almost lost our boat in consequence. Finally, however, we all got settled on board & started up the lake about 11.

We took photos unhindered of the lovely villas, & quaint spots we stopped at, & finally got off at Belaggio, which Brooksie picked as a place she'd heard a great deal about. Well—there was only 1 hotel, & that was not anything to brag of, but we had a good lunch & a bottle of white wine. The people in the outer dining room seemed a very rough sort. Then we wandered on, the sun getting hotter & hotter, & finally stopped & rested on the grass at a wonderful old church. When we got back to Belaggio, we bought a lot of satin wood souvenirs & postals. On the boat coming back we met Mrs. H. [Heilman] & Miss S. [Shaw] but they got off at Luino. We got back about 9.30 & had a big dinner, & then another row on the lake. I seem to have mentioned the meals most particularly on this trip but we were always so hungry that we ate & enjoyed them hugely.

.     .     .

8 LUNEDI                                       [*Monday, July* 8]

We got back to Milan this A.M. at 11. After lunch Miss MacDonald phoned to say I was to go on day duty at the Ospedale Maggiore with an English lieutenant in A.R.C. who was hurt quite badly in a train accident Sun. Miss Sparrow went on Sun. night, so now we are both busy. He is asleep or stupid most of the time, but I enjoyed trying to talk Italian with the sisters & the nurses, so it was a profitable day. I spent 2 hours hunting for the right hospital, & went to 3 before I got there. Some day!

.     .     .

9 MARTEDI                                      [*Tuesday, July* 9]

On duty at 8 A.M. & mighty glad to be working once more.

They moved my patient, & of course, me, too, to another padiglione—where the officers are. The first person I saw on the floor I am now on is my Italian Capt. of Luino [Serena]. Talk about Fate! He presented me with a letter he wrote me last week, the cutest letter in English asking if he might see me again. All the nurses here were lovely to me & most of them spoke Eng. Signorina Esengrini brought me home tonight in her carriage.

.　.　.

10 MERCOLEDI                            [*Wednesday, July 10*]

My patient seems to be improving, but, seems still very stupid, & has no memory for names or people. Capt. Serena has his one eye in my direction every time I leave my room, & I gave him an English lesson this P.M. while my patient was asleep. The nurses are lovely to me, especially Signorina Pirelli, whom I like very much. I lunched with the Capt. & 2 other officers in their room today—everybody talking with a dictionary.

.　.　.

11 GIOVEDI                              [*Thursday, July 11*]

Miss Sparrow left for Rome today, & I miss her quite a bit. I lunched again with the 3 officers. They seem to like having me & it certainly amuses me. I laugh so much at their expressions, I don't eat enough. Major Hamil from Rome, has been sev. times to see my pt. [patient], & made them do a spinal puncture today. I like his methods very much. Would like to work for him. Capt. S [Serena]—called on me at the Manin, with white gloves—green hat & a cane. I'm glad my Amer. friends didn't see him. That man is getting me scared. He gets as close as he can, & sort of drinks me in with his one eye. Lucky for me he hasn't 2, or I'd be hypnotized. And yet I feel so sorry for him, I can't be mean. He's nothing but wounds & yet as bright as can be & full to the brim with energy. Brooks came on duty tonight and seemed rather disgusted at being alone at night in a strange hospital. She's one spoiled child—& has always had her own way even in training.

13 SABATO [*Saturday, July 13*]

I do not lunch any more with the officers, as I think it is not right—and every day Capt. Serena comes for an explanation of the reason. They all make fun of him & even the Sister laughs, & yet they all like him. It's so funny, he tries to kiss my hand, & I get furious & go into my patient's room, & then my patient kisses my hand. It must be the air of Italy.

.    .    .

14 DOMENICA [*Sunday, July 14*]

The celebration of the French national holiday, & Capt. S. spoke in La Scala in the P.M. so I had quite a peaceful afternoon. At lunch, Signorina Pirelli & I were in the men's room, when he dashed in & asked for more wine so I made the Sister get a bottle of black coffee instead, & took it to him. Miss Fletcher went on duty tonight, as Brooks is going to Bologna, so the two of us went to see the doings in Piazza del Duomo, where we met Lt. Lambert—one of the aviators we lunched with last week.

.    .    .

15 LUNEDI [*Monday, July 15*]

I was dead tired this A.M. after being up so late, & walking so much last night, but I walked to the Hospital. I am getting ready tonight to move to 4 Cesare Cantu[12] tomorrow. Capt. S. asks me every day if he can call again, & I say no—for various reasons. Such an ardent suitor I thought existed only in books. He's positively silly to my Amer. mind. Signorina Esengrini gave me the loveliest bead bag this evening. People seem to be extra nice to me these days.

16 MARTEDI                                    [*Tuesday, July 16*]

Dead again, & I must pack up as I move "subito." My trip over to Cesare Cantu was the funniest thing. I felt like Rebecca of Sunnybrook Farm, as I had to carry so many parcels. I have collected a lot in the short while I've been here. Then the vettura almost collided with an auto & the drivers had words. My safe arrival was a miracle.

.   .   .

17 MERCOLEDI                                [*Wednesday, July 17*]

A letter today from Daddy & he seems to be rather lonesome. I somehow never thought he would confess it.

It is very nice being at home, or having a home to come to at night. My patient improves but very slowly. My days are long & I am trying to study a little Italian to pass the time. We walked home with the Capt.

.   .   .

18 GIOVEDI                                    [*Thursday, July 18*]

Tonight the Capt. walked home with me, & I promised to meet him later with Cavie in the Galleria. So Cavie and I, feeling like real sports started out before 10—the appointed hour—& walked through twice without seeing him—upon which we lost our nerve & sat down at a table near the center for a Gelati before we went home. Then he & Tenente Brundi, the artist, came along, & we had a nice ice & walked home. Respectable but still fun.

.   .   .

19 VENERDI                                    [*Friday, July 19*]

Nothing special to note. Mr. Rochfort talks a great deal, & keeps me busy with his questions, but I think he is better.

I sat up on the hospital balcony with the patients tonight. They are quite a cheerful bunch, at least the half-well ones. 2 are sick.

20 SABATO                                    [*Saturday, July* 20]

The Capt. walked home with me again, & came in this time. He
seemed delighted with our Hospital and took quite a fancy to Mr.
Hemingway[13]—who has the honor of being the 1st Amer. wounded
in Italy.[14] He has shrapnel in his knees, besides a great many flesh
wounds.

·    ·    ·

21 DOMENICA                                  [*Sunday, July* 21]

Mr. Hemingway's birthday,[15] so we all dressed up, & had Gelati on
the balcony & played the Victrola. Then Mr. Seely[16] brought him in a
large bottle of 5 star Cognac, & they did make merry. I simply can't
get to bed early these nights. Every night I start early, & get talking to
someone & it's 12 before I know it.

·    ·    ·

22 LUNEDI                                    [*Monday, July* 22]

This tempestuous Italian mode of wooing is certainly terrifying. He
tells me how much he loves me, & when I say but I don't love you, it
squelches him but a moment & then he begins again. And yet when
he is not talking like that I like him very well, & he sings beautifully,
a nice voice & lots of expression.

·    ·    ·

23 MARTEDI                                   [*Tuesday, July* 23]

Today, in the little dressing room where I sit when Mr. Rochfort
sleeps—Capitano did not frighten me, but he might have if I had
been far away from assistance. And yet, I can't get angry with him, as
he seems such a boy at other times.

He is going out to dine tonight & apologized sweetly for not being
able to walk home with me.

24 MERCOLEDI           [*Wednesday, July 24*]

This evening I was quite lonely, when I arrived home I found nobody, so I had to resort to the piano until Miss Shaw joined me & later on Cavie. Cavie thrills over all the tidbits of romance I tell her & it makes it more interesting to have an audience. Another letter from Daddy with a subtle air of proprietorship about it, & full of.loneliness. I feel quite guilty when I think of how little I remember him.

·   ·   ·

25 GIOVEDI           [*Thursday, July 25*]

A very tiresome day. I studied till I got a headache. Mr. R. was so restless & he talked nonsense incessantly. Again I walked home with the Capt. & he came in to call. Of course, as he & I & Cavie were going to the Park to eat Gelati & hear the music it began to pour. We waited until it stopped & then (at 11) dashed out, & found all Gelati gone. We had Grenadine in what would be a saloon in N.Y. & they began to turn the lights out, so we had to hurry. If C.J.B. could have seen us!

·   ·   ·

26 VENERDI           [*Friday, July 26*]

Today my patient seemed a good deal improved after he had a cigarette. Major Hamil & Capt. Post came to see him & I suggested his removal to our Hosp. so he is to go tomorrow.

Tonight the Capt. & Tenente Brundi came to call, & took Cavie & me to the Park, where we had Gelati, & then got quite reckless & had a little Champagne. It gave me a pain in my chest—but—otherwise nothing unusual. My Capt. grows even more ardent, & I am beginning to enjoy it, I believe.

27 SABATO                          [*Saturday, July 27*]

After all, Mr. Rochfort & I did not get over to Cesare Cantu. Too much red tape about getting out of the Italian Hospital.

I am getting very tired of being there all day, alone practically with a crazy man, with occasional visits from another crazy one. Then, too, I never get to bed nights and therefore am sleepy & hollow-eyed all day.

.    .    .

28 DOMENICA                        [*Sunday, July 28*]

Two letters tonight—1 from Daddy & 1 from my Belgian. I'm getting to feel rather confused. Here I've been practically 3 years without the least bit of sentiment or romance, & very little attention & all at once within the last few months, I have had 3 ser. [serious] affairs, and it isn't my fault either.

Its too deep for me—must be the effect of the War or Submarines.

.    .    .

29 LUNEDI                          [*Monday, July 29*]

Today, after much hustling about & excitement, we got away from Ospedale Maggiore.[17] All the nurses stood around to see me go, & were most cordial about urging me to return. After a jiggly ride in the I.R.C. amb. we arrived & I made Mr. R. [Rochfort] comfortable in a real bed. He seems to improve, & then gets off the track again.

.    .    .

30 MARTEDI                         [*Tuesday, July 30*]

Tonight I am to go on night duty, so I have the whole day off. Cavie had the P.M. and we went to a concert by mutilati at their Hospital. As usual we were very cordially welcomed.

After I went on duty who should arrive all smiles & bows but Pozzi the infirmiere of the Capt. & Ten. Brundi with packages of sugar, butter & flour for me to make a pie for them. I don't know whether it will get made or not—

⋅ ⋅ ⋅

31 MERCOLEDI                    [*Wednesday, July* 31]

Today while I was asleep, the Capt. called to say he was going to Verona for a couple of days. Cavie came in & told me, but, I didn't get up—was too sleepy. Had a very good night with nothing especially eventful. Last night I forgot to mention the wonderful sight I saw at 2 A.M. The moon shining vividly, & 6 searchlights on an aeroplane. It was a beautiful thing to see.[18]

This has been a fascinating month in some respects. I have gone pretty far in the emotional pathway. Somehow, things you read about, never seem quite the same when they become one's own experience.

Maybe these pearls of wisdom will sound like rot when I read them later, but, I know just what I mean & cannot describe it in an unhackneyed way.

⋅ ⋅ ⋅

# AGOSTO [AUGUST]

1 GIOVEDI                    [*Thursday, August* 1]

Night duty is so monotonous that I have really nothing to put down. Miss Pirelli[19] came to see me today. She is very nice, & I am sure we will be very congenial.

⋅ ⋅ ⋅

2 VENERDI                    [*Friday, August* 2]

The Capitano [Serena] & Tenente Brundi came to call after I went upstairs on duty tonight—ostensibly to call on Mr. Hemingway. The

Tenente left early—9.30, but, the Capt. left very reluctantly at 11.15. He is going to Paris in a few weeks—has a good position in a bank there. But he vows he does not want to go.

· · ·

3 SABATO                                    [*Saturday, August 3*]

I arose early this P.M. & went to meet the Capt. at 4.30 for tea—but, alas, he met me saying he was called to the Front—to take a banner to the Alpini, & make a speech. I was mean enough to say I'd never meet him again, tho' I don't know why, as it was not his fault. Females are so unaccountable in their actions sometimes—I was sorry I was so nasty after—as he said he would not enjoy his trip at all. But—

· · ·

4 DOMENICA                                  [*Sunday, August 4*]

Not feeling anything extra today, with a "cold feeling" in the middle of my stomach. Last night I had a lecture from Kid Hemingway[20] on the subject of my "meanness to the Capitano." I can't help laughing every time I think of it. In the P.M. I was quite sick, and Cavie out of the goodness of her heart, brought me a large dose of burned brandy—which I took trustingly. Really, I thought my heart was stopping 1/2 hr. later. There's no use talking, I'm not meant for alc. beverages.

· · ·

5 LUNEDI                                    [*Monday, August 5*]

Went to the Maggiore with Cavie. Everyone seemed glad to see me and it was nice to go and see them again.

Cavie was impressed by the Hospital, which is pretty up-to-date for an Italian one.

We also saw some of their new bead work, which is so beautiful. On the way home we found a very nice glove shop—beautiful hand-made gloves.

. . .

6 MARTEDI                    [*Tuesday, August 6*]

Signorina Pirelli called for me in her motor and took me to tea at the Margharita. Then we went back to my glove shop & then to her home. It is, of course, magnificent, but to me it seemed dreary & lonely. I would have been glad to see all over the house, as the rooms I did see, had beautiful things in them.

Funny the Captain has not come around yet. I wonder if he is back from the front.

. . .

7 MERCOLEDI                    [*Wednesday, August 7*]

Well tonight the Capt. showed up once more—just returned from the Front, where he was in an auto accident Mon. & barely escaped being killed. It made me rather remorseful for my treatment of him Sat. We had quite a long talk, in which he appeared to better advantage than usual. I believe there is a good deal of good in him, tho' is too accustomed to lack of self-control. Still, I'm dreadfully sorry that he cares so much.

. . .

8 GIOVEDI                    [*Thursday, August 8*]

I have asked for Sat. night off duty, having made a dinner date with the Capitano. Mr. Hemingway is devoted to that man—and they tell each other all their secrets. All my other patients are doing well. One, Lt. Darling—A.R.C. Amb. [Ambulance]—is what his name implies—a very nice boy.[21] He refuses to believe that I tell the truth about my age. This is not my reason for liking him, tho' it may sound that way. But, everybody else does, too. Mr. Hemingway is jealous of the attention he gets as he has been spoiled himself.

．　　．　　．

9 VENERDI                                    [*Friday, August 9*]

Signorina Pirelli came today, after I had spent a sleepless P.M. & I went with her to get almonds for Mr. Hemingway. Meanwhile it seems the Capt. arrived & Mr. H. [Hemingway] told him I had gone out. So I never knew he was upstairs until after dinner. Then he acted so funny—was evidently hurt, as he had come expecting me to go to dinner with him, & he would hardly answer when I spoke to him, so I got mad & stayed out of the room. Mr. H. finally rang for me, when the Capt. was going—& then he & I had an explanation, & I promised finally to go to dinner tomorrow night with him.

．　　．　　．

10 SABATO                                   [*Saturday, August 10*]

This A.M. Mr. Hemingway[22] was operated on bright & early—our first op. here. Everything went off beautifully. The Ital. doctor flashed smiles all around & learned a few Eng. words such as "needle—strong—enough." Then I had my 1/2 night off & the Capt. came for me at 6 P.M. We went to the Parco & saw the monument of Mt. Grappa. Then to a restaurant—Sempioncius—where at first we seemed to be the only guests. We tried 2 tables on the balcony, & finally it got cold, & he made me go into a little private room, much as I disliked the idea. However, I got home early and he seems to be more decent than I thought at first.

11 DOMENICA                    [*Sunday, August* 11]

Nothing to note—as they used to put on the charts at Bellevue. A new patient came in a friend of Mr. Hemingway's from Sec. 4—Lt. Horne.[23] He made himself quite at home and seems very jolly. He fixes his hair with water in the A.M. & then gets back into bed with his cap on. When I looked in he had the covers up to his chin & with his glasses—he looked a picture for Puck.

.    .    .

12 LUNEDI                      [*Monday, August* 12]

Being wide awake at 4 I got up & went strolling about the town. Silk stockings are the prohibitive price of 27 lire—and I was told before I came here that I shouldn't buy silk things in N.Y. as they were so cheap in Italy.

Mr. Seeley—our oldest patient (not in yrs.) is inclined to be spoony, I fear. He was looking for shooting stars this evening—so I had to quietly but firmly leave. Enough said!

.    .    .

13 MARTEDI                     [*Tuesday, August* 13]

I have bought a charming mandolin. Also Mr. Darling has bought a "piccolo" [small] mandolin & as Mr. Seeley has a mouth organ there is quite an orchestra evenings. There is quite a nice lot of patients, now.

This P.M. Miss De Long & I went to Maggiore to see some of the bead work done by the "feriti"—and to leave a few orders for bags. I have done quite a business for them in bag orders.

.    .    .

14 MERCOLEDI                   [*Wednesday, August* 14]

Mac had a P.M. today & asked me to get up & go out with her, so we went to Campari's for ices, & then looking for a vettura we ran across

Mr. Villard looking lonesome, so asked him to go, too. We drove in the Parco, & took pictures, & then went to the Manin Gardens, where he was so pleased with the prospect he invited us to dine there. I felt quite guilty, as I have not felt esp. kindly toward him as a patient, he being too sarcastic at times.[24]

.  .  .

15 GIOVEDI                                    [*Thursday, August 15*]

Cavie & Miss Fletcher began their classes today. I don't know what we will do if we don't get more nurses. Ten patients, now, & all wanting special attention. It's not so bad for me at night, as they sleep pretty well, but poor Mac gets the brunt of it in the daytime. The Capt. came tonight just in from Brescia. He came late & stayed late, saying it was his only chance to see me—after the patients were all asleep. He is all upset over having to leave Italy, & his mother is ill in Pavia, so I feel sorrier than ever for him. He is rather a lovable sort, after all, & seems to be more faithful than I gave him credit for. He, Mr. Seeley, & the Kid [Hemingway] had a great time talking of what they would do "dopo la guerra." I felt like a grandmother to hear their plans. In spite of my grey hairs & my assertion of 26 yrs. Mr. Darling insists I am bluffing & am only 20. He is such a nice boy. They tell me the last mail boat has been sunk. The worst of this going abroad business.

.  .  .

17 SABATO                                     [*Saturday, August 17*]

When I came back from an errand to the R.C. office & the bank this A.M. for Miss De Long I began to feel ill & was so sick all day I could not stand up by dinner time. And I was expecting Brooksie, so I felt rather disappointed. Cavie went down to meet Her & I took Spts. of Am. [spirits of ammonia] & braced up a little, but was not allowed to go on duty at 12. Quite a different evening from the one we had planned.

18 DOMENICA                            [*Sunday, August 18*]

This A.M. I got up feeling better, & helped with the patients for awhile. Then after dinner I began to feel less like a specter, so went out for Gelati with Brooksie & Capt. Rhodes—& then for a drive. Driving in a carriage is our chief amusement next to eating. It is such a lottery as to cab-men & you never know when you will get home safely. Twice they have just avoided collisions, twice horses have fallen & innumerable times there have been imminent run-overs. Brooks is having quite a flirtation with Capt. Rhodes. One of the many.

.    .    .

19 LUNEDI                              [*Monday, August 19*]

Last night was almost like one at Bellevue. We adm—5 patients yesterday, counting 2 I adm last night. 2 slept on the terrazza & one downstairs. Tonight, is not quite such a rush but at 1 I am expecting another from Vicenza. Mr. Darling & Mr. Horne are too nice for words about helping me all they can. The patient arrived at 7 A.M. this A.M. (Tues.) and at 6—I essayed to give Mr. Allen[25] a dose of Olio di Ricino. Ye gods! He was still asleep & just raked the whole tray of oil & coffee & malted milk off on the bed & the floor. I looked rather draggled when I came off duty. Oil of Castor is not an addition to one's costume, and my white shoes are not fit for further consideration. These Italian shoes are too queer shaped for words. How they would laugh in N.Y. over my circular rubber heels.

.    .    .

21 MERCOLEDI                          [*Wednesday, August 21*]

I have not written in the diary for a week, so now, I cannot place events exactly & will just put down things as I think of them. It has been such a busy week, and I have been trying to sleep daytimes in spite of the heat. Wed. I went to the Maggiore & saw Miss Pirelli. The bags were not all done, so I must go again next week. I waxed extravagant, & ordered myself a lovely bag at 65 Lire. Also a belt of blue & steel beads. Then I went through the Galleria, & fell for the lure of a handsome waist in a shop. Before I left there I had 2 waists, 1 chemise, & a lovely crepe de chine negligee. Horrible extravagance, but the negligee is so sweet I'm not at all regretful. When I got home with my purchases, Cavie wanted to know if I was going to Paris with the Capt. that I was laying in such a trousseau.

Mr. Hemingway & I expect the Capt. Wed. as he wrote a postal & said he'd be here, but he came not, & each night I was so busy I was glad he did not, but how the Kid worried. He was sure "we" had been jilted. Finally, 10.30 tonight (Sat.) he came in in "Borghese"— with a whiff of beer about his breath & a stronger whiff of perfume in his hair which was curlier than ever. He is terribly depressed over going Mon. & I feel sorry for him. He will be very homesick. My pet Mr. Darling left Friday. Also Mr. Michels, a paymaster in the Navy (Aviation) who was flirting desperately with me.

.    .    .

25 DOMENICA                                    [*Sunday, August 25*]

Now, Ernest Hemingway has a case on me, or thinks he has. He is a dear boy & so cute about it. It does beat all how popular I have become in the last 6 mos. Must be because I'm turning frivolous. Today I must attend the Tea given here for the Italian Red Cross by Miss Shaw.

.    .    .

26 LUNEDI                                      [*Monday, August 26*]

The old affair is over, thanks be! I felt like a dummy—with a mob of Italian nurses, & I couldn't say boo to them in their own language. At last I found 3 of my friends from the Zonda & then I felt more at ease Ernest Hemingway is getting earnest. He was talking last night of what might be if he was 26–28. In some ways—at some times—I wish very much that he was. He is adorable & we are very congenial in every way. I'm getting so confused in my heart & mind I don't know how I'll end up. Still, I came over here for work and until the war is over I won't be able to do anything foolish, which is lucky for me. I used to pride myself on my sense. I wonder if I'm getting foolish or if I can blame the romantic country for it's [sic] effect on me.

.   .   .

27 MARTEDI                              [*Tuesday, August 27*]

Here another week has sailed by, & I've neglected to keep up my daily stint of writing, and, by now I cannot remember just what happened from day to day.

All I know is "Ernie" is far too fond of me, & speaks in such a desperate way every time I am cool, that I dare not dampen his ardor as long as he is here in the Hospital. Poor Kid, I am sorry for him. Everybody seems to be down on him for some reason, and he gets raked over the coals right & left. Some of the heads have an idea he is very wild and he is—in some respects, but swears to me in a very honest way that he has always kept clean—& never been bad. I believe it, but the others—oh—no.

.   .   .

29 GIOVEDI                              [*Thursday, August 29*]

I saw my old friend Major Hamill this week. He is stationed at Milan as a headquarters for his inspection tours now. He seemed glad to see me again. I imagine the Maj. is something of a kidder with the ladies especially if young & not unpleasing to the eye.

.   .   .

30 VENERDI                              [*Friday, August 30*]

Mr. Michels left this A.M. & I'm not ashamed to say I kissed him goodbye—though I didn't dare tell the Kid. He seemed so blue & homesick & was going away for good & such things have a very different perspective over here, somehow. In the P.M. I escorted "mia ammalato["] on his first visit to the outside world in 2 months, which we both enjoyed hugely.

.     .     .

31 SABATO                                [*Saturday, August 31*]

Tonight, my 1/2 night off, as a very special dispensation I was allowed to go to dinner with Mr. Hemingway. We went to the Du Nord,

*Agnes von Kurowsky and Ernest Hemingway on the terrace of the American Red Cross Hospital, 1918. Photograph courtesy of the Ernest Hemingway Foundation.*

as a nice quiet place where the food was good, & had also a bottle of Asti Spumante—which is getting to be my favorite beverage. If the Doctor could only see me drink wine. Another nice patient came last night—Mr. John Miller, Sec II.²⁶

.   .   .

## SETTEMBRE [SEPTEMBER]

1 DOMENICA                                    [*Sunday, September 1*]

A great day for sleeping! It's funny how the weeks fly by when I'm on night duty. I asked Cavie to get me some anchovy paste for sandwiches for my evening meal, & she brought a something that smelled as tho' it had crawled in the alley & passed away in terrible agony. I put it out on the terrazza to save it for inspection in the A.M.

.   .   .

2 LUNEDI                                      [*Monday, September 2*]

Alas—she was sick this A.M. & I hadn't the heart to give her a whiff of the remains.

Great doings here tomorrow! They are going to take movies for propaganda work in the child welfare campaign, & Major Hereford is coming to superintend. And such a day of nausea as poor Cavie had to prepare her for the ordeal.

.   .   .

3 MARTEDI                                     [*Tuesday, September 3*]

Much excitement all day! The movie upset the whole house, & got everybody on edge. I escaped most of it, but, as I was starting out at 5 to the Kodak shop with Mr. Hemingway—Miss De Long told me I was not to go out with him again, which made me refuse to go, & got him all worried as he thought I was in Dutch. Then he went out to dinner, & Mr. Miller & Mr. Wheeler—another nice boy, went out @ 8.15 & did not come home until 11.30 to my great horror & worry.[27] It has not been spoken of as yet—but—

. . .

4 MERCOLEDI                    [*Wednesday, September 4*]

It was O.K. & nobody found out. They got me out of bed when I'd been asleep for less than 1 hr. to pose in the movies they took of the Hospital. My 1st appearance as a screen star. Maj. Hereford supt. the event, & it was great fun, except I felt so foolish.

I haven't had any mail for an age. I wonder why. Tomorrow night my 1/2 night off & we expect to make it a festive occasion.

. . .

5 GIOVEDI                      [*Thursday, September 5*]

It was—& then some—My first party here in the Home. Mr. Mc-Queen came with a Lt. of R.C.—a queer duck who gave an imitation of Louis Bernstein—pianist—"The Flight of the Grasshopper." Mr. Miller sang Harry Lauder songs, & we all sang the familiar songs. Then Hemingway & Miller went out for Asti & Mr. Wheeler got some crackers procured at the Y.M.C.A. & Lo—it was a spread—6 men, 3 girls.

. . .

6 VENERDI                      [*Friday, September 6*]

Cavie & Miss Fletcher left for Stresa, Lago Maggiore today. I meant to wake up & see them off but, most unaccountably slept through until 6. Poor Cavie, she was so disappointed because she couldn't go on her little vacation with me instead of Miss Fletcher, who is nice sometimes & at others very crabbed.

7 SABATO                                    [*Saturday, September 7*]

Lo'dy, Lo'dy, Goodness me—Mac found one of my yellow hairpins under Hemingway's pillow, & she & Mr. Lewis will never let me forget now.[28] I think both Ernie & I got through it pretty well. They are cutting off our allowance, now—& just paying our laundry bills & carfare. Also there is a printed notice about wearing only regulation uniforms—That means our old gray things. Che peccato!

.    .    .

8 DOMENICA                                  [*Sunday, September 8*]

Mac is not sleeping nights & it makes her so cranky daytimes it is terribly hard to get along with her. She picks on the poor Kid, whom she spoiled so at first, & as he says—"rides him all day." I've lectured him so much about being polite to her that he doesn't dare answer her back the way he used to. I think she'll either have to have a vacation or there will be a grand bust up.

.    .    .

9 LUNEDI                                    [*Monday, September 9*]

Capo Seeley[29] came back tonight brown & freckled, his hands in splendid shape. So now, he will not need an operation. He brought me a big copper paper-cutter that he made out of the band around a large shell. Very clever work. Miss Fisher also arrived from Genoa—full of regret at having to leave there, where she had a pretty good time, I guess.

.    .    .

10 MARTEDI                                  [*Tuesday, September 10*]

Miss De Long is sick with a bad cold. & was up last night 1/2 the night. Nothing worth mentioning during the day, as I haven't left the house since Sat. Tonight I admitted a soldier in the

M.P.S. with mumps. I fear we will have an epidemic of it, now, & where will we isolate them? Miss Fisher is going to special him. The Kid was sick tonight very much like Miss De Long. Mac says she hates him & doesn't care if he is sick.

. . .

11 MERCOLEDI [*Wednesday, September 11*]

I'm afraid she smokes too much. I gave my home ring[30] to the Kid— and was astonished to see how really pleased he was. It's strange to think how little an act will give a huge amt. of pleasure to someone. I'm getting more worried about what I should do about the Doctor. I feel like a criminal at times.

. . .

12 GIOVEDI [*Thursday, September 12*]

Today was a gay one. Mac, Fisher, & I & Lts. Lewis, Pay & Hemingway took in the races if you please. We had some time getting in, as it seems officers are always allowed in, but, only ladies of the first families & we had to have spec. permission. I didn't win a cent, & lost 30 lire—but, enjoyed it nevertheless. Brooks came back from Bologna, furious at having been called in here. Hem—Cavie & I met her—in the rain.

. . .

13 VENERDI [*Friday, September 13*]

I forgot to mention the bat fight Ernie & I had at 1 A.M. Wed. We finally captured it after chasing it around the room for 3/4 of an hour. It was most exciting.[31].

Hem. & Seeley went to the Club & played poker until late & the Kid told me he would only drink Anisette. Maybe I am "reforming" him after all, & if so I'll think I've done some good.

14 SABATO                                    [*Saturday, September 14*]

Tonight Miss de Long & Miss Fletcher went to the opera. Miss De Long was up before she went, & felt the very depressing atmosphere from the loneliness of the place, & was very sorry for me & the patients. If she'd seen us at 12 and later she'd have changed her mind. Capo Seeley got a crazy fit on, & walked on a ledge in his bare feet outside his window. I almost died of heart failure. He certainly was funny, too, but, scared—well I was cold.

·   ·   ·

15 DOMENICA                                  [*Sunday, September 15*]

Fisher, Brooks, Cavie & I all went to the races again with Lewis, Pay, Walker, Warehouser, & Robinson, (all aviators) & Ernie—in a new uniform. Mac was quite sick & could not go. I plunged & lost but recovered all but 8 lire, but Brooks & Fisher did some tall betting.

Then Brooks gets herself in Dutch by attempting to go to dinner & the opera. Miss De Long said she'd had enough gadding for one day.

·   ·   ·

16 LUNEDI                                    [*Monday, September 16*]

I hear Brooksie is in quite wrong with headquarters, & in imminent danger of being sent home. The crazy kid, she's always in bad with her foolishness. I'm certainly going to watch my step as much as I can.

We had another little party this evening. Even Mr. Allen came down & only one pt. was left upstairs, & he from choice. We played games, drank wine, & danced & had a really good time. Of course Brooksie spoiled things by monopolizing Cavie's man, but then—

·   ·   ·

17 MARTEDI                                   [*Tuesday, September 17*]

Some heavy party was pulled off tonight. Miss Shaw asked all the new nurses & a Mr. Brett who sang & executed the ukelele. I enjoyed

Mr. Tandy's amusement most of all. Dr. Horan came in the P.M. & stayed for dinner & after until 11—seemed to enjoy our society as a whole very much—as a change from the Front & the rough life. Mr. Allen is ill again. Seems as tho' we'd never get that boy home to his mother. Brooks is in a peck of trouble, & has to apologize to Maj. Collins for impertinence. Poor kid. She's fated.

.   .   .

18 MERCOLEDI                    [*Wednesday, September 18*]

I was a disappointed woman this day. Miss De Long gave me my 1/2 night to go to the opera & when I awoke at 3.30 I find there's not going to be any. I went with Cavie to have my hair shamp —& then to Campari's for gelati, where we struck the popular hour—6—& it was crowded. [32]

After dinner Cavie & I were urged by the Great Master to go somewhere which turned out to be the Parco. We wandered for an hour looking for the caffe & Asti—finally arriving. What with some lovely soft music, & the moon, & the Asti & the old castle—we were far gone.

.   .   .

19 GIOVEDI                       [*Thursday, September 19*]

I was so disgusted last night. When I got on duty I found Fisher having a high old time with Lewis in a chaise longue on the balcony. They told me it was too early for me—11.30 so I went out into the office & read until she went to bed which was 12.45. Hem. was furious—, & it was so common. I couldn't get over them. Tonight, we had a box for the opera at La Scala—"Ghismonde"—opening night & a ballet—"Le Carillon Magico" also new to Milan, & the most delightful I've ever seen. Mr. Hem—got sick in the middle & had to leave. Miss Fisher relieved me again, & was sitting with Mr. Lewis again when I came on duty. Dr. Horan went to the opera with us.

20 VENERDI                    [*Friday, September 20*]

Today is the Italian 4th of July & there were great doin's for the help
& tea for the girls from the store room. Such dancing & prancing!
And the Italian songs, my, my. In the evening the Kid said his shirt
was "getting a bit whiffy" so I washed it for him, after long persua-
sion. He & Dr. Horan & Mr. Lewis went to the races, & he really
came out ahead for once.

·   ·   ·

21 SABATO                     [*Saturday, September 21*]

I slept so much I was good for nothing when I finally got up for
dinner. Therefore there is nothing specially interesting to put in
here. I gave Mr. Lewis bacon for his breakfast & it made him so frisky
that later while I was standing at the casement 3d piano & he & Ern.
4th piano, he fired a paper book down & hit me on the noodle, thereby
causing great headache.

·   ·   ·

22 DOMENICA                   [*Sunday, September 22*]

Tonight, our old friend John W. Miller arrived, en route for Stresa.
He just came in for about an hour—& begged me for some pajamas,
so I sneaked him 2 pair. He strapped them to him with his belt, & put
on his overcoat, looking a very queer shape. Hem. & I laughed ourselves sick. The sequel, which we heard later, was that he was strolling thru the Galleria & the back pair fell off, stretching their legs &
showing strings etc. & he had to pick them up & carry them home
under his arm.

·   ·   ·

23 LUNEDI                     [*Monday, September 23*]

We had some party tonight! Enough to last me a long, long while.
Ernie & Jno. Miller went out & bought Asti Spumante with contrib.

from Rochfort & Tandy, & for a while the party dragged awfully. Then Mr. Lewis arrived with 5 aviators & as they'd all been imbibing (as we found later) things went merrily on. Lt. Walker & Mr. Brackett were both knocked out—not by Asti but Cognac which the B. boy brought down. It was a horrible evening. Those poor boys![33]

. . .

24 MARTEDI                          [Tuesday, September 24]

I have a nice cold in my face this A.M. as it poured all night, & I did not let Mr. Miller & Mr. H. go to Stresa in the rain. They left this P.M.—at 6. Ernie came dowstairs to say goodbye to me, & Miss De Long was close at hand, so it was rather formal until she went off & then I slipped into the elevator with him & we had a more real farewell.[34] Brooks was sent to Sicily again—Toramina[35] [Taormina] this time, but she was in tears & rebellious as usual. Wish I had her chances.

. . .

25 MERCOLEDI                        [Wednesday, September 25]

I wrote to the Kid last night at midnight as per order. It was the most dismal night I ever spent on night duty. I missed him so much, & it poured all night with thunder & lightening [sic]. And the mice ran back & forth, & everything was very dark & spooky, so altogether I was quite pleased to be rel. fr. night duty today. I spent the afternoon shopping with Miss De Long for a dinner given in honor of Cavie's birthday.

. . .

26 GIOVEDI                          [Thursday, September 26]

Today, Mr. Allen insisted on Mac going with him to the Races, & so she insisted I should go along. Capt. Harmon came with me, & I won 45 lire—my first big winning—or big for me.

How I do miss that boy. He would have enjoyed this afternoon so much. I've been counting up the letters I should write, & it's no less than 16——Awful thought!

. . .

27 VENERDI                              [*Friday, September 27*]

Today I had two letters from Ernie. The nicest letters I ever got. Mac was dying for a look (I don't know how she found out the letter was fr. him but she did) but I only gave her bits of quotations as it would never do to let her in on them. Of course, Cavie is my real confidante & knows all about me. How I wish Mac & I could go to Stresa tomorrow for over Sun. I'll pray for it.

. . .

28 SABATO                              [*Saturday, September 28*]

Well, my prayers were not answered, as they telegraphed for 2 more nurses in Rome, & Miss McCaffery & Signorina Lega went, so Miss De Long was afraid to let us go away just now. It is a good thing, too, as we hear there are some more patients—aviators—coming in. One Amb. man—Mr. Barlow came at noon today, so maybe things are getting busy. 2 more letters from my boy, & they surely do mean a lot.[36]

. . .

29 DOMENICA                              [*Sunday, September 29*]

Today was most strenuous. Cavie, Fisher & I went with Mr. Allen & Lt. Crisswell to the Races, where we saw a bunch of our aviator friends. I had 200 lire to bet according to a schedule for Mr. Brackett, & I had a small amt. of luck for him as I brought back 227 lire & lost 27 myself. Then we—Mac, Cavie, Miss Conway & I went to La Scala to hear "Mose." I was quite crazy over it, but, too tired to really enjoy it.

30 LUNEDI                                    [*Monday, September 30*]

Today we adm. 3 aviators[37] & Mr. McQueen fr. the R.C. Office.
Also, J. Miller came back fr. Stresa & says the Kid will return today,
Mon. Then more nurses were telegraphed for, so Miss De Long sent
the Misses Creelman & Fisher & I went on duty at 4 A.M. to relieve
her, after 3 hrs sleep, when I returned from the opera. Today I have
slept like a log all day, making up sleep.

My Kid came back tonight, & I feel so different. It seemed wonderful to be together again.

.    .    .

# OTTOBRE [OCTOBER]

I MARTEDI                                        [*Tuesday, October 1*]

Miss Markley was supposed to come today from Genoa, & go on
night duty, but, has not showed up—so I guess I'm in for it for a
while longer.

One of the aviators is very sick—Lieut. Colter. He is such a nice
patient too.

We hope to get rid of Mr. Allen this week, oh joy go with him.
Mr. Lewis is off for Stresa today, for 3 days & then goes to the Front.

.    .    .

2 MERCOLEDI                                   [*Wednesday, October 2*]

What happened of particular note today? I can't think of anything.
For awhile the place was so light that we were tempted to put an ad.
in the papers for more patients, but, it was not necessary. Now we
have almost every room filled—& one woman—an Amer. working in
the R.C. office. I am specialing Major McDonough these days. He
has lumbago, & I have been rubbing him a couple of times.

3 GIOVEDI                                    [*Thursday, October 3*]

Mr. Allen departed for the Races by him's lonesomes [sic] today with large sums of money of Mr. Brackett's, & 100 lire borrowed from Cavie. Mac & I went for a drive, & thinking the Kid had gone to the Races, we drove out there, only to find Mr. Allen sole. We invited him in, & then he said—"I'll pay"—in rather ungracious tones. Afterwards telling the patients sev. times that he was stung for a drive by us.

.    .    .

4 VENERDI                                    [*Friday, October 4*]

Mr. Colter[38] was so much worse last night & tonight that Cavie came on with me tonight. We were so in hopes we would pull him through. Dr. Jardine came @ 10.45 & said these cases were liable to go very quickly—& the Lieut. died at 11.30 almost in my arms. We worked over him like fiends & did everything we could think of but, it was no use. I cried for the first time over losing a patient, but it seemed so dreadful to die off in a strange land with none of his people near & he was so sweet!

.    .    .

5 SABATO                                     [*Saturday, October 5*]

I had a 1/2 night off tonight. I was just about done up this A.M. after that night of sorrow. Cavie stayed with me until 4. We laid him out & I shaved him, & I never saw anyone look so lovely & smiling.

Tonight I tried my best to go out & forget it—so I persuaded Cavie & the Kid to go for a drive—& we ran into Lieut. Lewis, who was going to Padua by the 12.30 train, so we all drove to the Parco & had a vermouth & then home. Very quiet.

6 DOMENICA                                    [*Sunday, October 6*]

The chief event of yesterday I completely forgot to mention—namely departure of Edward E. Allen, our patient since July 13 & one of our chief worries. The boy will never be forgotten in this Hosp. He's a by-word & our chief amusement has been "the sayings of Edward." Since Mr. C– died—there has been a sort of let-down in the work. It seems queer after we were so busy this past week.

.    .    .

7 LUNEDI                                      [*Monday, October 7*]

I am sorry to say the Kid has a jealous disposition. Every time I try to tease him I'm made sorry for it after, as he goes off at a tangent, without waiting to find out for sure. But, I'm forgetting the chief events of these days. Last night about 11 I began to hear a roar in the sts. [streets] like a multitude applauding & cheering. I got so excited, & tried to get Mr. McQueen to go out & see what it was all about, but, he wouldn't budge until I told him I heard a "Vive la Pace"[39] in the st. Then he threw on his uniform & dashed out. Miss De Long & Mac, Cavie & Miss Fletcher all got dressed at 12.30 & went out to get news. The Kaiser had proposed an armistice to Pres. Wilson, & the people were so excited they had regular riots. Mr. Tandy went out, & my Kid Hemingway—but he would not take the popular view that it was Peace, & sure enough he was right. He put up a royal battle with some of his Italian friends, & found out the people were being excited by the Red Guards, or Socialists. The next day, big bulletins were posted everywhere telling the people to go back to work, that it was all German propaganda. Very exciting times.

A nurse, Miss Noel came from Turin Mon. night, & got sick the next day. We thought she was going to have pneumonia—probably she has got a touch of this very infectious influenza or Spanish fever. She is much better today.

[*Thursday, October 10*]

I had a 1/2 night off & Miss de Long said I could get up for lunch as they were having tagliatelli [*tagliatelle:* ribbon pasta], which I am fond of. After lunch, Mac & I danced with Mr. Fielder, one of our aviator pts. a Southerner with all the wiles & graces of the type. Hem. came down & found us in the Salon, as he was going to the Races, and immed. thought I had a date with Mr. Fielder. When he came back at 6 I was walking downstairs with Mr. Fielder & he believed it when Mac said I had been out with him all the afternoon. So he refused to come to our fudge party. In spite of this disappointment I had a fair time. Mr. Maxwell & Landon came, & some patients, & we made it in the kitchen.

.    .    .

[*Friday, October 11*]

Was feeling so mean & cold today, & looked so miserable I guess Miss De Long had compunction [sic] for me. Anyhow, she told me to be sure & let her know if I wasn't able to last the night out. Brooks came back from Palermo, in wrong again, I guess—tho' one never would think it from her own story.

.    .    .

[*Saturday, October 12*]

Was relieved from night duty today—(Brooks went on) & really was glad, tho' of course the Kid was sad tho' he unselfishly said he was glad for me. We all (Mac, Cavie & I, Mr. Boodway, Fielder, & Ernie) went to a Y.M.C.A. entertainment. They had an Arabian dance by 2 Negro soldiers which almost broke up the party. The Y.M.C.A. went around apologizing for its vulgarity, & that made it even more wildly applauded than it was before.

13 DOMENICA                          [*Sunday, October 13*]

Brooks, as usual, has a heavy love she brought back from Palermo—
an Aviator. He is making use of a couple of friends who are patients &
stays up with Brooksie until a late hour at night. If she ever gets
caught it will be good-bye Italy for her. Mr. Seeley & Darling came
tonight & we had a little party for them. Mr. Brackett who was supposed to leave for the Front last night stayed for the Races today & lost
every cent he had—& got drunk in the bargain. So Ernie had to stake
him to a dinner, & he came back to the Hosp. after Miss De Long had
retired. Brooks had a fight with Miss De Long today anent going out
to tea with her Mr. Johnson. As she met everybody, naturally she was
discovered. I did not learn all particulars, but, the row they had in the
Hall was enough for me. She is certainly booked for hot water. Ernie
got sulky again tonight because I invited Cavie in the parlor, when he
wanted to have a private talk with me. He says he can't stand seeing
me all day like this, & not be able to say what he likes.

.     .     .

15 MARTEDI                          [*Tuesday, October 15*]

This A.M. at the breakfast table I was told I was to go to Florence by
the noon train, so I had some tall hustling to do. Of course, Mac
dashed in & woke up my Kid with the news I was leaving—he got up
& dressed at 9 A.M. an unprecedented performance, & then was so
rude to Mac, she nearly cried, & there was war in the air. I got after
him but he was so broken up I hadn't the heart to say much. I had an
awful trip in the rain—12 hrs—on the train—arriving at 12.30 at
night.

.     .     .

16 MERCOLEDI                        [*Wednesday, October 16*]

This A.M. Capt. Aikin called for me at the Hotel where I spent the
night & took me out in a car to the Amer. Hosp. up on a hill overlook-
ing Florence. Here I am to special an A.R.C. Lieut. nights while Miss

Jessup[40] has him days. An arrangement that pleases me, as I can see more of Florence that way. Lieut. Hough—the patient is very ill with the Spanish Fever—and runs a continuous temp. about 104.

·   ·   ·

17 GIOVEDI                              [*Thursday, October 17*]

It rains almost continuously, just now, being what they call the time of the sirocco.[41] Anyhow, it's no inducement to go to town. The nights are about the most doleful I ever put in, what with being alone in the building except for one other patient, and the rain pattering in a dismal fashion all night. Then, too, Mr. Hough is so restless. Miss Jessup & one of the other nurses sleep over here, or at least, they did last night.

·   ·   ·

18 VENERDI                              [*Friday, October 18*]

This P.M. in spite of the dark aspect of the sky I got up at 3.30 & walked in to Florence. I expected difficulty, but, found my way to the Duomo, more by good luck, or by instinct, than by deduction. From there, I wandered about, being careful not to get too far away from my starting-point, & I found such interesting old buildings, but, of course, had no one to tell me what they were. I did find an awfully good milk choc. place—the best & cheapest since I came to Italy. I also walked home—& was some bushed after walking 2 1/2 hours.

·   ·   ·

19 SABATO                               [*Saturday, October 19*]

Raining again. This sort of weather makes my old diary interesting & breathtaking to read over a year later. There's one good thing about this hermit's life. I'm certainly getting caught up in my correspondence, & by the time I get back to Milan I'll feel like a free woman. I like Miss Jessup, the day nurse, so much. She has only been home once since the war began, & has experiences by the bookful. A thoroughly good sport in every way.

.    .    .

20 DOMENICA                              [*Sunday, October 20*]

Really.[42] I hate to think how I may break out when this seclusion is over. Mr. Hough seems to be a little better, his temp. is not normal yet, but, is much lower than it has been. There seems to still [be] a controversy between his doctors as to whether he has Typhoid, or Spanish Influenza. I'm inclined to favor the latter, & so is Miss Jessup tho' it is not like other cases we've had at the Hospital. The poor man is beginning to talk very queerly—& seems confused.

# THREE

. . .

## Agnes von Kurowsky
# Letters to Ernest Hemingway

INTRODUCTION BY HENRY S. VILLARD

The many letters that Agnes wrote to Ernest Hemingway represent only one side of a correspondence that at times maintained the heady pace of nearly a letter a day, sometimes two on the same date. Then, after a three-year hiatus, there is one final communication, marking *finis* to the wartime episode. The collection is revealing in the affection displayed by Agnes toward a wounded nineteen-year-old driver of a Red Cross ambulance. The terms of endearment with which the letters abound stand out in sharp contradiction to her effort later in life to minimize the relationship and dismiss it as a mere flirtation.

It has always been assumed that the relationship was more fervent on his part than on hers, that while she reciprocated his sentiments it was by no means clear that she had fallen in love to the same headlong extent as he had. Indeed, without the corroboration provided by the diary and letters, it might be difficult to gauge the degree to which she had singled out Ernie from the other patients in Milan for her special attention. The letters, however, give ample evidence of her concern and devotion. Compared with the diary's relative restraint in chronicling the daily doings at the hospital, the letters pour out a veritable torrent of loving solicitude.

Besides the difference in tone and content, the letters provide another contrast to the diary. Whereas Agnes is writing in the journal for herself alone, jotting down thoughts she would not disclose to another person, in the letters she is opening her heart on paper: "I really never thought I could write what I feel so plainly & openly. . . . Once written you can't take back what you have said." Spontaneous, unaffected, caring, these are letters such as any young woman of that particular period in history might write to her sweetheart. They should be taken for neither more nor less.

It is a pity that we do not have the letters that Hemingway wrote in return. One can only assume that at the very least they matched the sentiments she expressed in hers. Late in her life she confessed that she had given Hemingway's letters to Domenico Caracciolo, her new love once Ernest had left for the States, and that he had burned them.[1] As a result, none of the Hemingway side of the correspondence is known to exist, not even the three epistles that Agnes, in the letter she wrote to me in 1962, said were given to her by Mary Hemingway.

.   .   .

[Sept. 25, 1918][2]

Kid, My Kid,[3]

I've just been in your room, & talk about chairs that whisper! That whole room haunted me so that I could not stay in it. So I just removed ye biscotti [biscuits] & other refuse, & in the A.M. will move the empties into Mr. Lewis' room as I hear Miss De Long is going to clean your house while you are away. My, but I wish you'd been here tonight cause I got ripping mad at Mac, & I wanted a shoulder to weep tears of anger on. You know, she would never let me come up in the daytime & fix anything for her patients.

Well she took a mean advantage of me, & came up & made a hot lemonade for Lt. Lewis, & when I remonstrated reminding her that she'd never allow me to do it in the day—she just said he had asked Miss De Long for it, so I walked out. Then she came out & said I could take it in to him & I said "Thank you, Mac. I'd rather not." She was so nice to me the rest of the evening that I think she was sorry, but it hurt me. It's such a little thing to lose one's temper over, but, it was so darned unfair!

Back to us—most important topic—if its anything like as cheerful an evening where you are as it is here you must be enjoying yourself. Cavie stayed up & we played 500 with Mr. Allen & Mr. Rochefort until the latter dropped out in favor of Miss Fisher. Then Lt. Mitlis came in & the game soon broke up as she & Mac escorted him down to the beau parlor below.

I wish you'd seen Edward. He was too funny playing with Cavie, who is not a scientific expert at the game, which he plays with his heart & soul in the cards & mathematical precision. She says "Now the joker is highest, isn't it? And the 2 knaves come next? What a pity I haven't any of those!" And she had just bid 7 on Diamonds. He remarked she'd do alright if she'd only use her head. Cruel youth.

It's a wonderful night for a big bowl of minestrone & I have enough here for two. Too bad I must eat all alone.

This P.M. I met Signors Walker & Maxwell. Great was the confusion but I pretended not to observe. Then Mr. Walker in broken tones apologized for the dreadful slip he made & I told him it was [not clear] & all forgotten.[4]

Well, if I write anymore I'll be in water marks as the paper not in the signal pattern is too lonely & lugubrious for words. The weather shore am helpin out the feeling.

Don't forget to come back to me, Boy O.M. [of mine]—cause I miss you most awfully.

Now, it's your turn and the test is on—so "on with the dance, let joy be unrefused."

> "Yours till the War Ends"
> (From love-letters of a Rookie)
> Aggie

(This is a dreadful hour to write, as it's all I can do to keep from being sentimental.)

[Sept. 26, 1918][5]

My dear Boy,[6]

I'm so sleepy I can hardly see, but, I must tell you the news as I certainly won't have time tomorrow.[7] I was relieved from night duty today, so I didn't go to bed, & as it was Sis Cavie's birthday, Gumshoe[8] & I spent the P.M. searching the town for favors for the dinner-party.

Everything went off with great éclat, & Cavie was quite happy, so now I feel I achieved my end, but, Gawsh—I'm tired. Miss De Long started the whole crowd on 500—so it was a hectic evening. Lt. Eckling (that R.C. man who played Louis Bernstein) called, also Lt. Mitchell. Very social occasion, indeed. Fisher went on night duty, & is in wrong already, as she was supposed to be sleeping this P.M. & she went out with Mac instead. So of course, Miss De Long & I ran right into them on the Corso.

If I hadn't been so busy today, I should certainly have cried from loneliness.

Cavie told me tonight she didn't think I missed you, as I seemed so carefree—so I rileived [sic] her of her mistaken idea, & told her I never missed anyone as much.

I'm so tired I can't write any more & be legible—or plausible. So A Riverderla, mia bambino [*Arrivederla, mia bambino*: good-bye, my baby]—& take good care of yourself. I may not write again if I find it takes very long for my letters to go.

Bless your heart—
Agnes

I've a letter for Johnny Miller.[9] I'm holding it.

·   ·   ·

[No date]

Dear old furnace man—

This is more bummier than usual but, consider the weather, my feeble imagination, the hour, & my courage in attempting light verse for the master, and then let your old stony heart be softened with pity.

For at times I can do even worse, and that is part of my dark past as yet unrevealed to your searching gaze.

Oh, Master, fain would I sit at your feet (after proper attention, & clean socks) and gather the pearls of real literature as they cascade from your typewriter. I'm picking out the discarded bits from the waste-basket & weaving them into some fancified tale.

Say, I'm cold just now & have need of a bit of a steaming. You can tell by the effect on my wandering intellect. Oh where is my wandering brain tonight? Put in the Storm like the 'lectric light. My word, it's getting to be a habit, y'know. I don't know how I do it but I do. I don't know how I say it when it's said, but there doesn't pass a day that I don't make someone gay, and I don't hear someone say "What a head!"

Dear bambino, I guess this is the last of the letters, as you'll never want a repetition of this ballyrot. But somehow, in spite of ye damp day, I feel not humid but [unclear] and you'll just have to forget to put it down on my record, as I can't help it spilling out. This is what comes of refusing, & turning you down. The Woman Pays. Ugh. But I l——[love] you just the same, so cherio & I'll see you dopo.

Agnes

"And what shall it be today
    My lad
And what shall it be today.
I must get to sleep,
And tonight I'll keep
You up till the break of day.
But, I know you'll not growl
        at me, my boy.
I know you'll not growl at me
For I'd soon be relieved
And then you'd be grieved
For then I'll be hard to see.
So tonight when you've gone to
        rest, my dear
Tonight when you've gone to rest,
While the rain it doth pour

I'll open the door
And ask for the loan of
        your chest.["]

.        .        .

[October 8, 1918][10]
Via Manzoni, 10
Milano

Oh—Brushwood Boy-o'mine—
'Most had a scrap with Cavie this A.M. because she wouldn't believe what I told about the demonstration last night—I having quoted from some of what you told me. But Casey—yclept the Gumshoe beleived [sic] all what I told her, & everybody else seems to bear it out in their latest statements, so "Allors" [sic].

Still, as there must be some foundation for the Amer. cable about the armistice being asked for, it is very nice to make wild plans for the New Year. So, I shall go to bed dreaming of happy futures, and won't let you be glum for ever so long, as you have been these last few nights. Then, maybe tonight we'll try & see who has the nicest—wildest—most impossible dream-plan for the Old Future we're going to jazz up together—n'est-ce-pas? And, Mister Kid, my dear—if you dare to once, let that expression of absolute desolation glitter in your beamish eye I'll lay off and—well—there's no telling what I'll do, but, it's most likely you'll be unable to appear before the Bellia's[11] [sic] when they come to town. (I don't want you to think that I've stopped being jealous, or you'll immediately suggest that I don't care for you anymore. Don't you sometimes wish we could skip a year? Then, I suppose we'd never stop regretting that lost time, and would say that all the nice things that didn't happen surely would have happened that year. And all the misery would be blamed on it, too. I wonder if I'm talking sense—or non-——.

Dear, promise me you won't get sick. Then maybe we can fool some of your hunches. And remember the terrible example of Capt. Graves. But, I didn't mean to remind you of him, even. As soon as you cheer up, & look at Life with your old-time rose-colored spec-kles

[sic] we will edit a new & richly embellished edition de luxe of a letter to the 3 original Campfire Girls—of Sec. 4—the ones that wrote us that pretty little letter with the aboriginal drawings of wild bird, & all. So instructive! Dear, dear, how times & manners have changed since I was a girl!

Your poco idiot—(but, yet—yours—so you can't kick.) Von— (otherwise know as Ag—Aggie—Agony—Artless—Curiosity— Vonny—

Agnes—Kid—Mrs. Kid
and a few others.)

.  .  .

[Oct. 15, 1918][12]

Dearest Kid:

My fountain pen is dry—the only dry thing in the coach—as there is a cute little leak in the roof—but I feel like talking to someone, & of course, the chief Someone is you—so I'll talk to you—with a pencil.

It's funny to feel that I'm going away from you when all along I was picturing how it would feel when you went away from me. We've just left Piacenza, and while the train is not exactly making great speed, still it is shaking from side to side in a most disconcerting way for one desirous of making pencil-talks. Across from me is the couple you saw—the Signora certainly has the fever & I wish I knew if it would be resented if I offered medicine & advice. Hubby seems to be taking very good care of her, tho' has her all wrapped up in his coat & hands her a cough drop from time to time. Perhaps that's why I like to imagine that you are here, offering me these little attentions, & putting my cape around me, etc.

I think if they hadn't been here I would have had a couple more Italian officer friends, from certain observations of my own—but niente—niente [no, no].

I've read your letter, of course, & I liked it so much—but do you think you should have given me your good luck, dear boy? Suppose you go back to the Front while I'm here, & have it not to guard you. But maybe you'll have a chance to come to Florence while I'm here—so I shan't worry any more than I have to. I only hope you can make out this raggedy writing—all the more promising for me if you cannot, as you have been so good as to admire my usual penmanship. I'm eating some choc—as a stimulant to my spirits. You know Miss De Long said I was the first one who had gone away cheerfully, so I must keep up the rep—even if it is camouflage of the first order—& you do hate camouflage so much.

I hope by this time you & Mac are closer than ever. I'm so sorry you—well, never mind I refuse to "bawl you out" by letter.

*Oh Sunny Italy.* Anyhow, when you get this you'll know I've arrived O.K. In my own mind my safe arrival is yet a disputed question as I don't know enough to even know where they put the names of their stations—on the roof, I guess, as I've looked all over & haven't seen any.

This is the most incoherent epistle I ever penned, being as I have to stop from time to time & meditate, & then lose my train of thought. But I hope you won't object to the confusion.

I'm so much sorrier for you than for me. I'm going to a new place to work—& you are left behind in the same spot—with nothing to occupy you. Dear Kid. Soon after I stopped writing I was informed by the couple across the way that I did not get to Florence until 11.15. Picture my dismay! Lucky I brought along that choc. Of course the train was late, & it is now 1.15 A.M. I wish you could see the grand apartment I am housed in for the night. It's 3 times the size of the library at the hospital where you & I were last night. I have counted 18 chairs, 5 stools & a setee, all gold & brocade. The walls are hung in red brocade & all the hangings are the same. Some room! I feel quite lost, but, am quite ready now to sleep. So buono notte, my beamish boy.

This pen is the worst yet. Hope you won't be disagreeably surprised at the untidiness of my scrawl. Oh yes, I forgot to say Capt.

Aikin met me, & I am to go to the hospital tomorrow at 9 A.M. My love I miss you dreadfully.

Yours—Agnes

I'll have another look at your picture ere I retire.

.  .  .

Oct. 16, 1918[13]

$M$y Spanish Mick—

This A.M. I mailed you the peroration of yesterday & last night just before Capt. Aikin brought me here in the car. As I am to go on night duty tonight, & I have the whole P.M. and not feeling sleepy, will dig into my piles of back correspondence. I was invited to go to the town, we are a little ways out, but it looked stormy again, & I had an old headache & wanted to write you—3 good convincing reasons. As I'm on night duty I'll have other opportunities & in fact it quite pleases me as, if on day duty, I'd be only able to see the town by night. This will only be while my patient is so sick, of course, & Capt. Aikin says he is going to keep me for awhile to look after the 7 or 8 other members of his staff who are sick with the "Floo"—so I'll be here for a while anyhow. This is all encouraging in case you get a permission with your 3 old pals. If you don't—it is rather discouraging, I fear, but anyhow, you said you couldn't stand seeing me around all day as you did for days, so it is probably for the best, anyhow. So be cheerful, old Kid of mine, & just remember missing you quite as much as you will miss me tho' maybe not quite as wildly.

When I saw that couple on the train yesterday I kept wishing I had you alongside of me, so I could put my head on that nice place— you know—the hollow place for my face—& go to sleep with your arm around me.

Miss Jessup—the only Amer. R.C. nurse here in Firenze, told me today about 2 aviators who were at the Hotel this week. They gave her a lurid account of Sam Walker's surprise party at the Ospedale that famous night. What do you know about the fame of our parties travelling over Italy like that? If I get a chance to see these young men—Mr. Farquharson & that blonde who sang in the quartette that night—I'll certainly give them something to think about.

This Hospital is a big one on a hill, with a wonderful view of Florence. There are quite a few English nurses here, but only one "trained" nurse. Everyone speaks Italian with great speed, so I, of course, am forced into silence.

I am so sorry I didn't bring Cavie's camera along—there's so many I'd like to have pictures of. (This is *not* meant for a hint, or a knock—Capito?) You so often take offense where none is meant. I keep looking at your picture & another one I brought with me, of you in bed, whistling, (the one Darling took) and hoping you are not behaving yourself badly, but, are sweet to everyone as I know you can be.

This is going to be a great night duty for me. I'm all alone in the building, with my patient & another—a British Tommy—with the Floo so I expect you'll get more letters than you'll know how to answer. I'll send some to the Club, because I don't want any suspicion cast on you. Dear old thing—you are so far away—but, 2 years is even farther, so I must be patient. All my love—& double.

As ever—your
Ag

·   ·   ·

Oct. 17, 1918

Kid, dear,[14]

I wish I could think up some new & original titles for you to surprise you with, but I always seem to come back to my first attempts. Of course, you are "Why Girls Leave Home," "The Light of My Existence," "My Dearest & Best," "Most Ernest of Ernies," "More Precious Than Gold in War Times," "My hero," & many more that I will not fill up the page with.

If you could see me on this night duty. I'm entirely alone with my patient. There is one other patient the opposite end of the building—he's asleep all night & 2 nurses are sleeping on this floor. Then there is an old soldier downstairs on guard at the door. Otherwise this building is absolutely empty & the other Hosp. buildings are about 1/2 block away. Gosh—if you were only here, I'd dash in & make you up about now, & you'd smile at me & hold out your brawny arms. What's the use of wishing?

The first part of the night it simply poured, & I sat & shook with terror over The Golden Triangle by Maurice LeBlanc, & you know his style. Then about 3 the rain had almost stopped & I peeked out of the window—& saw old Luna—a nice big yellowish one on one side, surrounded by thick dark clouds, & on the other side, below, were a few twinkling lights of the City. My, but you would have liked it and the rain just dripping enough to make a soothing sound.

My poor patient is quite sick & so restless, he has not been able to sleep all night—so I've been able to stay awake—& haven't had a chance to get cold—so I haven't really needed "my furnace" except for many other reasons than mere physical warmth.

Goodness, it's so quiet my pen sounds like a Caproni[15] going by.

8.30 I wish you could have seen the thrilling rescue I just pulled off. A poor little kitten was on the roof all night, & howling like mad. I found it when I came off duty & I climbed up on a bench & window sill & got it down to the accompaniment of much grateful purring, & the horror of an Italian soldier occupied in cleaning inside the window.

Well, I must hie me to my cold—cold letto [bed] & my chilly, chilly little 2 × 4—but, if the rain lets up enough I'll surely go to town this afternoon.

I love you still—ever—

Agnes

Oct. 17, 1918

Ernie, my dearest—[16]

That was such a nice letter I got today—& unexpected, too, as I didn't think I could possibly hear before tomorrow. I'll tell you one reason I liked it so much. I guess every girl likes to have some man tell her how nice she is, & how he can't do without her. Anyway—I am but human, & when you say these things I love it, & can't help but believe you. So don't be afraid I'll get tired of you. I haven't really started to worry yet over your forgetting to love me as you do now, but sometimes I do think of the possibility & I don't enjoy my thoughts at all.

Dear heart, don't go around looking so doleful. I like best to remember you as you so often were in the A.M.—smiling & bubbling over with real joy—& I always prefer to picture you with your famous grin. So don't spoil my picture & wear a long, tearful expression these days & write as often as you can afford the stamps, as I shall chiefly exist on what I get in the mail. I am very much disheartened about my patient tonight. 3 learned & pompous medicos held a consultation over him this evening but, we don't know yet what they decided. I only know that he is so restless & nervous that he is not able to sleep—& slept none last night—that & the spitting up blood are what I am worrying about.

So maybe I'll be back before you think. Tonight is clear for a change. It rained today just about the time I wanted to explore the town, so I stayed in bed instead. Here the night nurse is on duty from 7 P.M. until 8 A.M. Queer arrangement, isn't it? But I should worry, it isn't forever.

I've read your letter of today 3 times, & here goes for another look at it. To think I would ever become so foolish! You know you are rather wonderful yourself—you are so splendid & fresh-looking, & have such cheerful ways—except at off times, of which we will not speak. And then you have such good ideas in all the things that count. And, of course, you know you can write, so I do not have to tell you that. Take you all in all you're about the nicest man I know, or ever will know.

I feel terribly desolate—away off here far from you & my friends, & I haven't even discovered any Bellia's to help me pass the time. I am not in an American Red Cross Hosp. so just address me c/o Amer. Red Cross—& I'll get it O.K.

Good luck, my dearest—and don't forget me, nor that I love you.

Ag

.  .  .

Oct 19—[1918]

Dearest Mr. Kid,[17]

I'm sadly cheated—I got no letter from you yesterday, and I suddenly felt quite lost. Maybe today I'll get two. Anyhow, I'll try to keep cheerful until I know if I am to hear from you today—or not.

Yesterday, I went into Florence. I was told to take a tram in, but, I says to myself, it will be much more sporting if I walk in, & then I'm not nearly so apt to lose myself. So I followed the car tracks until they got too complex for me, & then, I just turned this way & then that— & came out at the Duomo as nice as you please. Then I found some fascinating looking buildings, & felt so ignorant because I didn't know what they were. Lots of statuary in front of some. Florence is certainly the most interesting place I've seen so far—it gives you the impression of antiquity & Middle Ages right away. I do wish I could remember all I have read about it. Next time I go in I shall purchase a guide book & learn something—there's so much to see. And I'm told the Pitti Palace is open, tho' the Uffici [Uffizi] Gallery is not. You know these by hearsay as well as I do, I daresay. I kept thinking yesterday as I rambled how wonderful it would be to have you here with me to help me find my way about, & explore. I walked & walked & finally found a place where I got some very good milk chocolate—a factory—like your Talmone in Turino. But, alas, when I was "stanco" & would take the tram home I didn't know where I should take it. After asking a few questions & getting unintelligible answers, I found the right track & my car dashed by me, so I proceeded to plod my weary way homeward. As the Hospital is at the top of a steep hill & quite a walk from town, by the time I arrived I was sadly bushed, as you would so aptly put it. I haven't done much walking here in Italy, & my poor old knees were caving in. The tram for me next time.

This letter is a la Sawhill—all about myself—but, dear one, I'm afraid to write much about you—or you & me.

Everything I see or read seems applicable to the Case of You & Me. I find a parallel in every romance.

My patient still seems about the same, & now they think he has Typhoid. Miss Jessup & I have our doubts about their diagnosis—but, time will show.

If you don't write to me every day—I'm afraid I'll have to stop dropping you one per day, & then I'd have nobody to talk to. I really care so much, Ernie.

Your own—
Aggie

.    .    .

Oct. 20–21[1918][18]

Dear Maestro Antico [Antique]—[19]

Yesterday I missed writing you, as I hadn't heard from you for 2 days, but this A.M. I found a letter that had been in the Office all day. Yesterday & this evening I got 2 more. A festa day! I'm told to tell you by them as knows that you should not say "Al" on my letters but "Alla"—("For the love of Allah" you know). Also, did I tell you this is not the Amer. Red Cross Hosp. but Amer. Hosp. under Italian Red Cross? Still, as I got your letters I should worry what you put on them's outsides as long as you put something nice on them's insides—& you just about do this, I'd say. I hope you are getting these letters I'm sending to the club, as I don't know the address, & am just taking a chance. You'd better date yours so I can tell when you do write. Your letters are beginning to cause a little excitement here already. In case I do not stay at the Hosp. very long, I'd rather you sent your letters to the Red Cross here & I'm quite as sure of getting them. If I left here I doubt if I'd ever get them, as they don't seem very careful about such things. These last 2 letters I got were certainly a little more cheerful. Maybe you were irrational, but anyhow I was sitting in my patient's room reading them, & almost roused him from his drowsy stupor by my sudden outbursts of hysteria. I had to have an audience so I read parts—humorous parts—such as that about mule meat versus brook trout—to Miss Jessup, who is just the sort of a girl you would like very much. She has had more world experiences—has only been home once since the old war began & went through the Typhus epidemic in Serbia, where she was the only nurse in the hospital. My paper is getting scarce, hence my seeming economy in writing on both sides.[20]

Dear boy, I don't want you to even think of getting me a camera & sending it down here. Such a foolishness. Still, its like your generous old heart & I preciates the idea.

I have to smile a tearful smile every time you write that "Have a good time" stuff. I'm leading more of a hermit's life than I ever did in Milan on night duty. I get up at 5.30 & have my dinner at 6.00 & go over to this very desolate building where we are incarcerated. Then I make chocolate in the A.M. for Miss Jessup & myself, & go off about 8 & go to bed again. Sometimes I see a few Italian nurses at the table at dinner & sometimes I eat alone. The only break since I came is my walk into Florence on Fri. & it has rained every day.

Still, I didn't mean this to be a complaint. I just didn't want you to think I was having a good time away from you. I think my patient is a little better, & of course, when he is really out of all danger, Miss Jessup & I may be able to get out together. I'm not as keen on doing the town by myself. If you & your trio were only here, not that I especially insist on the trio, but I was merely quoting your statements, oh Master Mine. Florence would be a very different place if I only had you.

You make me of a great stanco-edness talking about my forgetting & such. Do I bother you with any small talk of no import? I do not. Tho' I will say that my letters do not contain much of the humorous. Still I cannot be very humorous in these circumstances. Night duty, as I've before remarked, has a depressing influence on me—when I have nobody to talk to.[21] (I am just now holding sweet converse with a long lanky mosquito, who would fain kiss my hand. I missed him, by thunder!)

Well, I have nothing worth while to say except that I'll be a different woman when I see you grin again. Your last 2 letters are in the pocket of my apron, & during the long hours of the night whenever I begin to pine & fret I'll just take 'em out & re-peruse them, as I've done with all former missives. I'm afraid this is a very stupid letter. Forgive me. I have not the inspiration of your presence. Anyhow, I love you more & more, & I know what I'm going to bring you when I come home.

So kiss me good-night & go—(speaking to this letter—not you.)

> T[esoro]—M[io]
> [my darling]—
> oh most longed for!
> *Yours*—
> Agnes

. . .

Oct. 21–22[1918]

Oh, dearest Mr. Kid,[22]

No letter today, but, I won't worry. I'm sure you wouldn't neglect me so soon. I've sent you 2—or 3—c/o "British-American Officer's Club—Milan." I wonder if you have gotten them O.K. Today I wrote you a postal—a masterpiece of the camofleur's Art—which, as you will at once divine—is for the general public.

I had the first really enjoyable time, this afternoon, since I landed here. (That's a horribly constructed sentence—but I'm going too fast to stop & do it over.) Our patient is a little better, so Miss Jessup left him in the hands of another nurse & took me out on a shopping tour. I spent all my money in one day, but, I thoroughly enjoyed doing it. First, she took me into a real antique shop on the Ponte Vecchio,[23] where I fell for a ring.[24] First time I ever bought myself any jewelry—& the last, I guess, but it's a lovely ring. As I spent 130 lire on that, I began to fear I would not finish out the afternoon. Just wait until you see it—you'll be that jealous.

Then we went to a silver smiths where I got a couple of hand-worked spoons—& 2 chains of Roman pearls. All these are for gifts to take home, of course—not just for me. Also I got a little something for you—just a souvenir—so to speak. That wasn't from the silversmith's tho'. Everything here is much cheaper than in Milan. I haven't been to the embroidery shops, yet. I'll be ruined before I leave here, I guess. I'm down to 35 lire, now, & when I got back I found my traveller's checks for $50.00 so I'll have enough to go out again when they are cashed.

I suppose you'll think I'm an awfully extravagant person, but, I'm just afraid I won't have another opportunity like this, maybe. I also got myself a guide-book, & now I'm going to study it the rest of the night—& then I'll explore again. It's the first time I ever wanted to look at a guide-book, but, there's so much that's really worth while to see here, that I must take my chances & see it.[25]

Well, then, we had tea in a queer place that is supposed to be very smart—& then went over & sat on the steps of the Duomo until the motor came for us. The mosquitoes are being terribly attentive to me tonight. This morning one kissed me on the mouth, & it was quite lop-sided for awhile. I tell you this, for fear you might think it was not done by an insect.

This letter so far, is full of my doings & none of my thinkings, so I'll have to continue it in my next.

I hear that 2 of the nurses have reported to Miss Jessup that I was engaged. Miss Jessup thinks that you are merely an infatuated youth, whom I allow to write me, & I've let her think so—for reasons of state. You must never think I am ashamed of you. Why, some times I'm so proud of you, & the fact that you love me, that I want to blurt it all out, & just have to hold on tight so it won't get out. That is our war-sacrifice, bambino mio, to keep our secrets to ourselves—but, so long as you have no secrets from me, & I have none from you (at least, I can't think of anything you don't know already) why, we should worry about whether the old world knows. And, I'm afraid the world doesn't understand everything anyhow, & would make very harsh criticisms. But, dopo la guerra [after the war]—we should worry about criticism, shouldn't we? Won't it be wonderful to be free again? I can hardly wait. Peace is going to mean a lot more to us than it did when we first came over, n'est-ce-pas?

I'm so glad you are off of the hard drinks. It shows how much character you really have, that you can resist temptation, especially when low in your mind. I wish I could tell Gum-shoe that little fact—but—then she won't even be an item in our "dopo la guerra," will she?

Dear boy, I think every day how nice it would be to feel your arms around me again. And at night, lately, I've actually had to hug a hot-water bottle to keep myself from congealing entirely. Isn't that a fearful state of affairs? So far from my own furnace fire.

Oh, Kid, I do miss you—& more each day, I do believe—

> Your Mrs. Kid
> Aggie

.  .  .

[October 22, 1918]

[To Lieut. E. M. Hemingway][26]

I hope Mr. Tandy[27] did not get all set up over my sending him a card first. I just happened to run out of postals that day before I could send all the rest of you one. Still I suppose he'll never stop talking about it. I was at this very spot today—tho' not quite so high up.

> Yours very securely,
> A.V.K.

Oct 22–23[1918]

Ernie, *my* boy—[28]

Sounds rather patronizing, but, I meant it as proprietary—capito?

Having just bathed my hands in carbolic, regardless of my epidermis, I am now sterile & can talk to you awhile. No letter from you since the 2 Sun. afternoon, so I'll probably expire gaspingly tomorrow if none is forthcoming by noon. I am coming off night duty, & Miss Jessup going on for a week, as this may be a long siege if it turns out to be Typhoid. My patient is almost continually irrational now, & last night after I finished your letter I could not leave him for more than a minute at a time, as he was trying to get out of bed, & talking to people in his room—(or in his imagination) all night. I wondered what I'd do if he got violent, but, I was able to manage him very well, so I hope tonight we will get along as well. Just think I have all day tomorrow, & all tomorrow night off & nothing to do, & nobody to do it with. Miss Jessup will be off of course, tomorrow night, but, we are to have dinner with Miss Sheldon, the Directress of the Hospital (who is not even a nurse, by the way) and the tram out this way stops running at 9 P.M. So I guess we will have to be good.

Miss Nolan came through from Milan today with 6 letters & a postal for me, which I found when I woke up. One letter was from Capt. Serena, & he asked tenderly after you. The postal was from Mr. Fielder from Rome. Mama wrote me how terrible the epidemic was in America, & she hoped she wouldn't get it—giving me something else to worry about.

Jo Holdener, my classmate in England, whom you've heard me speak of, says they have 600 cases—25 of whom are nurses—& 5 of those have died already—(of the nurses). Cheerful, isn't it?

Today, I dreamed I was home in the U.S. & seeing all sorts of people. Among them I saw my doctor, & almost passed him by, then decided to speak. "Hello, Daddy," I said, & he remarked it was about time I recognized him. Then the rest of my dream I was all the time trying to get a chance to explain to him why I couldn't marry him, &

always some interruption came just as I was about to say it. He was so kind & sweet I felt more guilty than ever, too.

So since I've waked up, I've had it very much on my mind. If I could see him & tell him myself it would be so much less cruel than writing it. You have no sympathy for him, but you should. The dreadful thought came to me today, that, maybe my punishment for this treatment of him, would be to have you treat me in a like manner some day.

I certainly need a dose of your presence, dear—to reassure & comfort me. By the way—if by any possible chance you should come to Florence while I'm here, I hope you'll let me know in time so my letters won't be accumulating under Gumshoe's tender watchful care.

Not having a letter from you since Sun, makes a big difference. I feel rather far away & alone just now. What wouldn't I give for you & your favorite speech—you know the one I mean.

Except for missing you, I am quite well, & apparently—on the surface—cheerful, so don't worry so much about your Kid, tho' I love you for doing it.

Your faithful
Mrs. Kid

.　　.　　.

Oct 24, 1918

Ernie, my darling—[29]
I was just about getting discouraged, & all that, when today I got 5 letters in a bunch, after not hearing since Sun. I think they have been accumulating at the R.C. Office & they just haven't had a chance to send them up. Anyhow, I felt a lot better, until I read the last one, & heard you are going back to the Front without me there to bid you goodbye. I knew you'd have to go some time, but I did hope it

would not be while I was away, & I don't see much prospect of getting back for a week, or two, & that is doubtful.

I can certainly sympathize with your longing for action, tho', & if my prayers will do any good, I'm sure nothing can happen to you this time. But, oh, how I wish this old war was finito.

I can't remember now, what change I meant—but—if I said it—I think I must have meant a change in disposition—cheer— being difficult under the circumstances of last week. But yesterday Miss Jessup & I swapped & today I am on day-duty for a week, which is less lonely, maybe, but I don't have any time to see Florence or shop as I'd like to. Maybe it's a good thing as I can't help spending money if I'm out & see something I like. I just got letters from Cavie & Brooks & a card from K.C. De L.[30] Cavie advised me to write you—as you were very sad, & also told me to advise you to buy an overcoat. She doesn't know you have some already. I'll worry now about you going around without a heavy coat in this damp weather.

Brooks says she is trying to pet you on the q.t. as you are in the same boat as she is. But she can't make me jealous.

Dear Kid, I think of you so much & miss you so much since I came away—won't you believe me? In every letter you ask me not to forget you, or something like that. I don't think you realize that that is quite unnecessary. I dreamed of you last night.

I wonder if you have gotten all my letters. I've written every day except Sun. & will write every day as long as I'm here if I'm sure you are getting them & if you don't get tired of these stupid ones. I will confess I sometimes have a hard time reading yours, but, nevertheless I go over them often.

Thanks for the pictures, Kid mine, I'm returning them, as I imagine you would like to keep them.

Ernie dear, of course I wish I could keep you near me, but, I know too that you must go back, so I'll try & be as cheerful as I can, & write you very often—

Tesoro mia, I miss you so—

Yours only,
Aggie

Oct. 25, 1918
Alla 2 ore

My own Kid,[31]

Now I suppose I won't hear from you again until some kind friend calls at the R.C. office & gets me your letters, as I am tied here all day, & can't find the place anyhow. But as I'm sure you are writing I'll try & hold out until they come.

My patient slept for about 12 hours yesterday—his first real sleep, & since then has had practically no fever, and is rational & himself. We are so pleased that he is out of danger, practically (error using same word twice) and he will soon be a well man, I think, if they ever let him have food.

Some of the Americans in Florence told us the other day that the story they heard was—that the doctors had given up hope, & the nurses said they would pull him through, they were sure. I guess that's about right, as the doctors were very hopeless when I first got here. But, Miss Jessup gets the credit for all this, as she pitched in & took care of him before he had a doctor when he was sick in the hotel.

Do you know, that this week when I didn't get your letters, I imagined you had gotten sick & all sorts of foolish things—at least they seem foolish, now.

Today over a hundred ammalati [patients] arrived at the Hospital, & this building which was empty is now swarming with swarthy Sicilians and our peace is gone. In fact, more are coming tomorrow, & then not even this wing will be private.

In this book I am reading, one passage made me stop. Don't laugh at me if I quote it, will you? "It must have been beautiful to have begun life like that," she said. "Yes," he said, "at least we had our Spring." "To be together," said the lady, "and—so beautifully poor."

Now, don't make fun of that, but just tell me what you think of it?

Oh, my dear, how can I ever let you go without even seeing you? And, now, I suppose I won't even get your letters for several days, & won't know for a certainty whether you've gone or not. Miss Jessup was engaged to a British officer who has been missing since April, & she is wearing mourning for him.[32]

Don't let me gain you only to lose you, after I've just found out what I've gained. But, there don't think I'm whining or anything like that. I know very well you are going to live to a ripe old age, & no little war is going to separate us, so I'm not going to be cowardly about it any more—at least not to you.

I wish I had something more interesting to tell you. I guess I'll have to fill up with your favorite expression, which I can safely say I do *not* get tired of. I love you, Ernie, & I miss my boy. Thank you for your mother's message. I wish I knew her—but—you know your favorite song—"Elegy"? That expresses my feelings very well these days—for in spite of the sunshine, I am lost without you, & I thought it was the dismal rain that made me miss you so.

> Good luck, bambino mio
> Yours—only—
> Aggie

.   .   .

Oct. 26, 1918

My dearest Kid—[33]

This A.M. I got your letter of the 24th & I know now for sure that you have gone back to be in the thick of the action, so I know you are satisfied, & never would be if you'd been kept out of it.

If I send you a letter every day will you surely get them? And I wonder if you'll get a package if I should send you one.

Please note this paper. It is called "Frou Frou"[34]—& Miss Jessup & I bought it together because it was so loud in it's [sic] design. So now, I'm using it to show I'm trying to keep you cheered & not going to be mournful. Here everything is going very well. The patient is so much better that I fear I'll be back in Milan before you return, & then we would not have quite as free a hand in our confabs, etc. Capito? Oh—mon enfant, how I wish I could be along with you where I could be of a little use anyhow. Here, I fear your words to Cavie about the pleasure-trip are too sadly true. Goodness knows, I feel rather unenthusiastic about Florence now.

Still as Pollyanna would say, "I'm glad in a way I wasn't in Milan when you left, as I might have bawled, & disgraced the family." Likewise, you might have hugged me in front of Miss De Long, & then she would have been sure I was of your quality & breed. Still, I forget she's changed her mind about you—now. I'm glad, too.

I dreamed an awful dream about you last night, but, for superstition's sake I won't tell you today, as "Friday night's dream on Sat. told is sure to come true, etc." Anyhow, another superstition says dreams go by contrary—so I should worry. The main point is—as Rocky says—that I was upset over you in my dreams. But, I believed in you—& I do—so bring home the proverbial rasher [bacon], & do not disappoint me.

Something tells me this is the last offensive. Maybe, I'm wrong, as hunches often fail, but—

Today, everybody has been dressed up in their best & cleanest for the expected visit of the Duchess d'Aosta, but, ella non e venuto qui [she did not arrive] & she isn't coming now for a week or so.

You know, of course, that I'm hanging on the word I get from you so don't leave me hanging, or I may fall (anyhow—not fall in love—as I've already that, you know). Basta bambino mia [enough, my little boy], I love you so! Your Kid

Agnes

.　　.　　.

Oct. 26 [1918]

Dearest Pal—[35]

I've written you one letter already today, but, this pen is simply itching to start again, & I guess you don't care how many I write if I find something to say in each one. I never wrote so often to anybody before in my life—& I wonder how long I can keep it up, but, so far it seems natural, & they just shoot out as easy & spontaneous.

This is as far as I got yesterday, as I was interrupted, but, now, having laved the Lieut. & anointed him with sweet waters & good natured alcohol (Miss Jessup shaved him before she went off duty) made his bed, cut his little toe-nails, manicured his finger-nails, swept his room, fixed his flowers, dusted, made lemonade, & now while the cocoa is cooking for his next meal, I can recreate by writing you, as he has dropped off to sleep from sheer fatigue at so much excitement & fixing up. Let me tell you something funny about me. The mosquitoes have so bitten my countenance during my nocturnal slumbers that I look like a smallpox victim. Two mornings I awoke & beheld with rising wrath my speckled & again more speckled visage & last night I determined it was the hour for desperate measures. So I freely besmeared my face with Camphor Ice, as the strongest smelling stuff I had with me & slept with my head almost enveloped. Behold my horror this A.M. I look as tho' old Sol had pierced my skin with his most vicious rays & my poor face is a blaze of color, punctuated by small red spots, thus making me look more than ever like ye Smallpox. However, have no fear, it will all disappear I can guarantee. But just now I feel rather stiff in the smile joints. I should explain Camphor Ice burned my skin pretty nigh off.

I've just been down to lunch—(the first time I've left Mr. Hough that long—before this they have always brought a tray) & I feel a trifle "pesante" [lethargic] & feeble in intellect. I've had a lot of fresh figs lately—I'm crazy about them, & they know it, so whenever I go near the kitchen I'm offered more figs.

If you could see the service here that the nurses get you'd probably say you got better yourself up at the Front. The soup is put on a side table in a big kettle, & a pile of plates alongside & everybody comes along & fetches their own. Then when you finish the soup you remove the plate & help yourself to the next course.

Downstairs the soldiers are playing the Victrola—most squeaky operatic selections, & Mr. Hough has just been treated to his first chicken broth, & is basking in perfect content.

I don't believe I'll be here much more than a week longer,[36] & as the other patients I was to take are most of them well again, why I guess I'll be back in Milan soon.

I'll miss the Halloween party, but as you are not going to be there, I don't take much interest in it anyhow.

Miss Conway wrote me that "Brown-eyes" was heart-broken after I left—meaning you, of course. I'm so tickled over the success of the camouflage card. It was beyond my highest expectations. Now, maybe, Mac won't be quite so suspicious of me.

Dear, I hope to go to town tomorrow & will lay in a new stock of paper & stamps, so that I can keep on writing—even tho' I have nothing interesting to say.

This will be all for now, but, if I get the inspiration again this P.M. I will start off again. Good luck, Kid, & I love you, so don't do anything foolish.

Yours only—
Aggie

.    .    .

Oct. 28 [1918]
Monday

Kid, dear,[37]

As you see I did not get your letter mailed yesterday, as I had no stamps here, & was on duty & unable to go & get them. This afternoon Miss Jessup is going to come on duty early, so I can go to town, & I am to take dinner at her pensione with Miss Buck, a very pretty American girl here who has the dressings in the R.C. magazine. So I'll then have a chance to mail this earlier than if I had left it at the office of the Hosp.

I saw the paper this A.M. & the news sounded pretty good, & I thought of you when I read something about the battle of Grappa & wondered if you got there in time to be useful.

It's quite cold today, so I'm hoping you have a coat on. I'm glad you could use the old raincoat & don't bother about sending it back. Just let it go until you come back to Milan.

I'll bet Mac is pretty forlorn now that you've gone & left her, in fact, the old Ospedale must be a rather dead place without your scraps & "The wild, wild, woman." I'm not as keen on getting back as I was at first.

My patient is getting badly spoiled. He is very fond of hard back rubs, & says I'm some masseuse. Also, he likes me to manicure his finger-nails tho' I'll give him credit for this being the first time he's ever had them done.

He has an appetite that grows daily, & the doctor is so cautious he won't allow him anything but milk & such drinks. He takes it through a tube, & usually lies with eyes closed, gulping it down, & looks so like a baby with a bottle, I almost laugh in his face—but, this young man has absolutely a very slight sense of humor, & usually when Miss Jessup & I are chattering & laughing, he is as solemn as an oyster.

His kid brother was here to see him today, & he is quite an attractive boy. Tho' that need not make you at all concerned—he's not nearly as attractive as a boy I know—my boy, in fact.

Thank God, you've got a keen sense of humor! I can't imagine anything more awful than to have to live a life with anyone who hasn't got one.

I think you are just about the most companionable man I ever knew, and if you do fly off the handle once in awhile, why, even that is necessary to make life less monotonous.

Well, I do hope my letters will be a bit cheerful, but, I'm thinking you don't need cheering now, as I can picture you simply bursting with excitement a good part of the time, & I suppose—bursting with Brummy's Marteale [?] the rest of the time. I realize that in war, men have to drink, & especially when it is cold—so use your judgement, honey—& I'm sure you will come out alright.

> Goodbye, Ernie dear—
> Your own
> Kid

. . .

Oct. 29, 1918

Ernie dear,[38]
I've just written a letter by way of duty, to the medico [Dr. S.], the first in over a month, I think. But, I really believe he has forgot-

ten me, or is angry about something as I haven't heard from him in a dog's age.

Your letter came this A.M. from the Front,[39] & I was glad to hear so promptly. I went to the city yesterday P.M. as I said I would, but I felt so tired, & cold, & had the beginnings of a cold in the head which I desired to close up, so I did not stay for dinner, & the night as Miss Jessup had planned, but, hustled back to the Ospedale, & went to bed.

You see, I am growing very cautious for a trained nurse— because of your many strict injunctions to keep well. Today, I am O.K. except for slight sniffles, & nothing to worry about. Trained nurses are usually noted for being reckless about their own health, while trying hard to keep up that of others. Not, unselfishly, I mean, but, just recklessly.

I spent money recklessly tho' and can only attribute my extravagance to a slight wooziness from cold which dimmed my faculties, tho' I didn't get stung at all. I bought some lovely embroidered things which would not interest you at all, but, which feminine hearts take great delight in. Any casual observer would think I was buying a trousseau, & in fact, I have been accused of that, but, of course, you know it is not so, and, I intend wearing these.

Then I went in a leather shop, and wanted everything I saw, as they were not high, & make wonderful gifts, but, alas, I found my lire were low, and I had to leave behind a picture frame & a card-case that I had set my heart on. But, the next time I'm out, I'll cash my last 2 traveller's checks & get some more for Xmas presents for the nurses in Milan.

After my money is all gone, maybe, I can go sight-seeing. Anyhow, the galleries are always closed before I get into the town.

I'm telling you all this to show I am not always dependable, & sometimes have streaks, when I am greatly tempted. Now I'll go back to Milan, & live off of the income Cavie is going to pay me—monthly installments of her loan.

My patient is entertaining his kid brother so I gathered up my things and brought them out to the little kitchen where I can write without being disturbed. He doesn't understand why I write so many letters, and, says admiringly, "My, but, you certainly do tear them off!" And so I do. This is my 3rd today, & of the simply innumerable amount I owed when I came, I owe only 1 more, and then I write you every day, & my mother twice a week. So I've reason to pat myself, haven't I, old Master? But, I'm wondering how I'll manage when I get back to Milan, about your letters, I mean. However, I shouldn't worry until I have to, and, I'll do my best, bambino mio, to get you a letter every day, if possible.

Dear, I sometimes wonder at myself, because I think so much of you, and want you so badly to be here to talk to. It certainly is a new sensation for me. I never pined for anybody before in my life. In every book I read, I seem to find a parallel to you & me. Does it sound foolish to you when I write like this? I really never thought I could write what I feel so plainly & openly. Writing has always made me draw into a shell—it seemed so irrevocable. Once written you can't take back what you have said.

I guess if Dr. S——[40] ever saw a letter like this from me he'd think I'd gone mad. He never saw much of the Inner me, & you've seen so much. I'm ashamed to say I'm always comparing you with him in my mind's eye, & the comparison always comes out bene for you, & he is left in the dust.

Your letters are getting shorter, but, I hope it's because you are busy, so I don't mind so much. I'd hate to be opening my heart like this on paper, if I thought you were not responding in yours. But then, I'm almost sure I could tell by the way you wrote if you began to change.

I never imagined anyone would be so dear & necessary to me. What you say about the party going on in another room really astonishes me. Can you break out of things like that without causing comment? Of course, I'm terribly proud of your endurance, but, I certainly can trust you to do as you think best.

I do so wish I had a good picture of you. I've nothing but, a snapshot of you in bed, & another in the Parco with Lore—& I want one I can put in a nice frame. When I go back to Milan, I think I'll have my picture taken for your benefit.

I'm so glad the others in your section like me. I love to be liked, so it makes me happy to have my old patients commend me.

Give my best to all I know.

That's best regards—of course—my best love goes only to ye O.M.

> Goodnight—Tesoro Mio
> Aggie

I dare not read this letter over for fear I'll never dare to send it.

.    .    .

Oct. 30, 1918

My Old Master,[41]

This is a queer world, indeed. Since I wrote you yesterday P.M. much has happened. Miss Jessup came on duty with a temperature of 101 last night & insisted on staying on all night in spite of my entreaties. But, she gave in this morning at 5.30 & called me, & I came over & put her to bed with chills & a terrible cough. She's had the influenza twice already & this cough has been with her ever since the last attack and she needed a rest but stayed on with Mr. Hough—so I am not surprised, tho' I am worried. She has the Flu again.

I am to go on night duty again, tonight, and goodness knows who will take care of her & Mr. Hough in the daytime. I'm forced to change to a pencil because I have been put to bed for the afternoon, so I can be on duty tonight. As Miss Jessup & I had the same room, there was quite a discussion as to where I should sleep today, & finally I am put on a cot in an empty ward next to Mr. Hough's room. This sho' is war times, I says. I dreamed an awfully nice dream last night. I dreamed I was up at Section 4[42] at the Front, & having the time of my life. I seemed to be the only female present, & was a sort of guest of honor at a big banquet, which I enjoyed hugely but, all the time I had the feeling that if Miss De Long ever found it out, it would be my finish. Then you, who had been with me all along, disappeared, & I kept worrying about where you'd gone. All at once I spied you thru a lighted window shaving & fixing yourself all up in your best uniform. I was sitting on a bench outside waiting for you. Then

Miss Jessup sent for me, & I couldn't finish it. But I laughed over the shaving part—it seemed so natural.

Goodbye, dear boy, & take good care of yourself for me. I must tear off a little rest, now—

> Your own Kid—
> Agnes

·   ·   ·

Nov. 1, 1918

Ernie, dearest,[43]

I wrote you last night, while on duty, but, it was such a punk letter I was doubtful about sending, & couldn't post it until this P.M. anyhow. So now, at noon came your letter from Milan,[44] & I hasten to tear up last nights bromide & endite a fresher epistle. I was worried at first over your sickness, & then I read Cavie's letter & she guaranteed you'd be alright by the time I came back, so then I just buried my face in my pillow & laughed for joy to think I am going to see you in Milan when I get back.

When I thought it over I began to realize what a disappointment this must be to you, but, you've done your darndest as we all know, & surely God Knows Best, boy.

As you probably haven't rec'd my last letter yet, I'll have to tell you my news again. Miss Jessup has come down with her 2d or 3d attack of the Flu & is pretty sick. Everybody here has a cough, but, I think I had a light attack, which I succeeded in warding off by medicine & St. Anthony. Anyhow, my cold is much better, & would be gone if I was off of night duty. Miss J. got sick Tues. night & insisted on staying on duty all night, so in the A.M. she was pretty much of a wreck. Wed. I went on night duty with Mr. Hough, Miss Jessup—& about 30 soldiers—more or less recuperative. Of course they are not really my job, but they have no night nurse in this building & therefore take it for granted that I do the work, & so I say nothing—as I like to think I'm helping anyhow.

Today, I hear there's also a sick Y.M.C.A. man here for me to special—tonight.

Miss Jessup is a little better, I think, but, now I shall have to stay until she is able to be out, & probably will bring her to Milan with me.

I've been counting up, & must have sent you about 15 letters since I left Milan.[45] I only hope you have gotten them O.K. & none have fallen into hostile hands. I know they are not very interesting these days, as night duty has not developed my human side, & I think too much—especially of you.

Last night I was wishing I was with you on the big couch on the terzo piano. I had a grand old time yesterday A.M. giving Mr. Hough a perfect shave—my first attempt with a safety razor, but, I got full directions from him as I went along, & now feel fully qualified as a lady barber—having concluded with a facial massage, cold cream & powder.

Dear Kid, do write to me, & hurry up & get well so I shan't worry about you.

Just imagine yourself kissed goodbye

By your own Kid—<br>Aggie

·     ·     ·

Nov. 2, 1918

Ernie, dear—[46]

Good news today, wasn't it?[47] I think the "Dopo la Guerra" time is beginning to look less shadowy on the horizon. What would Life be without something pleasant to look forward to? Anyhow, I'm beginning to get homesick for Milan tho' I'd hate to say so here—it would look as tho' I couldn't stick out a few little hardships. But you know its not the food, nor the baths I want to get back to our own Ospedale for, don't you?

My hands are cold, so its rather hard to make the old pen slide. I have just finished reading over all of your letters, by way of pastime for the midnight hours.

My patients—I have 4 specials—& 6 soldiers—seem to be all sleeping, just now, at any rate. 175 new soldiers were expected today, the hospital having been emptied of all those able to go yesterday, but, so far they have not come, & I hope they will not arrive until next week so as to give everybody a chance to rest up for them.

Miss Jessup had a pretty good night last night, & her temp. was normal, so I'm in hopes it was the typical 3 day type—even tho' she had a little rise today. Mr. Hough & his kid brother sent her some lovely flowers—roses & chrysanthemums, enough to make anyone get better. I'm wondering if you are better, now. To think you had to go & be sick when I wasn't there to take care of you. But, I'm sure Mac took you to her arms & made much of you, so I hope you'll be feeling a lot better by now. I think I'm about O.K. or will be when I get off night duty, which is an indefinite prospect.

I feel so sorry for poor Brooks—it must have given her a terrible shock to hear about poor little Lt. Johnson. I can't seem to get him out of my head. By-the-way, remember asking me about a spoon marked A. v. K. T'is mine, & seems to be impossible for me to keep it, as I'm always finding it in public use. So you guard it until my return, will you, Kid dear? Ernie—I wonder if you like me to repeat—anyhow, I'll try it once for luck. I miss you so, dear, & I love you so much. I was picturing you the other night as you looked when you got off the elevator when coming from Stresa. I can remember every detail of your expression. I wonder—will you look like that when I come back, or more so maybe?

Now, I'll bid you goodnight, & begin to discuss my soup. Wish you were here to have a bowlfull with me. I do hate to eat alone.

Ever your Mrs. Kid—
Ag—

Nov. 3, 1918

Dearest Mr. Kid—[48]

Now there you go a-worryin' over me for absolutely niente. I got your letter tonight, & hasten to reassure you as to my good health. I'm really feeling quite fit again, & am quite proud to think I didn't fall sick in this place. As a matter of fact, they fully expected me to, I believe, but, I fooled 'em, I did. It was a funny thing but, a week or so ago Jessup & I were talking over the possibilities of our taking the Flu, & we both requested that the other take us straight to Milan if we did fall sick. But, we reckoned without the people here. They rather resented outside nurses being sent for Mr. Hough, but they'd be incensed if we tried to move either Jessup or Mr. Hough to Milan. Now, tonight, Miss Sheldon, the directress of the Hospital is down with the Flu, complicated with liver troubles, thus making 5 special patients for me, now.

I'm afraid when Capt. Aikin gets back there's going to be a rumpus, as both Jessup & Mr. Hough are rather wrought up over the way I am taken for granted as a part of the Hosp. But, as for me, I am not killing myself with work, & so I don't mind helping them out, as long as my own A.R.C. patients aren't neglected and I can certainly always keep peace as long as I think it better—& more profitable.

Such excitement today among the Italians over the news that Trieste is taken. I look forward now to seeing Mr. Hough's newspapers arrive in the mornings, and it seems wonderful to be alive in such stirring times, doesn't it? I thank my stars' wish every day that I came over, & won't be one of those who will say after it is all over—"Well, I didn't get a chance to do what I wanted, & thought I'd never be able to stand foreign service, so I just stayed home, & did private nursing." I know several like that & they sure are coming money.

But I can't say anything because you are just the same as I, only more so, Kid dear. Tell me something about that Publicity Dept. job. Will you be in Rome all the time, or travelling around through Italy? I guess you don't trust me much, as you are unwilling to place the old Atlantic between us, & I can't very well blame you, seeing what I did to the Doctor. Well, Ernie my darlin', some day you'll believe in me just as firmly as I now hold my faith in you.

Dear, Milan begins to look further & further away, & just when I want most to be there—when you are sick. Please hurry up & get your interior dept. in good running order again, or I'll be sure Mac & Cavie are not taking the proper care of you, & I'll be worried—dreadfully. Maybe, someday, I'll be where you can't shake me when you need a nurse.

> Goodnight—sweetheart
> As ever—
> Your Mrs. Kid

· · ·

Nov. 4, 1918

Kid, dear,

I fully intended getting up early & going into Florence this afternoon, but, only woke up at 3.30 with a bad headache & found it was cloudy besides, so I changed my mind. And the soldiers are so happy over the taking of Trento, & all, that they have been singing up at the other Hospital for a couple of hours, now, while the Victrola has been going at this one. The effect is not conducive to repose, so I'll just write to you now, & then it will get mailed this evening & probably get to you a day ahead of the usual time.

One of the Italian nurses was so excited she couldn't work, & had to go home. But, I can hardly blame her, as her home is in the captured district. Can you realize that the war is coming to an end? I can't.

I am told I have another patient tonight—a British soldier with the Flu, & Miss Sheldon, the Diretrice [*direttrice:* directress] is quite ill, & had to have morphine today, so I may be too busy to write you tonight.

She is a very nice lady, but likes lots of attention. Also, I'm told Miss Jessup is better. I'm doing my derndest to "cure 'em Kid," 'cause when Jessup & Mr. Hough are able to leave I can go, too, & then they'll find it wasn't so bad having American nurses here after all— tho' we were not very welcome at first.

Tomorrow will be 3 weeks since I came, & I don't know where the time has gone. When I sleep in the day, and am busy at night I find time flies.

Tell me something about yourself. Are you still in bed, & just how sick are you? Do they feed you on milk & Frotta[49] water? (How I dislike this fountain pen!) Are you in truth suffering from that famous & rare disease known as the Moroccan—?

If so you have all of my sympathy, as I fear the remedy has never yet been discovered.

A Rivederci, my dear one—

Yours—
Aggie

.    .    .

Nov. 5–6, '18

Ernie, dear,

Today Mr. Hough's brother brought me 3 letters from you, & I've just feasted. One of them—in the lively blue envelope was evidently held for postage, as I've already rec'd it's [sic] successor.

Anyhow, there's so much I'd like to speak to you about, that probably I'll forget 1/2 and that could all be prevented if it was a personal interview, & not such a long distance one. I usually get started on something quite different from what I meant to say, & then find, after the letter is mailed, that I've left out a lot.

First, dear, about your so-called confession. I'll talk to you when I come back—but please don't worry—it'll be O.K.

Then, I'm so awfully sorry to hear J. W. Miller, Jr. is so sick. Please tell him I said so, and I do sincerely hope he'll be less miserable by the time I see him. There must be a lot of sick ones at the Hosp. now. I wish every day I was back—mostly on your account, as I feel that you need me. But, cheer up, Kid, Miss Jessup & Mr. Hough are both getting up tomorrow, & I really hope to be through here by the first of the week. And I was told tonight that I'll probably come off of night duty tomorrow, & that certainly will help.

Today I was counting up & out of my 4 months in Italy, 3 whole months have I been on night duty. How's that for the simple life? However, I can't kick—you've been through a whole lot worse than I can even dream of.

I'm feeling quite fit again, now, as I'm sure I've told you several times. I'm so afraid you'll think I'm sick—or some such nonsense— & it's not a comfortable thought as I know from experience, you see.

I'll probably have to tell you in a day or so, to go slow on your letters, so I shan't have them come after I've gone back. It might gum the show, you see, much as I hate to have them stop. I'll miss them in Milan—especially as I won't have a very good chance to see you often—not being on night duty, & I remember how you burst out before I left. But my but I'm hungry for a sight of you even if you are Mongolian in cast[50]—cause you are still & more than ever, my love Ernie.

Tomorrow, if I'm really off of night duty, I shall go into Florence, & do some errands, & then take dinner, & spend the night at Miss Jessup's pensione as I was to do last week, only I came home early in the afternoon because I felt so queer in my head. Miss Jessup is so afraid I'm having a dull time, she makes all sorts of plans for my pleasure & edification. Thanks be, she has come through her attack so quickly & so well. Mr. Hough also, out of gratitude wants to show me Florence when he's well enough—but, I won't be here then, I guess. I would like a few days to really see some of the old churches & palaces, but, I guess it's going to be impossible. I told Mr. Hough, yesterday that Miss J. & I were going to Milan as soon as she was out, & leave him here to the tender mercies of the Ital. R.C. & he got dreadfully upset.

Oh, dear, I'm pinin' so for you. Will you be strong enough to hug me, Ernie, when I come back? You'd better be.

Your own Kid
Aggie

Nov. 7 [1918]

Ernie, my dearest—

Yours of the 4th (I believe) I got yesterday, & you scared the life out of me by your wild threats of disappearing before I get back to Milan.

My goodness, what would be the good of that? Capt. Ferguson, in charge here while Capt. Aikin is away, told me he telegraphed Miss Shaw that I would be back in 3–4 days, so I am setting my hopes & plans on Monday the 11th. And I hear my train arrives around midnight, as per rule for trains in Italy, so I won't see you at the station, but, I will probably have to have refreshments, so if you can sit up, I'll be able to come up & see you on the quatro piano. Dear Kid, I'm simply crazy to get back & out of this place. I'm off of night duty, now, but, things are none too smooth between the A.R.C. & the C.R.I. & I want to get away before I lose my temper.

So, ye old master can expect ye ancient maiden on the day of Mon—(would it were) by the rapid transit from Firenze.

I'll keep on writing you, but, of course, if you stop writing by the time you get this it will be better, n'est ce pas? Dunque, Tesoro mio, quando io le vista, io sono molto contente, per che io non ho domenticato niente. Capito?[51]

I guess I can spell Italian a little better than the Old Master, even if he can speak & understand it better.

Goodbye until domani. Carino [dear].

> Your own Kid—
> Agnes

·  ·  ·

[Padua]
Nov. 22 [1918][52]

Ernie, m'dear,[53]

I take my bum fountain pen in hand, at the first possible moment to give you the chronicle of my wild experiences since I left you. My—some day—I had yesterday.

In the first place—Mr. Barr must have forgotten to tell the soldier to come to the train, because we looked for one in vain. The facchino [porter] would not stay & we had 6 bags & such a mob. Cavie said she'd get on & hold a place, & a facchino said he'd come back for our bags when he placed some other ladies, so little me stood guard over our pile of luggage while the platform emptied. Finally, 5 min. before we were due to start, the British R.T.O. came along & offered help—& just then Cavie decided to look for me—so we landed in a densely populated corridor, & sat on our bags—all night. We had a rather nice Y.M.C.A. to talk to or rather Cavie did, as I endeavored to sleep with my head on a duffel bag. We arrived at Padua at 9 A.M. & found no one to meet us—& the facchino wanted us to take our baggage on a push-cart, & go in search of the A.R.C. but, while we argued a carozza [*carrozza*: taxi] turned up. The driver took us to the A.R.C. laboratory, where some people were in class. I butt in & asked for info—& finally was sent around the corner where I ran into an A.R.C. man, who gave us the address. Then cabby did not know where the st. was & had to find directions from the passersby. Finally, after a tour of Padua—old & new, we arrived at the Magazzino & Ospedale, & found Miss Shaw.[54]

She had sent a car for us, & we found later the chauffeur was taken ill, & fell in the st. & had been in an Italian Hosp. all the A.M. We were to start at once with 2 other nurses—Miss Warner & Miss Markley for Treviso—where the Amer. soldiers were—so, after lunch—about 2—off we went baggage & all.

Treviso was terribly interesting—with it's [sic] ruins, & full of soldiers. I think we must have been the only women in the town. We went directly to the Camp, & saw the Maj. who had sent for us—& he told us with deep regret that he'd been unable to get permission from Col. Persons for us to stay—tho' the soldiers are dying for lack of attention, so he would let us know for certain about the decision as soon as he heard from Col. Persons.

Here we were—7 of us—& they would have welcomed us, as we were sure from all that we heard, & one man, at the head refused to have Red Cross nurses for the Army men. Nothing left but to go the Magazzino in Treviso—where we met Miss Shaw. She took poor Cavie back to Padova with her—as they had sent 24 soldiers into the Hosp. there & have only 2 nurses—& the rest [of] us camped out. Miss Markley & I stayed wrapped up in the car & tried to sleep for a couple of hours, until they came for us & said dinner. We walked all around the town (which I was told was absolutely empty a month ago)—in the pitchy darkness & found our only restaurant "chuiso [*chiuso:* closed]" because there was no food. So back to the Magazzino—which was once a girl's convent school—& cooked Campbell's soup over a smoky little stove, which an Arditi kept going—chopping wood with his "poniardo" [sic]. At 8—two Army officers came, to tell us they had not yet heard from the Col—as they wouldn't let us stay at the one filthy hotel with [sic] permission from the authorities we came back to Padova—3 of us—& were told to go to a Hotel, as there were no beds at the ospedale—being full of soldiers. At the Hotel, there were no rooms—but Miss Shaw put me to bed in the room the night nurse had—& the other two went back to the Ospedale & put up beds in the office. Some wild life—but I like it.

Today—(I've just waked up at 8.30) we will know whether we are to stay at Treviso or not. It makes us sick to think of all we might be doing but for Army red tape.

I was unable to write yesterday, not having any baggage with me, most of the time, but, I'll try & get a chance every day. Ernie, my boy—(sounds parental but, I didn't mean it that way).

Dear Kid, I wish you were up here with me.

> With love, your stanco'd
> [exhausted]
> Aggie

·   ·   ·

November 22 [1918]

Dear Kid,

Just a note tonight as I'm *so* bushed—I've been unpacking & putting away supplies at the Hosp. all day. Also 24 more soldiers came, & we all pitched in to make beds, & feed them. Miss Crough does all the cooking herself, as the Italians can't. Supposing we had to cook the meals in Milan! Poor patients! But here they have hot biscuits & real home cooking.

We are to go to Treviso again domani matino, & this time I guess we'll stay.

I don't know yet what the address will be, but, will write tomorrow night & let you know.

Please excuse me, now, as I'm rather weary. I even opened packing cases & crates, & got very dirty—but, it was great fun.

Ever your
Kid (lonesome)

.   .   .

[Treviso][55]
Nov. 25, 1918

Kid, dear,

I know it's an age since I wrote last, but, for the last 2 nights I've just gotten off duty & dropped into bed, & hadn't the energy to even write you, which is some pep-lessness—isn't it?

I wrote you that I was leaving Padova in the A.M. for Treviso again. Well, we got off about 11 A.M. in a very bumpy ambulance, or something of the sort. Cavie & Miss Markley both stayed at the Hosp. in Padova as they had more than they could handle there. So Miss Warner & I, all of our baggage, some belonging to the other nurses, & 2 oil stoves jauntily went our way. We had an Ital. Driver who didn't know the way, so I had a great time directing him, from what I could remember of our last trip. We arrived & darn it my pen's gone dry—finally, & were ushered into a very snug little set of quarters with steam heat, if you please. We went on duty that afternoon, & found plenty of work to keep us busy for some time to come. For the first time in my life I slept between blankets without any sheets—that night & would have had no pillow if Miss De Long hadn't insisted on my taking a little pillow with me. I guess you think I'm crazy to tell you all the wild times I've had in the past week, but, I want you to know I've passed through some of the hardships of war, & you have no corner on the market—old dear.

Tonight, I'm very sleepy but I miss you so much, & haven't had a bit of mail since I left Milan, so I just had to write, anyhow even if it is rather incoherent.

I am very happy indeed, because I feel that I am doing some really worth while work, & my patients are so grateful, poor boys, for the slightest thing you do for them. There are 31 in my ward, & some quite sick, so you can see I'm a little busier than I was on night duty in Milan.

Well, I find myself dropping asleep over this. I wouldn't if you were here tho', dear Kid. I wonder when my mail will begin to follow me here. You see it's a long way—1st to Padova—then Treviso—then the Hospital, which is some miles from Treviso.[56] I'll try & write a bit every night, now, even if I can't mail it all at once.

With love from
Aggie

Agnes Von Kurowsky—A.R.C. nurse

·  ·  ·

Nov. 28 [1918]—
Thanksgiving Day

Best beloved—
I wrote to you 3 nights ago & carried the letter around in my pocket until it got worn out, trying to get somebody to mail it in Treviso for me, so it wouldn't go through the base censor here, but, I've given up now, & will mail my letters in the box downstairs, or I fear you'll be coming here on the double quick to see what's happened to me.

This has been some Thanksgiving Day alright. We had a little fun at the table finding out what we had to be happy about. We all said we should be glad we were not at the Hotel Roma in Treviso; also that we didn't die of the Spanish Floo. But, Miss Rittenhouse kept telling us what a good dinner they were planning to have in Milan, & I did wish I could have been there.

Yesterday I got a whole envelope full of 3 letters from—from the Medico [Dr. S.]—a nice one which I will let you see some day. Thanks so much for the pictures. I consider them fairly good, don't you? And what happened to the 8th one I only got 7. My other film is being developed here by one of the soldiers—& I hope to get it back tomorrow.

Dear Kid, I'd like to write a real letter, but there's a girl talking to me & I can't collect my thoughts—to say all I'd like to. Only this— I miss you & want to see you so badly.

Please don't think I'm ashamed of you—& don't dare to say it again. I thought I made you eat those words once, but, you said them again in your last letter, & it hurts me.

I wish I could tell you a little more of this place & my work, but, it's better to wait until we meet again.

So a riverdela, tesoro mio

Sempre il suo—
Aggie

.   .   .

[Treviso][57]
Nov. 30, 1918

Kid, dear,[58]

Wonderful to relate I'm taking a minute on duty to write this, by the light of two lanterns, or rather one—the other one's gone out from lack of wick. All the power's off so there's no water & no electric lights.

I am reduced to 13 patients from 31—& the ward is a mess, as there are no sheets, & so the empty beds are not made, but, the remaining pts. are happy. They are allowed to smoke, now that there are no seriously sick ones, & have the Victrola going.

I don't think I'll be here much longer.

The other ward, where the rest of the nurses are, is full of awfully sick patients. I lost my sickest boy, & felt so badly as he was a dear, & I worked so hard over him for days. One of the nurses, Miss Warner came down with the Flu, & we had to send her in to Padua today. There's no place here for sick nurses. I feel fine myself, & haven't had time to get sick. I'm living the life of a hermit, tho even worse than at Florence, as there's no way of getting in to Treviso, & we're too tired by the time we get off duty to do anything but go straight to bed.

I had a great time with my last letter. After carrying it around for 3 days, I finally sent it down to the censor here, to be sent thru like the soldiers' mail. But, the Lieut. brought it back, & said I could send my mail to Treviso. Says I who goes in to Treviso to mail it for me? Says he—only the mess sergeant, & he's not allowed to handle civilian mail. So I began to think I'll have to give up writing you this season. But, now, I've made a private arrangement, so hope it will work out O.K.

Dear, I miss you so, but, I mustn't start talking about it as I must maintain my cheerful disposition—but, you know, don't you, & believe me. I get to thinking about you sometimes when I'm working & almost forget what I'm doing. And today making rounds with the Capt. I just began to hunger for you, & wish we both could home subito—ensieme—capito [immediately—*insieme:* together—understand?].

Basta!

I must go & take the temps. or I'll get shot at sunrise. Don't say anything about the writing of this. I hate to write with a fountain pen.

Goodbye—love—

Aggie

December 1, 1918[59]

$M$y own dear Kid—

I was sure I felt too sleepy to write a letter tonight, but, I knew I must brace up & tear off one to my mother & I might as well stick pins in myself to keep awake, so I can send you at least a line to say I'm still your Kid. And thank you for the pictures of you & of me, which I got today—4 letters from Padova & I took them over to the ward—with several others from the States—and had such a good time reading them all—& yours last—that the patients all said that I must have been reading a letter from my "fellow" to wear such a broad grin as I did.

You certainly are the champion love-letter writer, old furnace man, and I sure do admire to read them, Mr. Hemings-way.

Dearie me, how nice that trip to Madeira sounds—but, I'm afraid you'd never want to go & be somebody worth while. Those places do get in one's blood, & remove all the pep & "go" and I'd hate like everything to see you minus ambition, dear lad. You certainly have changed since I first saw you. I often wonder whether I've done you harm or good, but, whatever it is I am responsible, so I must stick by you.

I sometimes wish we could marry over here, but, since that is so foolish I must try & not think of it. But, I'm really afraid to face the doctor, & tell him I don't care for him & never will. I'm trying to let it die out of itself.

So glad you've gotten some money, but, don't do anything so foolish like buying the Duomo, & don't let anybody sell you a nice little fat Italian wife for that money. See if you can save it, Kid, to celebrate with when you hit Nuevo York. And whaddayoumean by saying I'm broke. Here I am here in the cold—far far from temptation, & nothing to buy, so I'll probably come back to Milan with the same money I took & then some—which will be nice for Christmas.

One of the soldiers was nice enough to develop one of my films for me, & I believe another one is printing them tonight, so in my next I may send you the films, & let you have some good prints made, as these will be amateur stuff. The one of you & me came out very bene I think.

Good night, dear boy, & be good.

I'm afraid you're hitting it up in the Cova since I left—a wild boy—indeed.

Your own
Aggie

. . .

Dec. 4, 1918[60]

Dear Old Master,

Good news today! They are going to evacuate this place about the 16th of this month. But, whether I will come back to Milan, or stay in Padua I don't know.[61] I feel terribly anxious to be back in my "Home Town" for Xmas, somehow. I wonder why.

I'm so glad the Cure is progressing, even a slight squeak will not be a drawback. Then you can never sneak up on me & give me a surprise.

I'm a tired woman the [sic] night—having taken a hike with Miss de Graw[62]—the first time I've been out in the day-time since I came here. We walked up the road, and saw barbed wire entanglements, reserve trenches with cement dugouts. All very guerre-like & interesting. It's hard to believe that one month ago the shells fell all around here thick & fast.

We essayed to return by the field—I leading the way 'cross country. Of course it was rather muddy & very slippery, & every field was bordered by little ditches, so travelling was not all it should have been, but, all went well until we were about 50 yds from the Hosp. grounds when we couldn't seem to find a bridge across the little brook. Finally I found a place where someone had thrown some cross-stalks across and, delighted at my find, I started over. After cascading down a slippery bank I stept on the cross stalks & went kerlap to the bottom of the stream. Such feet as I brought home with me! I must stop this now & begin to clean my shoes, or I won't be able to go on duty tomorrow & that would be fearful.

Thanks for the pictures, dear boy. I can hardly believe you are the same boy you were before you were shot to pieces. However, I think I like you as you are so it's all right isn't it? The Y. man gave me a book to read by "R.D. Hemingway." Any relation of the distinguished journalist E.M.H.?

Here are the films which the X-ray sargeant developed for me. Old dear, consider yourself severely hugged & a kiss implanted on your left eye.

Your missis
Aggie

.   .   .

Dec. 8, 1918[63]

Dear, old dear,

Your letter came by Miss Smith herself the night before last, & this P.M. another written just after you had sent them. You certainly are good to me in writing, & I'm ashamed I can't get a letter to you oftener. But, dear, it's so hard to write here on the ward, & I'm too tired to collect my ideas when I go off duty nights. Now, I am not so busy here—only 4 real sick men—& 15 up patients, & now I have another nurse. T'is ever thus—when there's lots of work, you can't get help, then when things begin to clear up along comes lots of assistance. The men have a Victrola going, so I find myself writing all sorts of things I didn't mean to, as you can see by the erasures.

I have so much to say to you, too. But, I'm not sure yet that you are getting my letters as I have to go to such out of the way means to get them mailed. The Victrola is playing "When you're a long way from Home." Cheerful, isn't it, for these poor boys who are so home-sick & so tired of Italy. But, they're a funny lot, & keep me so amused—especially one whose sayings should be put in a book. I wish you could hear him when he gets started. He went out the other night & got lost, & didn't get in until 11.45 P.M. & was reported, & I spoke to the Captain about him, so he feels that I am responsible for his getting off without anything being said about it, & I can't make him believe anything else.

Pause of 1 1/2 hours while I served afternoon tea. Some service, it was—tea in glasses—on a tray with a can of sweetened condensed milk, & those Red Cross crackers. The other nurse followed me with the milk & crackers, & we stirred all the milk into the tea with the same spoon.

When I first came there were 3 glasses in the whole ward. I don't know why I tell you so much of what I do here, because I don't really think you are terribly interested in people you will never see.

Since your letter the other day, when you spoke of possibly coming up here to see me,[64] I keep looking out of the window & every now & then I jump because I think I see a familiar stalwart figure in a good-looking English uniform & overseas cap with a cane. It's a mighty queer thing, & I've been sadly disappointed several times.

I'm sure I don't know how long I'll be here, now, because, a case of spinal meningitis was discovered yesterday & it may mean a serious epidemic if we have any more. I have no case of it in my ward, but, if there are any more they will probably quarantine the whole place. Don't get scared of me, now, 'cause I seem to bear a charmed life, & even the Floo doesn't harm me.

If you were only here to take some walks with me—it would be great, because the whole country is full of interesting things & very attractive.

Oh, Kid, I wish I could look ahead & see how Fate is going to treat us. I've got such a lot of patient faith in the old girl I'm sure she won't throw me down. As to the medico, I am at a loss. He hasn't answered the letter I wrote about the Capitano [Serena] yet, so I am still at sea. But I think my neglect of him will do the trick as well as anything I could say—& not quite as cruel as hard cold facts on paper. That's one reason why I don't want to go home this winter, as Time will teach me much.

I fear by that time nobody will be enfolding me on the dock, as you will probably be at your country seat recuperating from this "dreadful war."

[unsigned]

.  .  .

Tues. night
Dec. 10, 1918

Honey, Kid—[65]

I've just had my 1st chance to look at the letters you left me last night[66]—& I see you say you've only had 2 letters from me since. I left. That doesn't seem possible as I've written a good many. Why I wrote & mailed two before I left Padova. It doesn't seem like a reality at all, that you were here yesterday. In fact, it already seems like a long time since I last saw you. And I wonder when you will get back to Milan, & just what sort of a reception you'll have there.

I began this last night—the 10th but was unable to keep on writing, as Miss Hummel[67] had to go on night duty at 12—& as she rooms with me, I had to put my light out so she could sleep for awhile. So here it is Wed. p.m. & I should be taking the 3 o'clock temps.

I had good news this a.m. The sergeant in charge of the building said they were hoping to close up my ward by Sat. if I could get the men all well enough by that time. Miss Shaw was here yesterday & was very nice to me. She said, our pay was raised, & we could get the extra 10 per since Sept. when we went home. Also to let her know when we wanted to go home, any month after January being open. So, all things being considered—I'm going to ask for 1st of March— as that will get me home in the Spring—& I won't have to go home with Gumshoe. Then she also said we would have to sail from Italy— not allowed to go thru France, which is a bitter disappointment as I'd hoped to get back to Paris for a few days anyhow. Do you think we'll be able to get over again some day? If so, I shan't worry about seeing everything now.

Then, I've been thinking over what you said about Xmas, & I just guess a nice big picture of you, now—(not last year) would about fill the bill, & be as much as I'd want—old Master. Can it be obtained? In case you go home before I do, I want your representative to keep me from desperation.

Well, dear heart, I'd like to write more, but, I dassent, as I've lots to do. I have no stamps but, will try & get some this P.M.

Your ever lovin'
Aggie

. . .

Dec. 13 [1918]

Dear old Skeezicks—[68]
I began a letter to [you] this P.M. on the ward, & didn't have a chance to finish it, so goodness only knows who is reading my address to you. Why should I worry—nobody would ever know from the way we begin & end a letter who was the author? That sounds as tho' I didn't want anyone to know & I suppose you'll say I'm ashamed of you—but, I'm not, and some day I'll prove that to you.

I wrote to my mother that I was planning to marry a man younger than I—& it wasn't the Doctor—so I expect she'll give me up in despair as a hopeless flirt. I'd hate to think I was fickle. Don't let's talk about me. I'm not worth it—so now, we'll speak of you & us—as you usually prefer such speakings.

I haven't had a letter—for why I don't know—since before I saw you—and patience—it is a great virtue, but, it is also very hard to keep virtuous mitout letters. Now, don't get eggsited from de sounds of dot speechs [sic].

Oh, Kid, I'm sleepy & foolish, but, I would not be the former if you were here, altho' I'd be more so the latter.

Last night, Miss DeGraw & I did some baking. I made 6 "punkin" pies & she made 2 cakes—and one of the doctors today said—not directly to us, but we heard it—that he didn't see why the nurse that made those pies was still a widow. We suppose he thought Mrs. Heilman[69] made 'em but, anyhow, you won't starve, 'cause your prospective frau knows enough cooking for one man, anyhow.

Oh, my dear, I forgot—nay—neglected—to ask you what did you want for your Xmas? From the looks of things I'm afraid you're going to get nothing as I'm not seeing any progress towards Milan, but, I'd like to know anyhow.

Well, Kid, the group's all here, & all talking at once, & I can't make any headway, so addio.

Yours (some day)
Aggie

.   .   .

Sun—Dec. 15 [1918]

Dear—[70]

I seem to have lost out on mail—even worse than you now, as I'm sure some of your letters have been lost. I've received none since the day before you were here, & you told me then that some were on the way.

And I'd sure admire to know what is going on in Milan. They tell me the Hospital is closing, & that Mac & Brooks have gone on vacation—so it looks as tho' I would not be going back there. Especially as Cavie has gone with Miss Shaw to start a hospital over the Piave. I think I told you that in my last letter.

It begins to look as tho' we'd spend Xmas here—and except for Miss De Graw & Miss Smith[71] there isn't anyone I can find anything like a kindred spirit in. You made an awful break when you spoke about Miss Rittenhouse before Miss Smith—she's her best friend, & I simply shuddered. But tapping on your foot didn't seem to stop you at all. I fear you're going to have sore feet for the rest of your life if I'm there, and you continue to be so brutally out spoken. But then, I think if you were faultless I'd not care a snap about you. Perfect people are not nearly so lovable, & of course you have some very fine qualities, also, but, you seem to think I see only ye mistakes, etc.

Do you know, I believe that your promising to go home right away, & these homesick boys always talking of getting back home & hating this country so, that I'm getting downright anxious to go home myself? It's strange how circumstances can affect one. When I was with Jessup I wanted to do all sorts of wild things—anything but go home—and when you are with Capt. Gamble you felt [sic] the same way. But I think maybe we have both changed our minds—& the old Etats Unis are going to look tres tres bien to our world weary eyes.

Last night 3 Y.M.C.A. entertainers sang for the boys—& it really was good—the first social evening since I came here.

We were supposed to bake pies, but, played off & went to the show instead. Yesterday Miss De Graw & I took a lovely walk. We went into the grounds of a big villa here—the Villa Margarita. Do you know anything about it? We believe it used to belong to the Queen as it certainly was a pretentious place once. Every walk was lined with busts—artists on one—musicians another—all sorts of famous folks. Most of them were off at their pedestals, & one old codger was fitted out with a "tin derby" which looked so funny that I took his pictre.

I must go to lunch, now, & as I'd rather not have anybody read this I'll seal it subito.

Goodbye—old Kid dear—
Your
Aggie

.　　.　　.

Dec. 16 [1918]

Kid, dearest—[72]

Today I had 4 letters from you, besides 8 others, & some postals. I was so excited I couldn't work, but, sat right down to read them—leaving yours for the last, of course.

Two were addressed here, one Padua & one Treviso. I couldn't find the dates on the latter two but I think they were of an early date.

Your news was somewhat startling—about going home I mean. And I do hope I'll get to Milan for Xmas, or it will be a miserable day—at least I'm afraid so. I've tried hard to find out where we'll be, but, as yet nothing can be decided.

They are expecting to send all the sick ones to Genoa in a Hosp. train, & now, I've only 10 patients—5 bed patients—& 5 up—so you can see I'm not overworked.

One day I hear we won't be needed after the end of this week, & then I fear they'll never get all the patients out before Xmas. Besides I think the officers want us to stay to make things a little more cheerful & homelike for them.

Last night after the movies—I came out at 8.30 half asleep—Miss De Graw & I baked eleven (11) pumpkin pies—& were working up to 12. I was 1/2 dead—when I dropped on my lumpy couch, but, it will see me early tonight.

I am going to enclose a letter I rec'd in answer to the one I wrote about the Captain.[73] It may make you understand my worries—& yet my assurance. Also a clipping my mother sent. By the way she tells me she doesn't want me to come home as long as I can find interesting work over here, as I will probably never have another chance. But, just the same she'll be glad to see me. That's her way of being a Spartan mother!

I simply loathe this pen—& am forced to give up in disgust.

> Your own Kid
> Agnes

·   ·   ·

Dec. 19, 1918

Ernie, dear,[74]

I am sending you a whole story I cut out of—now don't laugh—Snappy Stories.[75] But, it sort of struck my fancy. And I thought you'd like it, too.

I haven't [written] for 2 nights, because—night before last I was shining my shoes to go to Venice, and yesterday I spent there. It was some full day, but, so worth while. I'll never forget it. We got up at 5 A.M & the ambulance took us in to Treviso for the 6.40 train and we got to the City of waterways by 9 A.M. We saw the Cathedral—San Marco—and the Doges' Palace—Bridge of Sighs—had a couple of gondola rides—did some shopping, and ate & came home by the 5.40. Something didn't agree with me, & I was rather an ill woman on the way home, but, it was the only dim part of a bright day. Of course, it would be much more to remember if you'd been with me, but, I find I must not expect much, & then I will be more contented.

I had such a nice ton of mail last week, & hear I am getting a Xmas box from home, which I didn't expect. I hope it comes through O.K.

Dear Kid, if this hits you about Xmas time, just make believe you're getting a gift from me, (as you will some day,) & let me tell you how I love you, & wish we could be together for our first Christmas. May you be cheerful & contented, anyhow.

Of course, I'm still hoping I'll see you here or maybe in Milan. Nobody knows for certain where we'll be, & it will certainly be hard to make a celebration here, as all these boys, & officers are as home-sick as they can be, & we don't begin to take the place of their wives & sweethearts, tho' we may help as mothers & sisters.

So long, sweetheart. I'm praying I'll see you before you go, in fact I'm sure I will. I hear you're sailing with Mac, Fisher & Miss Sparrow[76]—the one I came over with.

> Your own
> Aggie

.　　.　　.

Dec. 20 [1918][77]

Kid, dear(est)—

I've a sort of feeling this will probably miss you, as you may be coming up here for Xmas—perhapsly—but, anyhow, when I feel like writing & have the time I should never neglect the opportunity as they do not come any too frequently.

We are trying as hard as we can to make a Christmassy atmosphere—& time for these poor boys, and it's rather difficult going, as they have not the spirit, & we have not the material to put it into them.

As for myself, I've been away from home for 4 years, now, but somehow, I always could find someone I cared about to have a little fun with—among the girls at Training School, I mean. But this year I wish the whole thing was over—a very selfish wish, I know, as everybody else feels about the same way.

How about you? I wonder why it is I don't get your letters regularly, now that you are writing to the Hospital direct.

Dear heart, I have nothing new to tell you. I'm just writing 'cause I want to, & it seems excessively stupid of me not to be able to make up any items of interest. I told you about Venice, didn't I? Did you ever see Venice yourself? You should go there on your permission.

I am going to make pancakes this afternoon, for the patients, on my little smoky stove—some job. We've been making fudge several times lately, in fact, they are living as high as tho' they were home—almost.

Be nice, now, & don't get rash when you hear I'm not coming to Milan—as I'm afraid it looks that way. By this I mean don't lap up all the fluids in the Galleria.[78] But I don't really believe it is necessary for me to give that little advice, you're learning fast, & soon will be caught up with me in years—of experience & wisdom.

> Your faithful old guide,
> Aggie

Kid, I miss you more & more, & it makes me shiver to think of your going home without me. What if our hearts should change? Both, I mean, & we should lose this beautiful world of us?

Dec. 21, 1918[79]

Dear old Cuss—

I'm getting pretty regular these days, don't you think? I got a letter from you addressed to Padova & dated the 11—just 10 days in coming. So I guess it comes quicker by the Treviso & F. H. 331 route.

So you are really going—can't hardly realize it, but, I think you are doing right. Only, Kid, dear, is it necessary to forego your vacation with Bill? Somehow, I think your family will advise you take at least a month's vacation in the wilds you are so fond of. Now as for my news—Miss Shaw was just here, & said Cavie was beseeching her to send me up the line to work with her at some forlorn little ruined place where she is setting up a little Hosp. & dispensary.[80] It sounds awfully interesting, & will be a good experience for me, & it is just temporary, so I am rather glad. As long as you are not in Italy, what diff. does it make where I go—& of course, it is much better for me to be working & not having too much time for brooding, & introspection.

I'm afraid we are a mad pair, but, I rather like being mad, when I have such good company.

However, Miss Shaw says I am to go back to Milan to collect my things before they close up the house there, after Christmas some time when I am no longer needed here.

This has been mighty interesting, but, I am beginning to feel that my usefulness is about over here. Miss De Graw has been wonderful to me, & seems to feel sorry at the prospect of my leaving her to go to Cavie, and that always gives one a nice satisfactory feeling.

And I hear Miss De Long is going to Rome—which means that I will be able to see Rome some day. So now there's only Naples & Sicily left that I want to see—after Rome. I'm certainly a mighty lucky girl—'cause I've had a great variety of experience in the short while I've been over.

I have my Ardito knife now. One of the men—an ex-patient, heard me say I wanted it—& he sent it on to me from Treviso. Wasn't that nice? But, they've all been pretty nice to work for, & I've had a good time.

For Xmas they are planning a great entertainment and fine eats.

Tonight Miss De Graw & I are planning to make lemon pies for tomorrow.

I think I'll have to stop writing for a few days, now, or your mail will surely miss you. Goodnight, dear,

> your own Kid—
> Aggie

·   ·   ·

> Dec. 31 [1918]—and then some.

Dear Boy:

This is the hardest letter I ever tried to write anyone and goodness knows I don't usually have much trouble slipping you a few lines. But—if I'm doleful you'll cause the boat to sink—and if I'm troppo [too] cheerful you'll blow up in your very characteristic style and get the old boat all full of smoke, thereby causing consternation among those of an elderly order. So the only solution I can find, is a happy medium (if you know what that is) and I shall endeavor to dispense cheer & yet give the impression of subdued spirits. Does that sound too jovial, Kid? 'Cause if you don't like it, of course I must take it back & converse in a very ordinary & commonplace manner.

I'm in hopes that when you are really at last started on your return trip that everything will begin to look ten times brighter, and you'll find that little things that have looked very big will resume their normal proportions. And how envious we all are of your arrival in N.Y. My, but, it will be pretty good to see the old town again. I don't think I've seen any place yet that comes up to it for living in, that is. Imagine living in Venice all the time & going down cellar in the dark, missing your step & falling into the canal. Or your clothes getting moldy from the dampness. And all that sort of thing.

Capt. Moore was teasing me today about my fondness for Italian officers. Brooks was praising up the British, but, I said, "Well, we all come back to a perfectly good American just the same." Of course, my mother married a foreigner, so I shouldn't be the one to brag of Amer. true bonds—but, you understand, I'm sure.

Now, Kid dear, and Kid mine, will you take some advice from your superior officer?

I wouldn't offer you advice ever if you weren't such a good sweet kid about taking it from me—most of the time, & I won't dare write you any after this one—'cause I know what it is like to get letters full of advice. My mother used to write me yards of those when I was in training.

*Don't* no. 1. Don't chew tobacco in the presence of ladies. It's a filthy habit wot I can't endure notting.

*Don't* no. 2. Don't wear loud neckties in the States just 'cause the Italian ufficiali can't dress decently in mufti. You hadn't orter copy their styles.

*Don't* no. 3. Don't use no perfume, curling irons, nor tooth-picks. Don't like 'em—that's all.

Dots enuf. Now what I was going to say when I was interrupted was that I don't want you to work so hard you wear your nervous system raw on the edges, thereby undermining your health, which is now one of your chief assets. Please use your good judgment & take that vacation with Bill Smith if you feel it is needed. I'm not the one to put a stop to that and I certainly don't want to be responsible for your going into a decline early.

Jan. 1, 1919

I'm beginning the New Year right in one respect. I'm writing to you. And that's a sign I'll write this whole year—to you. So now when you get blue & can't find your ideas as fast as you'd like & things look particularly low & hellish (scuse me) just remember I'm looking to you for my future life. You've got to make good, and things never stay low for long. To then cheer up & square your shoulders and jump in with both fists clenched.

Do you want me to telegraph you—wherever you are—when I arrive in New York? I suppose you won't be able to come & see me then, but, you will want to know when to write & where. Somehow, I'm not a bit anxious to get home. I won't see you anyway, & the work at home looks particularly dull & uninteresting. But, you made me promise not to stay here on this side of the water, so I must needs go. This has been the most eventful year of my life. I know I've had more experiences and I've met more nice people & I've known & grown very fond of my Kid Ernie. What more could I ask?

Happy thought just came to me. "Well think one thing—Ernie never is sarcastic or angry in his letters, so I won't have any cause for worry for quite a while." Isn't that a good thing? You were a dear last night tho', and I shouldn't complain of things in the past which must be forgotten & forgiven—on both sides, of course.

Dear Ernie, you are to me a wonderful boy, & when you add on a few years & some dignity & calm, you'll be very much worth while. I only fear all the Chicago femmes will be wiling you away from your night nurse. If I only had your gift of expression I could write a lot longer & nicer letter, but, I always feel self-conscious when I get foolish on paper—silly of me, isn't it? But I've always been that way & can't stop it suddenly. So read between the lines & find out all the nice things I can't find the words to say.

Now, Ernie, I'm looking to you to do big things. Don't worry & fret over me & get silly ideas in your imaginative brain, but carry on and you'll get farther than you would if you sat down & thought of me all the time.

If you see any of my friends, such as Bill Horne, Capo, Brummy or Jenks or any others—give them my blessings & tell 'em to look me up in N.Y. through the Bellevue Registry, 426 E. 26th St.

You can write to me after I come home c/o Trust Dept. National Savings & Trust Co. 15th St. & N.Y. Ave. Washington, D.C. That's the safest way, & I don't know my Wash. address.

Now, goodbye, Ernie dear, & do your best for both of us.

With all my love,
Your own
Aggie

[Milan]

Jan. 6, 1919

Kid dearest,[81]

Altho' your other letter is not mailed yet, as I have no stamps, I am going to write again. I know you won't care how often I do that. Yesterday was the big scrap at the Palazzo Reale for to see our Presidente.[82] Ma Che, but, it was some occasion. 1st. We wait all day for ye biglietti d'invito [letters of invitation]. Then we tear into our entire outfit plus white gloves. Then we solemnly parade down to the Palazzo, feeling terribly big about the hands—try to get in about 5 different portes & finally achieve the right one. Liveried flunkies of a great gorgeousness line the velvet-carpeted stairs. One perfectly stunning person in red & gold comes out, as we pass up the stairs, with a broom & dustpan and removes any slight trace of our pedestrian commonplaceness we may have inadvertently left behind us. That kind of got my little goat—as I'd just polished to the nth degree my best shoes. Then we were ushered into a boiling hot room where we met the Stuckes (spelling possibly incorrect) & others of the Amer. Colony. Of course, as we were dressed "cap a tout" for inspection, nothing—not even the gloves—could be removed. Hence, we suffered for our country as never before.

Mac began to get peevish then, & has been so ever since. Finally the President & family dashed through to take off their wraps. Another long wait—the room being full by this time of high dignitaries, & generales of great rank. Finally, we form a line headed by Capt. Patrick & are pushed into the presence. But, no he is not here. We wait once more—leaning comfortably on those about us. Finally again there is an uproar & I can see his ear & Mrs. W.'s hat. Emotion overcomes me, & I lose my presence of mind. While the rest raise their new white gloves to be shaken over the heads of those in front, all are horror stricken because I didn't even get a finger. I am too overcome to realize my failure, & I try again. The Y.M.C.A. is pouring over me in serried ranks to get the last look. (I don't know what kind of ranks those are, but you ought to—you're in the business.)

Gasping, we then sought air—fresco [fresh]. Also home. Oh,

no, Miss Shaw & I had tea with Capt. Eckland & then he stayed to dinner again. And such a fuss as we had after dinner about the Scala tickets. It seems there were only about 1/2 enough to go around—so they had to make a distinction & they made it on the passport. Mac having a British one, woe's me, they left her out—& sent her a ticket with Miss Bertassi in the Gallerie de Peanut. Whoo—then the fun began. By dint of great diplomacy, Miss Shaw got her to go with Capt Eckland, Miss Larkin[83] & Miss Strycker. There being only 4 seats anyhow, & Miss Shaw insisting on Capt. E. going instead of herself. I, wisely insisted on staying home on account of my cold & cough. Well, Mac went finally, & somebody told her that Capt. E. said he gave the seat to her because she was good-natured. Ma Che—but his name is more than mud—adesso [now]. And for some unknown reason, Mac is peeved with me, & rises with dignity & leaves the room when I come in—etc. I tried to get away on tonight's train, but as today is a Festo—Epiphany—I can't get my trunk to the Station. So I must wait another day & am trying to spend it in my room as much as possible to avoid worrying the Spaniard.

My, I'm glad I'm not a sensitive person. It certainly takes a lot of joy out of life. You sort of fly off the handle, but, you come back very nicely always, so it's alright in the end.

It seems funny to be writing a letter that you won't get until the news is quite stale. And to think how long it will be before I'll hear from you.

I may keep these letters & mail them in Padua to escape the R.C. censor here, anyhow. I'll be able to write you a few lines every day after I once get settled in my winter hibernating quarters.

Wish you'd been here yesterday, but, then I also wish you were here now, so that doesn't do me much good, does it?

This paper is very appropriate of my feelings just at present, so I guess I'll stop. Jan. 12 Kid, dear, I found this letter in my box of paper, unfinished, but, I don't suppose you'll mind if it's a bit late so I'll send it on anyhow.

> Your very own Kid,
> Aggie

[Padua]

Jan. 7, 1919

Sweetheart mine,

In spite of my fears, so far I am doing better than I had hoped—in my correspondence, I mean. You know I wouldn't promise because I wasn't sure I'd be able to fulfil my oaths.

Now, I'm in Padova—having started with Miss Shaw last night. I was not supposed to come until today or tomorrow on account of not being able to get my things to the station as Mon. was a festa—but, at a half-hour's notice I came.

The old train was 2 hrs. late starting. 2.30 A.M. & of course we didn't get seats. But we piled blanket rolls & bags in the racks & they rolled down at intervals during the night on the fat somnolent officers below. That really pleased us, as we were sitting on very delicate suitcases, expecting a collapse any minute.

Today I found quite a little bunch of mail waiting for me—4 letters from you—3 Sicily[84] & one on the way down there. They said at the office that I got more mail than anybody else around here. Good reason why—isn't there?

I wonder if they will worry when they begin to decrease—for awhile, anyhow. I forgot to tell you I saw Brundi again on Sun. in the St. Margherita tea room, which you turned up your nose at, when I took you there. He hasn't seen nor heard of Capt. Serena, and if he didn't turn out in Milan when Pres. Wilson was there—why the man's not anywhere in this vicinity—that's all.

They tell me the Piave is so swollen, nobody can get across. It would be a funny thing if Cavie & I were over there & all communication was cut off—as they say happens in the winter time for weeks at a time. But, just think of the money I can save up there. I'll have all kinds of dough for my permission & home-coming clothes.

Goodnight, old dear. I'm a sleepy woman—as I had very little slumber in the aisle last night, & only a short nap this P.M.

Love you just the same. How about you?

Your own,

Aggie

Jan. 9 [1919]

Kid, dear,

I'm startin' domani matina [*domani mattina:* tomorrow morning] for Tore [Torre] di Mosta, and goodness only knows when I'll get my letters mailed from out there, but I'll do my best.

Last night I missed writing 'cause I went to a shindig at the Ospedale—a minstrel show given by the boys, & afterwards we danced—not with the men this time (remember the mail clerk's ball) but, with some very nice officers.

Oh, & yesterday I had some day. Having nothing else to do, I asked Miss Shaw if I couldn't go out to Treviso with her. Of course, it began to pour, & we had no curtains on the car, & what with the wind & speed we surely got a drenching, arriving with mud-encrusted faces. We went out to the F. H. 331, & I enjoyed seeing all my old patients. I believe the nurses are all leaving there tomorrow. And I saw Jones, the soldier who is the dentist's asst. who told me a little tidbit which might be of interest. The day after I left he was talking to one of the patients from Miss De Graw's ward, who said he knew you well & corresponded with your sister. By name Bill Hutchins—of the Oberlin quartette ("spelling not verified").

What with the rain & all of Miss S——'s errands we got back in Padova at 6.30 P.M. And oh, what mud.

Today it was quite sunny so I don't think the travelling will be half bad tomorrow.

I got Gumshoe's letter the other day written before Xmas. I quote from it—"Your steady is here but going away tomorrow for a nice trip. Now don't laugh when I say I am going to miss him very much. He is a good boy & has been so kind & thoughtful for me. I am glad tho, that he is going to America, for I do not want him to waste his time—he is too fine!" How's that for a eulogy, old dear?

Anyhow, it's been my own opinion for a long time & shows I have good judgment.

Today—I got your last letters from these shores. Thanks for the pictures but I would rather have had the films you took. Miss Larkin is very anxious for some prints of those taken in Milan, & I want the film of me badly to send some home to the madre & friends.

Goodnight, squeezicks. I'm quite tired, but joyous still, in spite of all.

Your cheerful kid,
Agnes

.   .   .

[Torre di Mosta]
Jan. 12 [1919]

Dear Old Man—

That's just an experiment, because I want to see how it's going to sound. You'd laugh if you could see me just now. I'm sitting on the side of a bed in our Hospital—(1 ward of 11 beds) with my feet propped up on a little stand. We have a nice assortment of patients— one lady who has had pneumonia, & who speaks so indistinctly I can't understand a word, & have to have the ward-maid tell me what she has said.

Next comes Assunta, a baby who has been here since the Hosp. started who is very much spoiled & awfully cute. Next is a little villain who arrived in our family today. He has a very sore mouth, and is howling continuously, now, because I won't allow him to have bread with his milk, which he has refused to eat therefore. Then comes Ugo—who is cute, too, & has lost some front teeth, but, he has no vanity & grins clear around just the same.

Then Nona—or, Maria, the Vecchio, who sits up in a bunch all day, with a shawl over her head. Can't you see her? You know the type. She seems to admire me immensely, which is often embarassing [sic], & says I am troppo giovane [too young]—only 18 from my appearance. All of which is comforting even when the source is considered.

Then there is one very sweet girl about 14.

The girls around here are simply stunning. I never saw better-looking, nor healthier looking anywhere—as a general rule. Of course, we have many visitors besides who are all very polite. The place we are in was the headquarters & hosp. for the Austrians for a whole year & more—so we can see ghosts, I'm sure, if we sit in the dark. They say there were 5 generals here, then. Interesting, well, I should say. I expect to ask all kinds of questions as soon as I get acquainted and can make myself understood. Still you'd be surprised how well I can get along with my Italian patients, and I'm learning all the time.

Besides Cavie & myself there is a social worker, American, who is rather staid, & has no sense of humor—Lieut. Rose of the A.R.C. who is leaving for America tomorrow—an Ital. doctor—tenente, & I don't know his name, but, he seems nice tho' quiet—2 Ital. nurses— one rather nice, the other Cavie says is a pill. This morning—she's supposed to be on night duty—she came in about noon, & started giving me orders, & I honest to goodness, lost my temper, just like Mac would have—altho' I didn't answer at all. Now you have our complete family—tho' I suppose you'll say you're not interested in the family. Sounds just like you—can almost hear you.

I've just discovered what a foolish trick I've done. I've written on this page before I've finished the other sheet—Scusi [apologies].

It's getting very dark, & our only light is lanterns but, at that we're luckier than the people around here, who have no lights at all. I'm going to try & write a little bit every day & mail it once a week. Will that satisfy your 'ighness[?]

I had the most interesting trip down here from Treviso. We didn't come over the same bridge you showed me—but one they called the Ponte dei Piave, or something like that. There we had to wait quite awhile, because there was a long column of camions [trucks] coming from the other direction. It was noon time & I heard one soldato say he hoped they'd hurry because he was hungry—so I gave him the crackers I had for lunch—as I had eaten choc, & wasn't hungry.

Then I gave out some oranges I'd bought for the Hosp. & told my driver when they gave out, I'd have to use the onions & cabbages I was bringing for the soup kitchen. Every now & then on the road someone would stop us, & ask for a lift. When it was lone soldati my driver said "Hop on behind"—in wop—but, when it was ufficiali & their whole escort he refused them. Beyond the river I saw so much destruction it is really hard to realize they were once villages. And talk about mud—& bad roads—well, I nearly left the camion several times when we bumped very high.

Every town with inhabitants we came to, the driver asked the direction & distance & it began with 5 kilometers, & rose steadily to 20 as we got nearer & nearer.

I was the worst-looking mud-bespattered object you ever saw when I arrived. But Cavie gave me a royal reception & made me quite at home. She's had an awful time of it, & has simply done wonders. She was so pleased with the book you sent her. As far as I can see, it is the only literature up here. So hurry up & write some, so you can send me copies, so I can improve my mind.

Tonight, the Sindaco [Mayor] & Priest & another dignitary are paying their respects to Lt. Rose, so I made my escape with a lantern to the stanza I share with 3 others, to indite a few lines to you first & later, maybe, a few letters to other ordinary folks. All the maids just came in to bid me Buona Sera. Aren't they nice? I think that's a sweet custom. (Sounds gushing doesn't it? I hate gush—too.)

This house is the biggest & most prominent in the town. You can't miss it. In front of us is a square which seems to be the gathering place for the people who come after milk & soup—and if you could see the mud it is chiefly composed of—Ma Che—but, we have mud here.

Well, goodnight dear Kid, & how I wish I knew how you are at this moment—but, I know you're O.K. I'm afraid I'll be writing you in wop pretty soon, as I find myself thinking in it, these days.

> A riverdela—
> carissimo tenente
> Suo cattiva ragazza
> [your naughty girl]
> Agnes

Jan. 21 [1919][86]

Dearest O.M. [Old Man]

Yesterday I got 4 letters from Gibraltar—some joyful surprise, oh Kid! The one about my cough tickled me so, I simply roared until Cavie wanted to know what on earth was the matter, so I read parts to her—carefully expurgating but she still remains suspicious that I will finally end up by being Mrs. Hemingstein—and I haven't denied nor asserted anything—just smiled knowingly. I think the Dr. has stopped writing me, as I haven't had but that one letter since Nov. I have one devoted admirer here. Domenico—aged 14. He guides me on my pilgrimages to the sick folks around here, & has hurt Cavie fearfully several times by refusing to go with her, & then insisting on going if he finds out I am to go. He also presents me with villainous looking Austrian sabres & guns & shells. How I'll ever get them home goodness only knows.

My nice Austrian knife that I got at Treviso I loaned in the kitchen one day to cut up the kindling & it is now "rotto" & no good as a souvenir. My own fault, so I can't say a thing.

We had a frightful day yesterday. Just after dinner, they brought in 4 children (in an oxcart) bleeding from head to foot & looking—as Cavie said—as you must have when you were wounded. They were playing in their yard & found a bomb. 2 other children were killed outright & 2 of the ones brought in were badly hurt. 1 in the intestine, & the other in the eyes. We all worked like mad over them for about 2 1/2 hrs. Cavie & I—the Ital. dr. & nurse. Just as we were about through dressing them, Bruno our little chauffeur hove in sight with a Ford ambulance—the first since I came as the other ones are broken. We looked on him as a direct gift from Providence & packed in the poor little things to go to S. Stino Hosp. about 5 kilometres from here.

Then last night I & Cavie & Domenico went about 3 kilometres to give a morphine hypo. to a sick man who never can sleep. This certainly is the life. It's great to go along the road & meet a buxom lassie with an R.C. bathrobe over her skirt & waist & festooned up like an overdress. Also it's great to have people so anxious to do you a service. I'll be more spoiled than ever. Sometimes I think I'd rather enjoy living in Italy some day, and, then, I get disgusted again and change my mind.

I had a glorious day today. In the A.M. having the ambulance I took a bed, mattress, bedding & gowns to a sick woman about 1 1/2 kilometres from here.

I had a great time fixing her all up nice & fresh. Then in the P.M. I also went to a house in the village here & fitted out one of our old lady patients. Her only household goods being one iron bed & mattress for herself son & grandchild. Then Bruno suggested we take a run to S. Stino, but conscience forbade me to go without an excuse, so we got Cavie to take a box of goods the priest in S. Stino wanted. Some roads around here. You bounce up & down furiously while jerking from side to side, & the poor little Ford can't stand it at all.

Bruno, by the way, told me today that when I first came everybody said I must be his sister because we looked so much alike. So we will have our picture taken together to see if it's true.

This was the first swing day since I came, so I was able to finish up that film we started in Padova.

I took some pictures of Luigi, our cook. He is a most delightful character, the exact image of the comic paper Weary Willies—with one eye out of focus and a perennial smile. Cavie says it's worth coming to Italy to hear him say "oh poveretti!" The serving women made him a chef's cap, & in an R.C. gown he is terribly ornamental. He is so proud of our new cook-stove he tells the entire neighborhood of it's [sic] wonderful properties & all it can do. It's a treat to hear him.

Well, Kid mine, picture me as happy & contented & don't worry about me but go ahead. These ups & downs of mine are really life & I enjoy them.

By this time you're ["there" deleted] I mean home, & must have received some of my letters or will soon. Don't forget your promise to send me your stories.

Your Signora Kyde,
Agnes

Feb. 3, 1919

Ernie, dear Kid—

I guess you'll think it's a regular excuse to say I'm in the midst of confusion, but, honest to goodness, boy, Torre di Mosta is by far the most confusing place I ever was in.

Our family is enlarging, which means more to cook for, & we have some very sick patients, so that means more work in the Hosp. and both Cavie & I jump from one thing to another so much that we never know what we are supposed to be doing.

Then, too, we are getting more society all the time. The little tenente I spoke of before, is giving me a desperate rush—now don't get excited. Today he brought a hare for our dinner. Food here seems to take the place of flowers & candy.

My little boys come every evening & sit around an oil-stove in the magazzino and make music on reed pipes which are constructed fresh every night for the especial purpose of earning cigarettes & chocolate. They all smoke furiously from the age of 12 up, & I can't refuse them cigarettes, tho' I've tried & tried.

Just now, I am writing with a veritable Kewpie sitting on my lap, & have one eye—another lapse of 10 minutes. Goodness only knows what this muddle will sound like to you.

We've been having wonderful weather. I really believe the sunny Italy part, tho' it sure is cold, especially just at the present.

The future is a puzzle to me, & I'm sure I don't know how to solve it. Whether to go home, or apply for more foreign service is the question just now. Of course, you understand this is all merely for the near future, as you will help me plan in the next period, I guess. Cavie has been very cruel to me lately accusing me of being a flirt— which is putting me in Brooksie's class. You know I don't do anything like that, don't you?

Feb 5 [1919]

Now just look—2 days since I started this. Yesterday I was out most of the day, we had company for dinner & I had to go out after to give a hypodermic about 2 kilometers away. Then an old woman in the

Hospital died, so I was late getting to bed. Today was a very sad one, as 2 of our little patients—brother & sister 14 & 16 yrs. both died of Influenza & pneumonia very much like Colter. We sent all of our other patients home, so tonight we have an empty hospital. Tonight I'm going to pound the pillow as soon as I finish this,. as tomorrow our cammion [sic] is going in to Treviso with the mail.

It'll be a month Friday since I hit this town, & it certainly has been full of experiences. I'm getting fonder every day of life in furrin' parts, & every time Miss Conway tells my fortune she tells me I'm going to travel a lot. How do you like the idea?

> Goodnight old dear,
> Your messy but cheerful
> Aggie

.   .   .

Feb. 15 [1919]

Dear Kid,

My, but it's hard work writing letters when you have none to answer. Do you find it so, too?

We've had a lady writer visiting us here for a couple of days. I think Mrs. Vorhee, or Vorse. They tell me she writes for the Home Journal so I suppose your nose will elevate itself. Anyway, she's been studying the country & us, for material, & the mental strain on us, fearing any moment to find our pet faults in print—has been terrible.

I was in Padova for 2 days this week, but, didn't feel very lively, & was a dead weight. They had only 4 patients & 4 nurses, so they felt quite free, & were furious with me because I insisted on coming back to what I call home. I promised, however, to come back Friday (yesterday) with Cavie for a big Valentine dinner given at the American Mission by Gen. Treat. Quite an [sic] swell affair. But when I came back & saw how things were I gave up the idea "subito."

The woman with typhoid that we've been going to see for over month, got suddenly much worse, & we've been almost living there. I spent one night & Cavie spent last night with her. Then our Ital. nurse has been sick for about 4 days, & we had this lady visitor with Maj. Fabbri, our chief up in this section. Then last night they had invited 2 tenenti for "cino" [*cena:* dinner], & it was an elegant one, too. I'm learning all kinds of Italian cooking from our Luigi, the apple of our eye. I do hope the writing lady will put him in her story of Toere [sic]. He's worth a whole book. We have an Arditi Capt. who comes here to sleep until he finds a room. The ladies all liked him until they heard he beat the prisoners so. The ones (Arditi) we have here are the wildest of them all. You'd certainly adore them.

It sure is surprising what a happy family we are with our Italian & American & English mixture. Of course, we have to talk Italian because they won't or can't speak English. Our tenente medico is the funniest & brightest one I've seen yet. He has the strongest sense of humor, & yet at first was so quiet & serious. Now he's turned into a perfect imp of mischief. Last night we had a regular pillow fight—the most undignified performance I've witnessed in this country.

Cavie is to go to Rome very soon to take charge of the Hosp. there when Miss De Long leaves in March. Then when I've closed up this place & turned it over to some Italians, I'll join her there. I have a chance of staying a year in Rome, but, I'm thinking strongly of going to the Balkans—so I'm rather undecided as yet. Mama wrote me not to come until I really felt like it & work is going to be very dull at home after this life. Maybe you are finding it so now.

But I'm afraid if I stay a year more in Italy I won't want to go home at all, &—I've seen some samples of Italian Americans, & they are not what I care for.

I am interrupted again & I'm discouraged so will stop.

Ever afftly—
Agnes

Excuse the smooches—I have no blotter.

Torre di Mosto
Mar. 1 [1919]

Dear Kid,

I got a whole bushel of letters from you today, in fact haven't been able to read them all, yet. You shouldn't write so often. I can't begin to keep up with you, leading this busy life I do. I'm sorry you got the idea I'm not having a good time, 'cause its not true. I'm having the time of my young life, & never lack for excitement. I also like my work well, in spite of all the mud, & difficulties I mentioned before.

Now Cavie has gone to Rome, & left me in charge of the Hosp. & housekeeping—not a very large affair, but, we feed about 35 to 45 at noon time, & that's no laughing matter.

They—meaning our most frequent visitors—call me the Directrice, which makes me wild. Among the aforesaid visitors is an Alpini major, an old friend of our Italian nurses. He has spent 5 years steadily at the Front, minus 40 months at Hospitals in that time. One arm is paralyzed, but, he's full of pep—30 yrs. old, & very small. He's only been here one week, but, already he's an old friend of everybody here. He also speaks English, which is an advantage. Then there are several tenentes' [sic] that I don't like, & some I do. Two Amer. officers came from Oderzo to see us the other night, because Cavie had invited them. They arrived the night after she left, & their first question was "Do you run an Italian mess?"

Don't send the shells to my mother, as I've got so many I don't know what to do with them, & you might as well give them to someone you know.

I also have a star-shell pistol & lots of cartridges, which gives us one of our chief diversions—shooting them off on dark nights.

By the way, I've learned to smoke. What do you know about that? Also I've learned a fascinating gambling game, 7 1/2. Do you know it? I won 10 lire the other night. Oh, I'm going to the dogs rapidly, & getting more spoiled every day. I know one thing—I'm not at all the perfect being you think I am.

But, as I am, I always was, only it's just beginning to creep out.

I'm feeling very cattiva [wicked] tonight, so goodnight, Kid, & don't do anything rash, but, have a good time.

Afft,
Aggie[87]

. . .

March 7, 1919

Ernie, dear boy,

I am writing this late at night after a long think by myself, & I am afraid it is going to hurt you, but, I'm sure it won't harm you permanently.

For quite awhile before you left, I was trying to convince myself it was a real love-affair, because, we always seemed to disagree, & then arguments always wore me out so that I finally gave in to keep you from doing something desparate.

Now, after a couple of months away from you, I know that I am still very fond of you, but, it is more as a mother than as a sweetheart. It's alright to say I'm a Kid, but, I'm not, & I'm getting less & less so every day.

So, Kid (still Kid to me, & always will be) can you forgive me some day for unwittingly deceiving you? You know I'm not really bad, & don't mean to do wrong, & now I realize it was my fault in the beginning that you cared for me, & regret it from the bottom of my heart. But, I am now & always will be too old, & that's the truth, & I can't get away from the fact that you're just a boy—a kid.

I somehow feel that some day I'll have reason to be proud of you, but, dear boy, I can't wait for that day, & it is wrong to hurry a career.

I tried hard to make you understand a bit of what I was thinking on that trip from Padua to Milan, but, you acted like a spoiled child, & I couldn't keep on hurting you. Now, I only have the courage because I'm far away.

Then—& believe me when I say this is sudden for me, too—I expect to be married soon.[88] And I hope & pray that after you have thought things out, you'll be able to forgive me & start a wonderful career & show what a man you really are.

Ever admiringly & fondly
Your friend,
Aggie

.   .   .

Dec. 22, 1922

Dear Kid—

Well, when your voice from the past reached me—after I recovered from the surprise, I never was more pleased over anything in my life. You know there has always been a little bitterness over the way our comradeship ended, especially since I got back & Mac[89] read me the very biting letter you wrote her about me. (The mean part of that was that she had already read it to "the Doc"—whom you may recall hearing of in those dim days.)

Anyhow, I always knew that it would turn out right in the end, & that you would realize it was the best way, as I'm positive you must believe, now that you have Hadley.[90] Think of what an antique I am at the present writing, and my ghost should simply burst on the spot, leaving only a little smoke that will evaporate.

Oh, gosh, there's so much to tell you I can't tell where to start. The past 3 years have certainly been full of interest for me. I don't think Life (Capital) will ever be tame if I have anything to say about it.

In the first place—to dig up the ruins—I came back from Italy—a sadder but a wiser girl—feeling that I'd like to break something & preferably somebody, & life wasn't really worth living. I was ruined for America, & when the poor Doc—much fatter—ambled around I was as nasty as possible, tho' he stuck fast until I sailed the 2nd time, when he promptly married, & now is struggling along & has a young son.

I worked in Miss Shaw's Tuberculosis Social Service Department for 6 months, & then went home for a visit, and came back to

N.Y. just when things were beginning to stir up again in Europe—so I was slated for Russia & sailed in March 1920. I didn't dare tell my friends & relatives it was to be Russia, as they all had an idea it was certain death as a suspected spy to venture over the borders of that poor land. But, darn it all, when I got to Paris, Russia was closed, especially for women workers, & I went to Bucharest with 2 other nurses to do some Baby Welfare work—as I was *not* a specialist in that line. I will never forget that trip on the Simplon Express— maybe you know it. When we landed after 4 days of the train at 1.30 A.M. in May—nobody to meet us as telegrams never arrive in that benighted land, nobody who spoke even French, and no street lights beyond the station & no cabs, even. We had picked up an attractive young Roumanian on the train who proved our life saver. We found a tiny cart & a small boy in charge of it who took our bags & then the parade started & walked miles in the pitchy dark town to a hotel where the chief nurse lived.

Bucharest, after the war, simply could not & still cannot accomodate [sic] it's [sic] guests. We were refused there and wandered to another where there were supposed to be some Red Cross rooms but they were occupied, and as it was nearly 3 A.M. we begged & finally were given an attic hole with 2 beds. As I was the smallest I had to spend the night on a bench fenced in by duffel bags.

I certainly didn't intend to go into detail but the memory of that dreadful night always makes me eloquent. Since then I've slept on a bench in a station, ridden on an unlighted train, and, well you know how bad those countries can be. Italy during the war was luxury compared to what I've found since the war in Roumania.

I spent that summer in Bucharest—rather lonely as I lived & kept house with a devilish chief nurse—the other girls were scattered. She kept me because I learned Roumanian & spoke French & was therefore useful.

We turned over our Baby Work to Lady Paget's unit from the League of R. C. Soc. in Sept. & sailed from Constantsa on the Black Sea, via Constantinople & Athens—the Corinth Canal & finally— Naples. And there, I was surprised & relieved to find that I landed without any of the feelings that tormented me on previous visits—

Naples being the home of a certain dashing young Artillery Officer.[91]
I had a wonderful time showing my pal & a y.w.c.a. girl about to all
the spots I knew,—& then on to Rome, Florence, Milano, Switzerland, & finally Paris in much straightened [sic] circumstances finan-
cially. After 4 months in Paris—Oct. to Feb—many rumors that we
were to go here, there, & the other place, & an assignment to a very
special Hospital train that was to go to Poland—(we had such fun
getting it ready from curtains for the windows & bunks to silver for
the table, and then the a.r.c. after spending about 25,000 francs on
the fitting up found the tracks in Poland were too wide & it was taken
apart & put away—). I went back to Roumania for the Junior Red
Cross, and by special request, & then I spent months in a little town
in the Carpathians among peasants. We—my pal & I lived in a peasant cottage, whitewashed & simple, and really life was good, even if
we did have a hard job. Then after a summer at a Tbc. Sanitarium in
Constantsa—a wonderful experience—I asked for release & came
back home Nov. 1921—after a vacation in Budapest—Vienna (a city
of cities) and Prague.

In January I went on duty as night superior at Bellevue & stuck
it out for 9 long months, and then when a girl friend from Roumania
arrived here with a scholarship for the N.Y. School of Social Research, we took a tiny box of an apartment together, furnished it
halfway, & now I am doing private nursing as a shortcut to wealth tho'
certainly not fame.

Last month I had a very tempting offer from the Red Cross to go
back to Europe—either to Warsaw—or Sofia, and—I turned it
down.

Let it be said that never before have I turned a deaf ear to old
Dame Opportunity when she suggested travel, but, I really began to
fancy my little apartment, and couldn't rush right off and leave
Christine Golitzi my Roumanian friend alone in a strange country.
I've been there myself & I know.

But, sometimes I get lonesome, and then I kick myself for not
going, & I dream of Paris—that dear old place, where I had so much
time on my hands, and roamed about in so many funny places. If I

could only stand just now—at early twilight—at the Place de la Concorde, and see the little taxis spinning around those corners, & the soft lights, & the Tuileries fountain—oh, my. I'm homesick for the smell of chestnuts on a grey, damp Fall day—for Pruniers, the Savoia (Noel Peters) and my pet little restaurant behind the Madelaine—Bernard's, where I ate crème chocolate every night. Maybe I'd better stop, or the paper will get soft & blurry out of sympathy for my sorrows.

If you ever go to Roumania, let me know beforehand, if you can, & I can send you all sorts of addresses & contacts.

Europe will always draw me—any part of it, but, I think I'll always remain true to my first love Italy. Even France fades into the background, & the first time I went through Italy en route to Bucharest, I hung out of the car window from Domodossola on the Swiss border to Trieste, that night, when it was pitch dark, & my eyes were full of cinders, that had collected during the day. We left Padova early in the evening & from then on I was particularly on edge with excitement—going through the Veneto—Venice—excuse me for letting go again. Old age makes people sentimental, anyhow.

It is so nice to feel I have an old friend back because we were good friends once, weren't we? And how sorry I am I didn't meet & know your wife. Were you in Paris when I was there a year ago this Nov.? Is there any chance of knowing when your book will be out? How proud I will be some day in the not-very-distant-future to say "Oh yes, Ernest Hemingway. Used to know him quite well during the war." I've always known you would stand out some day—from the background, and it is always a pleasure to have one's judgment confirmed.

May I hope for an occasional line from you? Friends are great things to have, and I appreciate them more every year—but, oh there's a woeful waste of them—and some disappear as fast as you collect new ones.

I'm not reminiscing on Milano, Padova, etc.—on purpose, because I really must stop, but, it's been great—"priceless" to have this long talk with you—tho' I haven't said any of the things I meant to when I began.

With my best wishes to you & Hadley—if I may speak of her so—and a strong grasp of the hand—as they say in Roumania.

Your old buddy—
Von
(Oh excuse me, it's Ag)

142 East 27th St.
New York

# FOUR

. . .

## Ernest Hemingway
## *Letters from Italy, 1918*

INTRODUCTION BY HENRY S. VILLARD

While no letters written by Ernest Hemingway to Agnes von Kurowsky have come to light, a number of those which he wrote to his family after being hospitalized in Milan have been made available to scholars by the Lilly Library at Indiana University. These letters from Italy speak for themselves; fourteen of them are reproduced herewith.

Although Ernest deals with the hospital experience in some detail, mention of his romance with Agnes is conspicious by its almost total absence. In a letter to his mother on August 29, 1918, Ernest says, briefly, "I'm in love again," but she is not to worry about his getting married. He is not—as he told her "once before"—he is not even going to get engaged. Obviously, the relationship had not yet ripened to that point.

A hint as to how far the affair had progressed and the future responsibilities he had thereby incurred is contained in a letter of November 11, the day the war was over. He is planning to go to work to "make the world safe for Ernie Hemingway," and if one assumes that by then he was contemplating marriage, it follows naturally that he expects to be a "busy man for several years," by which time he will

· 169 ·

have accumulated his pension payments and will bring his children over to see the battlefields.

The only other reference to Agnes is in a letter dated December 11, which describes the trip Ernie took to Treviso "to see the girl" in a field hospital there and at the same time informs the family that he is booked to sail on January 4. He realizes he ought to get home and start to work instead of going to Madeira with Captain Gamble, a decision for which Agnes could claim the credit. Marriage must have been on his mind, as it appears to have been on Agnes's, for in her letter to him on December 13 she says she had told her mother she was planning to marry a younger man, not the doctor.

. . .

Via Manzoni, 10
Milano
July 21, 1918

Dear Folks:

I suppose Brummy[1] has written you all about my getting bunged up. So there isn't anything for me to say. I hope that the cable didn't worry you very much but Capt. Bates[2] thought it was best that you hear from me first rather than the newspapers. You see I'm the first American wounded in Italy and I suppose the papers say something about it.[3]

This is a peach of a hospital here and there are about 18 American nurses to take care of 4 patients. Everything is fine and I'm very comfortable and one of the best surgeons[4] in Milan is looking after my wounds. There are a couple of pieces still in. One bullet in my knee that the X-Ray showed. The surgeon, very wisely,[5] after consultation, is going to wait for the wound in my right knee to become healed cleanly before operating. The bullet will then be rather encysted and he will make a clean cut and go in under the side of the knee cap. By allowing it to be completely healed first he thus avoids any danger of infection and stiff knee. That is wise don't you think Dad? He will also remove a bullet from my right foot at the same time. He will

. . .

*The terrace of the American Red Cross Hospital in Milan. Hemingway would spend his afternoons here in the late summer of 1918.*

probably operate in about a week as the wound is healing cleanly and there is no infection. I had two shots of anti tetinus [sic] immediately at the dressing station. All the other bullets and pieces of shell have been removed and all the wounds on my left leg are healing finely. My fingers are all cleared up and have the bandages off. There will be no permanent effects from any of the wounds as there are no bones shattered. Even in my knees. In both the left and right the bullets did not fracture the patella; one piece of shell about the size of a Timkin's roller bearing was in my left knee but it has been removed and the knee now moves perfectly and the wound is nearly healed. In the right knee the bullet went under the knee cap from the left side and didn't smash it a bit. By the time you get this letter the surgeon will have operated and it will be all healed, and I hope to be back driving in the mountains by the latter part of August. I have some fine photographs of the Piave and many other interesting pictures. Also a wonderful lot of souvenirs. I was all through the big battle and have Austrian carbines and ammunition, German and Austrian medals, officer's automatic pistols, Boche helmets,[6] about a dozen Bayonets, star shell pistols and knives and almost everything you can think of. The only limit to the amount of souvenirs I could have is what I could carry for there were so many dead Austrians and prisoners the ground was almost black with them. It was a great victory and showed the world what wonderful fighters the Italians [are].

I'll tell you all about everything when I get home for Christmas. It is awfully hot here now. I receive your letters regularly. Give my love to everybody and lots to all of you.

Ernie

Write to the same address.

·    ·    ·

A.R.C. Hospital<br>Milano<br>July 29, 1918

Dear Mom—;

I just got your letters of July 2 and June 22. Hurray for nun bones and three rousing ones *for* Ma and Uncle Georges. Tell the Ivory [Marcelline][7] for me to regard Sam in the Cold light of reason and not to get too enthusiastic and also to remember ye old proverb about the great magnitude of the unhooked inhabitants of the ocean. Also what was the Pater doing enroute to Georgia? I got his cable of congratulation yesterday. There is nothing new to report on the Hemingstein Front. The latest dope is that I will step forth from the Hospital on or about the 1st of September. The wounds are coming on in rare shape. However from present indications I will never look well in kilts as the old limbs present a somewhat cut up appearance. They look a bit disgruntled. For a time now I resembled a walking blacksmith shop. Nearly everyone in Northern Italy has some souvenir from the wounded Stein. Never mind Maw while the Master woodsman was putting in his week in the trenches he managed to strike several slight blows towards discouraging the Austrians. Also I have glimpsed the making of large gobs of history during the great Battle of the Piave and have been all along the Front from the mountains to the Sea. Oh Yes I've had to speak Italian ever since I've been over here and so I just naturally learned it. I can now carry on a conversation for just as long as the other fellow wants to talk. I've also got a pretty good working knowledge of French. It may seem funny after my showing in Latin but languages have been a cinch for me. And I can get by as an interpreter in Italian now. The trouble is I have it all by ear and cant write it a bit. But I can read the Italian papers easily.

Milan is a peach of a town. It's about the most modern and lively city in Europe.[8] It sure does get hot though. We have lots of cool drinks though and they pull my bed out on the veranda under the awning. From our porch here we can see the dome of the Cathedral. It is very beautiful. Like a great forest inside. The columns seem to go way up into the sky like the "murmurring Pins [pines] and the Hemlocks." However I prefer Notre Dame. They are going to send me down to the Riviera to convalesce after I get so I can walk so I'll get some sea fishing and boating and swimming in September. All the advantages of Foreign travel. Eh? A lot better than waiting to be drafted Eh Robert?[9]

If you can mother we would appreciate it if you could send us some magazines. There isnt any U.S. Reading matter. Also ask about three of my kid sisters why they dont write to me?

Well good night old dear and god Bless you. I'm a good boy.

Much love.
Ernie

August 7 [1918]

Dear Folks and Ivory—;
Your Epistles of July 9th and 13th received today. I greet you.
The July 13th letter from Dad beat the July 5th from Ivory. Such are
the wonders of the Postal system.
Gunnar Dahl was one of my best friends and played Tackle next
to me on the old Light weight team. He was a peach of a jolly good
scout. I hope God will give me a chance at some of the German Swine
that killed him. I'm glad Pop had such a good time with the drafted
men. If they're anything like most of the contingents I've seen off he
must of had a busy time.
Ed. Welch[10] who was Sous chef, or in English, Second Lieut,
second in command of our section[,] is leaving for home next week.
He lives in Royes [?] Park and will come out to see you folks as soon as
he gets home. He is a peach of a fellow and will tell you all about me
and our bunch. He is a Catholic so dont pull any boners. Charles
Griffin, a chef, or head of the section, is also going back to the States.
He lives in N.J. but may come to Chicago to see you folks. He and
Eddie are both fine fellows.
Day after tomorrow I am to be operated on for my right knee
joint and right foot.[11] I'll tell you all about it afterwards. I've been in
bed a month tomorrow and it is getting pretty darn tiresome. However
I ought to get out in a month now so as to be on crutches. I'll convalesce at Riviera where I can get some good swimming and fishing.
Then in the last of September I get a two weeks "permission" or
leave with all railway travel free. So Brummy and Jenks[12] and I will
probably go down to Naples and Rome and cover Southern Italy. I've
seen all of northern Italy and Southern Italy will have to show some
pep to come up to the North.
You would be surprised all right family to hear me talk Italian. I
really can by the hour. I'll show you when I get home down at the
fruit stands. I also have my French down pretty well. I write a letter
or so in Italian every day.
I think I'll stay down here this winter. Maybe I'll go to Mesopotamia. It all depends on how strong I feel. Mesopotamia nice in the

winter. But reputed to be hell in the summer. It would be fine to take in Bagdad and Jerusalem etc. during the winter though. If I can enlist for Six Months I'll go down. But not for a year. Some of us may go down into Serbia too. I'd like to get a Serbian medal.[13] Well have a good time while Papa is away children,

> Much love
> Ernie

P.S. You see we're in the Italian not the American Army. Don't address my mail Lieut. That confuses it with the American Army Ambulance. What our rank is is Soto Tenente, abbreviated S.Ten. or Soto Ten. That is the Italian for 2nd Lieut. Our mail is separate from the U.S. Army. Use my new Italian address too.

. . .

> American Red X Hospital
> Milano
> Aug 18, 1918

Dear Folks,

That includes grandma and grandpa and Aunt Grace. Thanks very much for the 40 lire! It was appreciated very much. Gee, Family, but there certainly has been a lot of burble about my getting shot up! The Oak Leaves[14] and the opposition came today and I have begun to think, Family, that maybe you didn't appreciate me when I used to reside in the bosom. It's the next best thing to getting killed and reading your own obituary.

You know they say there isn't anything funny about this war. And there isn't. I wouldn't say it was hell, because that's been a bit overworked since Gen. Sherman's time, but there have been about 8 times when I would have welcomed Hell. Just on a chance that it coudn't come up to the phase of war I was experiencing. F'rexample. In the trenches during an attack when a shell makes a direct hit in a group where you're standing. Shells aren't bad except direct hits. You just take chances on the fragments of the bursts. But when there is a direct hit your pals get spattered all over you. Spattered is literal. During the six days I was up in the Front line trenches, only 50 yds from the Austrians, I got the rep of having a charmed life. The rep of having one doesn't mean much but having one does! I hope I have one. That knocking sound is my knuckles striking the wooden bed tray.

It's too hard to write on two sides of the paper so I'll skip.

Well I can now hold up my hand and say I've been shelled by high explosive, shrapnel and gas. Shot at by trench mortars, snipers and machine guns. And as an added attraction an aeroplane machine gunning the lines. I've never had a hand grenade thrown at me, but a rifle grenade struck rather close. Maybe I'll get a hand grenade later. Now out of all that mess to only be struck by a trench mortar and a machine gun bullet while advancing toward the rear, as the Irish say, was fairly lucky. What Family?

The 227 wounds I got from the trench mortar didn't hurt a bit at the time, only my feet felt like I had rubber boots full of water on. Hot water. And my knee cap was acting queer. The machine gun bullet just felt like a sharp smack on my leg with an icy snow ball. However it spilled me. But I got up again and got my wounded into the dug out. I kind of collapsed at the dug out. The Italian I had with me had bled all over my coat and my pants looked like somebody had made current jelly in them and then punched holes to let the pulp out. Well the Captain[15] who was a great pal of mine. It was his dug out said "Poor Hem he'll be R.I.P. soon." Rest In Peace, that is. You see they thought I was shot through the chest on account of my bloody coat. But I made them take my coat and shirt off. I wasn't wearing any undershirt, and the old torso was intact. Then they said I'd probably live. That cheered me up any amount. I told him in Italian that I wanted to see my legs, though I was afraid to look at them. So we took off my trousers and the old limbs were still there but gee they were a mess. They couldn't figure out how I had walked 150 yards with a load with both knees shot through and my right shoe punctured two big places. Also over 200 flesh wounds. "Oh," says I in Italian. "My Captain, it is of nothing. In America they all do it! It is thought well not to allow the enemy to perceive that they have captured our goats!"

The goat speech required some masterful lingual ability but I got it across and then went to sleep for a couple of minutes.

After I came to they carried me on a stretcher three kilometers back to a dressing station. The stretcher bearers had to go over lots because the road was having the "entrails" shelled out of it. Whenever a big one would come, Wheeeee—whoosh—Boom—they'd lay me down and get flat. My wounds were now hurting like 227 little devils were driving nails into the raw. The dressing station had been evacuated during the attack so I lay for two hours in a stable, with the roof shot off, waiting for an ambulance. When it came I ordered it down the road to get the soldiers that had been wounded first. It came back with a load and then they lifted me in. The shelling was still pretty thick and our batteries were going off all the time way back of us and the big 250's and 350's going over head for Austria with a noise like a railway train. Then we'd hear the bursts back of the lines. Then would come a big Austrian shell and then the crash of the burst. But we were giving them more and bigger stuff than they sent. Then a battery of field guns would go off just back of the shed boom, boom, boom, boom. And the Seventy Fives or 149's would go whimpering over to the Austrian lines. And the Star shells going up all the time and the machines going like rivetters. Tat-a-tat, tat-a-tat.

After a ride of a couple of kilometers in an Italian ambulance, they unloaded me at the dressing station where I had a lot of pals among the medical officers. They gave me a shot of morphine and an anti tetanus injection and shaved my legs and took out about Twenty 8 shell fragments varying from [drawing][16] to about [drawing][17] in size out of my legs. They did a fine job of bandaging and all shook hands with me and would have kissed me but I kidded them along. Then I stayed 5 days in a field hospital and was then evacuated to the Base Hospital here.

I sent you that cable so you wouldn't worry. I've been in the Hospital a month and 12 days and hope to be out in another month. The Italian Surgeon did a peach of a job on my right knee joint and right foot. Took 28 stitches and assures me that I will be able to walk as well as ever. The wounds all healed up clean and there was no infection. He has my right leg in a plaster splint now so that the joint will be all right. I have some snappy souvenirs that he took out at the last operation.

I wouldn't really be comfortable now unless I had some pain. The Surgeon is going to cut the plaster off in a week now and will allow me on crutches in 10 days.

I'll have to learn to walk again.

You ask about Art Newburn.[18] He was in our section but has been transferred to II. Brummy is in our section now. Dont weep if I tell you that back in my youth I learned to play poker. Art Newburn held some delusions that he was a poker player. I won't go into the sad details but I convinced him otherwise. Without holding anything I stood pat. Doubled his openers and bluffed him out of a 50 lire pot. He held three aces and was afraid to call. Tell that to somebody that knows the game Pop. I think Art said in a letter home to the Oak Parker that he was going to take care of me. Now Pop as man to man was that taking care of me? Nay not so. So you see that while war isn't funny a lot of funny things happen in war. But Art won the championship of Italy pitching horse shoes.

This is the longest letter I've ever written to anybody and it says the least. Give my love to everybody that asked about me and as Ma Pettingill says, "Leave us keep the home fires burning!"

Good night and love to all.


Ernie


I got a letter today from the Helmles addressed Private Ernest H — what I am is S. Ten. or Soto Tenente Ernest Hemingway. That is my rank in the Italian Army and it means 2nd Lieut. I hope to be a Tenente or 1st Lieut. soon.

Dear Pop—; Yours of July 23rd Rec'd. Thanks very much. But you need the kale more than I do. If I ever get really broke I'll cable. Send any money that others send me Pop, but don't *you* give me any unless I cable for it. I'll cable if I need it.

Love, Ernie.

·   ·   ·

Agosto 29, 1918

A . R . C . Hospital.

Milan, Italy

Dear Mom——;
I haven't written before for quite a while because I aint got no pep. The old limbs are coming along fine. My left leg is all healed up and I can bend it finely [sic] and I now get around my room and this floor of the hospital on crutches. But I can only go a little bit at a time because I'm awfully weak yet. My right[19] leg was taken out of the cast a couple of days ago and it's still as stiff as a board and awfully sore from so much carving around the knee joint and foot. But the surgeon, whose name is Sammarelli, he's the best in Milan and know's Beck of New York, now Dead, and one of the Mayo's. Says that eventually it will be all right. The joint gets better every day and I'll be moving it soon.

I'm enclosing a picture of me in bed. It looks like my left leg was a stump but it really isn't just bent so it looks that way.

They have been wonderful to me here. All the Americans have made an awful fuss over me. A Mrs. Stucke who has lived here some years has been particularly indescribably nice. Brought me books, and cakes and candy and with her daughter visits me about 5 times a week. She is a peach and is writing to you about me. Then there is a Mrs. Siegel, a nice dear old jewess who has been up to see me a lot and a Mr. Englefield, a brother to one of the Lords of the Admiralty, who is about 52. He has been younger sonning it in Italy for about 20 years and has adopted me. He is very interesting and seems to have taken a great fancy to me. He brings me everything, from Eau de Cologne to the London Papers and a peach of a Catholic missionary

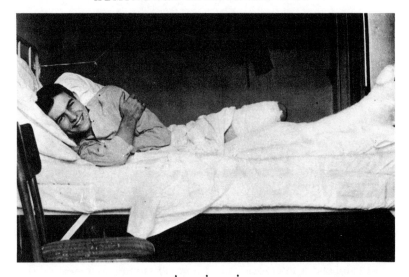

*Ernest Hemingway in the American Red Cross Hospital. He sent this photograph, taken by Henry S. Villard, home to his parents.*

Priest from Italia, a regular good old scout like Mark Williams, comes in to see me very often and we have great old gab fests. And there are a number of jolly good Italian officer pals of mine that blow in all the time. One of them a Tenente Brundi is a famous artist and wants to paint a portrait of me. It will be a darn nice souvenir.

Now Mom you may not believe it but I can speak Italian like a born Milanese. You see up at the trenches I had to talk it, there being nothing else spoken. So I've learned an awful lot and talk with the officers by the hour in Italian. I suppose I'm shy in grammar but I'm long on vocabulary.[20]

Lots of times I've acted as an interpreter for the hospital. Some body comes in and they cant understand what they want and the nurse brings 'em over to my bed and I straighten it all out. All the nurses are American. This war makes us a lot less fools than we were. For instance Poles and Italians. I think the officers of the two nations are the finest men I've ever known. There isn't going to be any such thing as "foreigners" for me after the war now. Just because your pals speak another language shouldn't make any difference. The thing to do is learn that language! I've gotten Italian pretty well. I've picked up quite a lot of Polish and my French is improving a lot. It's better than 10 years of college.[21] I know more French and Italian now than if I'd studied 8 years in college and you want to be prepared for a lot of visitors after the war now because I've got a lot of pals coming to see me in Chicago. That's the best thing about this mess, the friends that it makes. And when you are looking at death all the time you get to know your friends too.

I don't know when I'll be back. Maybe for Christmas, probably not. I can't get in the Army or Navy and they wouldn't take me in the draft if I'd go home. One bum lamp and two shaky legs, so I might as well stay over here and play around the old conflict for a while. Also Mom I'm in love again. Now don't get the wind up and start worrying about me getting married. For I'm not; as I told you once before. Raise my right hand and promise! So dont get up in the air and cable and write me. I'm not even going to get engaged! Loud cheers. So dont write any "god bless you my children" not for about three [?] years.

Your [sic] a dear old kid and your still my best girl! Kiss me. Very good, now goodbye and God Bless you and write me often.

I heard from you last letter of July 27 about a week ago. Send B.L.T. often. The papers Pop sent came. 2 packages. Much obliged to him. Also the two money orders from Gramp and Uncle Ty. I'm going to buy diamond studded radium dumb bells with the Kale.

> So long old dear.
> I love you
> Ernie

.  .  .

> September 11, 1918
> A.R.C. Hospital
> Milano

Dear Dad—;

Your letters of Aug 6th and 11th came today. I'm glad you got that one from Ted [Brumback] and know he will be glad to hear from you. He came in from the front as soon as he knew I was wounded and at the Base here and wrote that letter to you in Milan. It was before my leg had been XRayed or operated on and so I don't know just what he told you about it all because I was too sick to give a darn. But I hope it was all right. I had a letter from him from the front a couple of days ago and they are having a good time. Mother wrote me that you and she were going up North and I know you had a good vacation. Write me all about it if you did any fishing. That is what makes me hate this war. Last year this time I was making those wonderful catches of Rainbow at the Bay.

I'm in bed today and probably wont leave the hospital for about three weeks more. My legs are coming on wonderfully and will both eventually be O.K. absolutely. The left one is all right now. The right is still stiff but massage and sun cure and passive movements are loosening up the knee. My surgeon Captain Sammarelli, one of the best surgeons in Italy, is always asking me whether I think that you will be entirely satisfied with the operations. He says that his work must be inspected by the great Surgeon Hemingway of Chicago and he wants it to be perfect. And it is too. There is a scar about 8 inches long in the bottom of my foot and a neat little puncture on top. Thats what copper[22] jacketted bullets do when they "key hole" in you. My knee is a beauty also. I'll never be able to wear kilts Pop. My left leg thigh and side look like some old horse that has been branded and rebranded by about 50 owners. They will all make good identification marks.

I can get around now on the street for a little while each day with a cane or crutch but can't put a shoe on my right foot yet. Oh, yes! I have been commissioned a 1st Leiutenant and now wear the two gold stripes on each of my sleeves. It was a surprise to me as I hadn't expected anything of the sort. So now you can address my mail either 1st Lieut. or Tenente as I hold the rank in both the a.r.c. and Italian Army. I guess I'm the youngest 1st Lieut. in the Army. Anyway I feel all dolled up with my insignia and a shoulder strap on my Sam Brown Belt. I also heard that my silver medaglia valore is on the way and I will probably get is [sic] as soon as I'm out of the Hospital. Also the [sic] brought back word from the Front that I was proposed for the war cross before I was wounded because of general foolish conduct in the trenches I guess. So maybe I'll be decorated with both medals at once. That would not be bad.

I'm awfully glad that Hop and Bill Smith are going to be near where you can be nice to both of them. They are the two best Pals I have about and especially Bill. So have him out often because I know you will like him and he has done so much for me. I will probably go back to the ambulance for a while when I get out because the gang want me to visit them and they want to put on a big party. I got a long letter the other day from every fellow in the section. I would like to go back to the ambulance but I wont be much use driving for about Six months. I will probably take command of some 1st line post up in the mountains. Anyway don't worry about me because it has been conclusively proved that I can't be killed. And I will always go where I can do the most good you know and that's what we're here for. Well, So Long Old Scout,

Your loving son<br>Ernie

P.S. If it isn't too much I wish you'd subscribe to the Sat. Eve Post for me and have it sent to my address here. They will forward it to me wherever I am. You need American reading an awful lot when your [sic] at the front.

Thanks,<br>Ernie

.  .  .

Sept. 26, 1918[23]

My Dear Pop.

We can see Switzerland from here. Convalescing with some awfully nice Italian People. Back to the front in about a month. Electrical treatments given foot.

Tenente Ernesto Hemingway:<br>Croce Rossa Americane

*Hemingway on holiday in Stresa, September 1918. In the background is the Grand Hotel. Photograph courtesy of Maurice F. Neville.*

Sept. 29, 1918[24]

Dear Folks—;

I'm up here at Stresa a little resort on Lake Maggiore one of the most beautiful of the Italian Lakes. I have ten days leave from the hospital and am resting up here. After 4 more days here I must return to the Milan hospital for more electrical treatments for my leg.

This is a wonderful place. The hotel is about as big as the Chicago Beach on the South Side.

In spite of the war it is very well filled with an awfully good bunch. There are several countessas or Countesses and one the Contessa Julia has taken a great fancy to the Old master and calls me "dear boy" etc.

Also a Signor Bellia, of [not clear] one of the richest men in Italy is here with three beautiful daughters. He and mother Bellia have adopted me and call themselves my Italian mother and father. He is a very jolly old scout and looks kind of like Grandpa [not clear]. They and the daughters take me everywhere and don't allow me to spend a cent. They have invited me to spend christmas and my two weeks leave with them at Torino and I think I shall probably go. The girls are named Ceda, Deonisia and Bianca and want to be remembered to my Sorelli Marcelline Ursula Sunny and Carol. They all ask questions about my sisters and my "piciolo frattellino" [*piccolo fratellino:* small younger brother] Leicester.

The second night I was here the Old Count Greeo [Greppi] who will be 100 years old in March took charge of me and introduced me to about 150 people. He[25] is perfectly preserved, has never married, goes to bed at midnight and smokes and drinks champagne. He told me all about his dining with Maria Theresa the wife of Napoleon the 1st. He has had love affairs with all the historical women of the last century it seems and yarned at length about all of them.

He took me under his wing and gave me a great send off.

I limp pretty badly but can row on the lake and sit around under the trees and listen to the music and go on trips up the mountain in the cog railway. We went up the Mattarone and saw Monte Rosa. From the front garden of the hotel you can see Switzerland. The mountains just a few Kilomets away.

Gee I'm afraid I wont be good for anything after this war! All I know now is war! Everything else seems like a dream. I speak Italian all Day long and write two or three letters a day in it. It really is awfully easy for me now just like English.

You see at first I only knew the Italian of the front—all the language of the trenches and camp. But being with a crowd like this and being three months in Milan with Italian officers I have learned "polite Sassiety" Italian now and can flirt and fish in Italian with great ease.

I know you will have a good time up north and I hope next September that I will be at home and we'll all be up north. Probably not though. But by next Christmas it will be all over and there wont be enough Germans left to wind the Watch on the Rhine.

Love to you all and to Grandma and Grandpa and Aunt Grace and P. L. Slamd Family

Love
Ernie

. . .

[Milan]
Oct. 18, 1918[26]

Dear Folks:

Your letter of September 24 with the pictures came today, and family, I did admire to hear from you.[27] And the pictures were awfully good, I guess everybody in Italy knows that I have a kid brother. If you only realized how much we appreciate the pictures, Pop you would send 'em often. Of yourselves and the kids and the place and the bay—they are the greatest cheer producers of all, and everybody likes to see everybody else's pictures.

You, Dad, spoke about coming home. I wouldn't come home till the war was ended if I could make fifteen thousand a year in the States—Nix, here is the place. All of us Red X men here were ordered not to register. It would be foolish for us to come home because the Red X is a necessary organization and they would just have to get more men from the states to keep it going. Besides we never came over here until we were all disqualified for military service you know. It would be criminal for me to come back to the States now. I was disqualified before I left the states because of my eye. I now have a bum leg and foot and there isn't any army in the world that would take me. But I can be of service over here nd [and] I will stay here just as long as I can hobble and there is a war to hobble to. And the ambulance is no slacker's job. We lost one man, killed, and one wounded, in the last two weeks. And when you are holding down a front line canteen job, you know you have just the same chances as the other men in the trenches and so my conscience doesn't bother me about staying. I would like to come home and see you all, of course. But I can't until after the war is finished. And that isn't going to be such an awful length of time. There is nothing for you to worry about, because it has been fairly conclusively proved that I can't be bumped off. And wounds don't matter. I wouldn't mind being wounded again so much because I know just what it is like. And you can only suffer so much you know and it does give you an awfully satisfactory feeling to be wounded. It's getting beaten up in a good cause. There are no heroes in this war. We all offer our bodies and only a few are chosen, but it shouldn't reflect any special credit on those that are chosen. They are just the lucky ones. I am very proud and happy that mine was chosen, but it shouldn't give me any extra credit. Think of the thousands of other boys that offered. Dying is a very simple thing. I've looked at death, and really I know. If I should have died it would have been very easy for me. Quite the easiest thing I ever did. But the people at home do not realize that. They suffer a thousand times more. When a mother brings a son into the world she must know that some day the son will die, and the mother of a man that has died for his country should be the proudest woman in the world, and the happiest. And how much better to die in all the happy period of undisillusioned youth, to go out in a blaze of light, than to have your body worn out and illusions shattered.

So, dear old family don't ever worry about me! It isn't bad to be wounded, I know, because I've experienced it. And if I die, I'm lucky.

Does all that sound like the crazy wild kid you sent out to learn about the world a year ago? It is a great old world though and I've always had a good time and the odds are all in favour of coming back to the old place. But I thought I'd tell you how I felt about it. Now I'll write you a nice cheerful bunky letter in about a week so don't get low over this one.

I love you all.
Ernie.

AMERICAN RED CROSS
Nov. 1, 1918

Dear Family—;

Back to bed again for a little while. Dads and mothers letter of Oct 12 came today. Also ones from Bill Smith and Frances Coates.[28] Frances doesn't mention being engaged and so I guess she thinks I don't know it. Well I might as well tell you why I'm in bed again. Nothing bad. You see I got a leave of absence from the Hospital the day the offensive started and flew for the front. Worked hard day and night where the worst mountain fighting was and then came down with jaundice. It makes you feel rotten and look like an inhabitant of the flowery kingdom but is nothing to worry about. I had the satisfaction of being in the offensive anyway and now I can rest up in the hospital and get cured and finish the treatments on my leg. Then I'm going to take my two weeks leave down "licenzia" [licenza: leave of absence], in Italian; "permission" in French down in the South of Italy Somewheres. Give Rome and Naples and Sicily and Florence the once over and get lots of pep for the next [word unclear] at the front. Brummy and I were working together during this last offensive. And the Italians have shown the world what they could do. They are the bravest troops in the Allied Armies! The mountain country is about impassable to skilled Alpine climbers and yet they fight and conquer and by the time you get this they'll have the Austrians all the way out of Italy. Italy has been fighting her own war all along and deserves all the credit in the world!

It is getting pretty chilly here now and quite rainy. But I have my old Mackinaw and am going to get it fixed up with some very jazzy buttons. At the front they had never seen a mackinaw before and I wore it all the time. They figured it was some kind of camouflage coat for sniping.

Well Lots of love to all,

Ernie.

breast pocket and I'm getting quite a railway track. But it is kind of embarrassing because I have more than a lot of officers that have been in three and four years. But then "for what we are about to receive may the Lord make us truly thankful" as we used to hustle through before flying into the pan cakes. But seriously I did come very close to the big adventure in this last offensive and personally I feel like every body else about the end of the war. Gee but it was great though to end it with such a victory! And by Gese I'm going fishing all next Summer and then make the fur fly in the fall. The living allowance for a 1st Lieut. is 800 Lire a month or about $160. I don't receive that while in the hospital but $20 a week insurance after 1st four weeks. This has been held up and delayed and I haven't had a Chit for four months dead broke but the first payment of 500 lire was transferred through today. There is about 1500 more coming. So when it all comes through I will have the world by the tail with a down hill pull.

This payment I received today helped me pay off my debts and left a small surplus which will last until it all comes through. I don't believe that you can get any Christmas presents through to me. So if anything is coming from outside the family or anybody have them buy me Am. Ex. Money order as presents. Then I can get the presents over here. It is[32] useless to try and send a Xmas box the way things are going now and besides it is prohibited unless you have a ticket sent from me. And we being with the Italian army don't have the tickets. I'm enclosing some pictures taken while on my convalescence. I've been hearing from you folks pretty regularly and I'll try and get you a letter oftener. The jaundice is all cleared up and I'm pulling through my annual[33] tonsilitis now so feel bohoo rotten. Pop can experiment on my one tonsil after I get home if he wants to. I'll save it for him. The other night feeling around in my leg I located a bullet but it is in a comfortable place and quite unobjectionable. To be exact; the back of my lap. So I'll save it so Pop can take one out. Keep on writing me at the same address and be very good all of you and eat lots on Thanksgiving for me and it is 100 to 1 shot I'll see you this Spring. I want to see some of Italy and Austria now as I'll not be back for several years. Because about next fall I am going to commence the real war again. The war to make the world safe for Ernie Hemingway and I plan to knock 'em for a loop and will be a busy man for several years. By that time my pension will have accumulated a couple of thousand lire and I'll bring my children over to view the battle fields.

Well toodle-do family,

Lots of Love.
Ernie.

.  .  .

[Milan]
Nov. 14, 1918

Dear Pop—;

Yours of October 21 and the check for 40 L. came through today. Thanks very much and It came in very handy. One months insurance of 509 Lire has come through. But I used it nearly all paying off my debts. There are two more payments to come and may be a third it has to go from Rome to Paris and then Back to Rome and then to me and they are slower than Dinky Dyle. First payment over 3 months late. It will take about one more payment to put me entirely clear. Then the third will have me sitting pretty. The tonsolitis is still pretty bad but I'm over the jaundice and 3 or four more days and my throat will be all cleared up. Then I'll start on my treatments again at the big Italian hospital.³⁴ I walk over about a half mile every afternoon and the treatments take about an hour and a half and then I have a good massage. Grandma's big Illustrated Thanksgiving letter came today too. Give her and Grandpa my dear love and thank her very much. When my Doctor heard about my latest medal, the Croix D'guerre, he kissed me tonsolitis and all. My "Italian Father" Papa Count Bellia, sent me a wonderful big box of Choclate [sic]. I haven't been able to eat it but the nurses like it very much. About a ten lb. box must of cost 150 lire. He and the family are very good to me.

You see I didn't get any living allowance all during my time in hospital and all my convalescence because I was supposed to be getting insurance. But the insurance was so blasted slow I had to borrow quite a little to live on.

But now that the first payment has come it will all be through soon and everything will be all O.K. You see I figure it this way Pop. I will have to work so hard when I start in for the next few years that it may be quite a time before I see Europe again. So now while I am here with the privilege of free railway travel, we can have an order of movement written to any place or places in Italy, and all the privileges accorded an officer and honored by the Italian gov't and people I ought to see as much of Italy as possible. Rome and Naples and Sicily etc. It wouldn't be fair if I didn't. And you'll be just as glad to see me in May and June as you would be in February.

So after I've finished the cure for my leg in a couple of months. And the Doc said today he was going to take my tonsils out after a while, why I'll have a look around Italy. Also that will be a nice trip to Abruzzi for Christmas and the Count Bellia wants me to spend a couple of weeks with them at Turino. He has an awful lot of dough and is a peach of an old scout. The whole family are great and they treat me just like a son or like a prodigal son! I got the Oak Leaves of Aug 31st and Trout & Stream today. Thanks. The Oak Leaves with my letter hasn't come through yet.

Good luck Pop and I'm glad your [sic] doing so well.

Much love.
Ernie

.    .    .

Thanksgiving night 10.30
November 28, 1918

Dear folks—;

There was a very good dinner and we all ate turkey, pumpkin pie and [?] and trimmings downstairs tonight. I imagined the dinner you were having with all the folks at dinner and I sure would like to have been there. There certainly is good cause for Thanksgiving this year. Probably you are all wondering when I will get home and really I don't know. About 7 weeks more treatments are necessary if I'm to have a fairly good leg.

Then I have so many invitations to various parts of Italy that I'll maybe take a month to fill them and to see the country. The Bellias want me to stay a couple of weeks at Turino. And I've promised Nick[35] to go shooting with him in Abruzzi and there is a chance to go pig sticking in Sardinia. They have wild boars there and you ride them down with a spear on horseback. It is regarded as quelque sport. Captain Gamble wants me to go to Madiera [sic] with him for two months. It is tropical there and very cheap living and a wonderful place. He paints and thinks we could dodge the rotten weather there. The weather is foul here. Fog today worse than London and snow day before yesterday. In the south of Italy, the weather is great though they say. My blame leg is worse than a barometer, it aches with every change in temperature and I can feel snow two days in advance. That's why I hate to think of a Chicago winter. By the last of Jan. I ought to have about 1200 or 1500 lire and can take a good trip on that. It's impossible to obtain sailings now for the States. Everybody held up.

A lot of Chicago fellows from my old section have left for home and they have all promised to come out and see you. Also Brummy will be going through town. So probably by the time you get this letter you will see some of them. They are Howell Jenkins, Fritz Spiegel, Jerry Flaherty and Lowry Barnett and they'll all be out to see you. They're all good pals of mine and Jenks especially. They'll give you all the dope about me.

If I get a chance I'll go up into Trieste and Trento and I may be able to. Most of my souvenirs were stolen but I still have some good ones. I'm sure to be in Milan for Christmas and would like to send you all Christmas presents but with the present state of the mails you'd be sure never to get them so I'll just try and bring somethings when I come.

How is everybody? I hear from you about every week or so and Oak Leaves come through every once in a while. The flu epidemic is finished here. Thousands died—but I didn't have it. All I've had is jaundice, Tonsilitis and Vincents angina.

My girl's up at the front now and so I'm very lonely here.—only about 3 other human Americans in town and nothing to do. I go to the opera though at the Scala. Have seen Aida, Glusmarda, Mose, Barbiere Di Seville and Mephistophele with Toscanini conducting. Going to see D'Annunzio's Lo Nave Sua [sic]. Wish they'd give Carmen and La Boheme or something interesting. I know lots of the singers who hang around the American Bar. Real chocolat Frappes there.

I'm feeling fine now and my knee is a lot better—I can bend it quite a bit—The machines are very good.

Well Cheerio and I'll write next Thanksgiving,

So long
Ernie

Uncle Ty writes and asks me to write a "nice original letter," to him. Wonder who the devil he thinks I crib my stuff from.

. . .

December 11 [1918]

Dear folks—;

I've booked passage for January 4th via Genoa, Naples and out through Gibraltar. So maybe I'll see you before you get this letter. Don't know how long the boat takes but ought to be home by the middle or last of January.

Your last letters were those of November 12. I've just returned from a peach of a trip. Today is Wed. Saturday morning I left Milan and rode in motor trucks and Staff cars up to Padua. Stopping over night at Verona. Its a 12 hour run on the train and I reached Padua Sunday aft. Then I blew out to Torreglia to visit some British officers at the artillery camp there. They gave me a wonderful time and I rode the Colonel's hunter Monday morning. I ride pretty well now and got along great. We took fences and ditches and everything. Then in the afternoon we took the Staff car "Vauxhall" and Lieut. Hey and I went up to Treviso about 50 miles to see the girl [Agnes]. She is in a field Hospital there. We picked up her and a Miss Smith a friend of Hey's and went all up over the battle field. And walked across the suspension bridge and saw the old Austrian front line trenches and the mined houses of Nervressa [Nervesa] by moonlight and searchlight. It was a great trip. After we came back the four of us got a big midnight supper cooked ourselves at the hospital and then about 1 oclock Hey and I started back to Torreglio. I had a great time while I was staying with the British and they treated me royally. We had horses and I inspected the guns and had a good servant to do me. With the car we went all over the country. It's the 105th Siege Battery. Capt. Shepard who invited me up is a famous artist for Punch, you may have seen some of his stuff. Hey is a Canadian and quite a famous engineer.

I'd like to stay over here and bum a while as I may not get another chance for a long while. But I really feel as though I ought to get back and see you all a spell and then get to work. For a while I was going to go down to Madiera and the canaries with Capt. Gamble but I realize that If I blow down there and bum I will never get home. This climate and this country get you and the Lord ordained differently for me and I was made for to be one of those beastly writing chaps y'Know. You know I was born to enjoy life but the Lord neglected to have me born with money—so I've got to make it and the sooner the better.

So                          So Long and Good Luck
                            Ernie

# FIVE

. . .

# James Nagel
# Hemingway
# and the Italian Legacy

When he came down the gangplank of the *Giuseppe Verdi* on January 21, 1919, a reporter from the *New York Sun* was waiting for him. Ernest Hemingway had just returned from the most dramatic adventure of his young life, one that had inadvertently cast him as hero, and people wanted to hear more. He told it to them. In the story that ran the next day, Hemingway was described as a young man who had joined the Red Cross in France and showed the effects of 227 wounds from pieces of shrapnel, most of which had been removed, "but he still retains a hundred or more." The article went on to describe the wounding, how Hemingway had been hit by a shell from an Austrian trench mortar and then by machine-gun bullets, "one of which got Hemingway in the shoulder and another in the right leg," and how in Milan "surgeons extracted thirty-two fragments from his head and body. . . . Weary of doing nothing, he obtained permission to go to the front again in October, staying there until the armistice."[1]

The broad outlines of this story were true, but the specifics were not. The story was misleading on where Hemingway joined the Red Cross, how many wounds he suffered, where his wounds were, and what he did after he left the hospital in October. And it said nothing about one of the most important aspects of his service in Italy, how he had met a nurse in the hospital, how he had fallen in love, and how they were planning to be married. There were reasons, family reasons, why Hemingway would not have wanted people to know about his romance, but it would turn out to be, in many ways, a formative experience. The Italian journey would eventually provide the background for ten of his early short stories and one of the great novels in English, *A Farewell to Arms*.

The relationship between Hemingway's life and the fiction that grew from it is a problematic and complex matter. His popularity and a flood of scholarly books and articles about him notwithstanding, the identity of the nurse, Agnes von Kurowsky, was not known until 1961. Despite *Hemingway's First War* by Michael S. Reynolds, published in 1976, an excellent study of the background of *A Farewell to Arms*, and a series of lengthy biographies by Carlos Baker, Peter Griffin, Kenneth S. Lynn, and Jeffrey Meyers, among others,[2] questions persist about the extent of Hemingway's wounds, whether he was ever in the Italian Army (as he later claimed), the nature of his romance with Agnes, and what medals he was awarded. Related to these issues are a host of factual matters about which hospital he was in, whether he spoke fluent Italian, as he asserted in several letters to his parents, whether he had an aluminum kneecap, as he told his family.

Hemingway has not made it easy to understand what really happened to him in the war. What dominates the imaginations of most people is the story of Frederic Henry and Catherine Barkley, caught in war and desperately in love, who escape to Switzerland to await the birth of their child, only to have Catherine and the baby die in the hospital. It is a crushing and moving tragedy, one that lives in the mind of anyone who has read *A Farewell to Arms*, but it is not, of course, what actually happened. Nor can Hemingway's comments of 1919 be relied upon. When he spoke to the students at Oak Park High School in March of that year, he gave a romanticized account of war that was published in the *Trapeze*:

> Several hours after their initial engagement with the enemy, Lieutenant Hemingway saw a wounded captain being brought back to a field-hospital in an ambulance.

He had been shot in the chest but had plugged the holes with cigarettes and gone on fighting. On his way to the hospital he amused himself by throwing hand grenades into the ditch just to see them go off. This illustrates the spirit of these men.[3]

The article went on to say that Hemingway was first in the ambulance service and then in the Italian Army, a myth that has persisted, and gave a similarly heroic rendition of his wounding, with Hemingway carrying an injured man after the trench mortar explosion and with the King of Italy personally decorating him with a medal. Inspired by this story, the student body responded with a song:

> Hemingway, we hail you the victor,
> Hemingway, ever winning the game,
> Hemingway, you've carried the colors
> For our land you've won the fame.
> Hemingway, we hail you the leader,
> Your deeds—every one shows your valor.
> Hemingway, Hemingway, you've won
> —Hemingway!

It must have been a satisfying moment for a boy who had never been a hero while in school.

The truth is that Hemingway had served with the American Red Cross as an ambulance driver and, for six days, as the head of a rolling canteen unit serving refreshments to Italian troops. He was returning to an Oak Park that had sent twenty-five hundred of its sons to the war, fifty-six of whom were killed in the army.[4] There would have been little incentive for him to have set the record straight. Theodore Roosevelt, one of Hemingway's boyhood heroes, had recently said that every American boy should do his duty:

> Let him, if a man of fighting age, do his utmost to get into the fighting line—Red Cross work, Y.M.C.A. work, driving ambulances, and the like, excellent though it all is, should be left to men not of military age or unfit for military service, and to wom-

en; young men of vigorous bodies and sound hearts should be left free to do their proper work in the fighting line.[5]

If the students at Oak Park High School were willing to believe that Hemingway had been a combatant rather than an ambulance driver and dispenser of refreshments, he would let them.

The story of how Hemingway got involved with the Red Cross begins in Oak Park, Illinois, a suburb of Chicago. Born to Dr. Clarence and Grace Hall Hemingway on July 21, 1899, Ernest graduated from high school on June 13, 1917. The United States Congress had declared war on Germany on April 6 of that year, but Hemingway was below draft age and showed no initial interest in military service. He spent the summer at the family cottage on Walloon Lake in Michigan and, to the disappointment of his parents, decided not to go to college. Instead he chose to pursue his interest in journalism. His uncle Tyler lived in Kansas City and was friends with Harry Haskell, an editor for the *Kansas City Star*, at the time one of the best newspapers in America.[6] Haskell arranged a cub-reporter position, and in mid-October Ernest took a job he would hold until the end of April of the following year.[7] Basically, Hemingway started by writing obituaries, the classic agony of beginning reporters, moved on to a letter column, and then was assigned to the "short-stop" run, covering police activity and the local hospital.[8] He seems to have succeeded as a reporter, but before he could work his way up any further, something came along that was to change his life forever.

About the time Hemingway arrived in Kansas City, the Austrians were attacking on the eastern front in Italy, and the Italians suffered a devastating defeat, an event he would later make a central element in *A Farewell to Arms*. The medical units assisting the Italian Army were overwhelmed; it was evident that by the late spring of 1918, when the period of enlistment for most of the American Red Cross volunteers would expire, there would be a shortage of ambulance drivers in the five sections serving the front lines in Italy.[9] The Red Cross initiated an active recruitment drive that spring.

One of Hemingway's colleagues on the *Star* had already served in

*Ernest Hemingway with Theodore Brumback, his friend from Kansas City. Hemingway is wearing the standard Red Cross uniform. Photograph courtesy of Maurice F. Neville.*

the ambulance corps. Theodore Brumback, the son of a judge in Kansas City, had lost an eye in a golfing accident at Cornell University in 1915 and was not eligible for service in the military. Instead, he had spent four months of 1917 in France as a Red Cross driver and was in a position to encourage Hemingway to get involved.[10]

Hemingway had his own eye problem, with only partial vision in his left eye, a condition he had from birth and not from a boxing accident, as is sometimes reported. This limitation, however, did not prevent him from joining the 7th Missouri Infantry, a "Home Guard" unit that had been formed when the National Guard in Kansas City was called for duty in France on August 5, 1917.[11] By December Hemingway was duly enlisted, as he wrote home to his parents:

> We got our Woolen O.D. Winter Uniforms and overcoats, and they are the regular army stuff, we ahve [have] the Black and Gold hat cord of Missouri state. (I had to go out there and am continuing now[.]) Our overcoats surely are good. Tehy [they] are Regulation like the unilform [sic] and are warm as the dickens. If it ges [gets] much colder on the sleeping porch I am going to have to wear mine to bed. OH Gee I forgot something good. My army shoes arrived and I am wearing them Now so they will be good and comfortable for hiking. They are great and I am much obliged to you for sending them Dad. I got another Army thing the other day too that is great. An Army slip on sweater. Khaki wool. Marge Bump[12] knitted it for me, and it is a peach of a sweater. She and Pudge are making one for Carl[13] too. They adopted us to supply with knitted stuff and Carl doesn't get his until he is drafted, or enlists, but I got mine sooner because of the Guard.
>
> Now I have got to say So Long
> My love to every body
> Ernie[14]

By its very nature the Home Guard would remain in Kansas City, so Hemingway took advantage of the opening in the Red Cross ambulance units to get involved in the war in Europe. As would have been true of all recruits, he needed the approval of his parents, a driver's license, and a physical, which he took on May 13 in New York.

At the end of April of 1918 he resigned his position on the *Star* and enjoyed a brief vacation in Michigan before leaving for Italy. He left Oak Park on May 11, arriving in New York the next day. Outfitted with the standard uniform, he joined the other men waiting to sail to Europe. What is remarkable about this brief interlude for Hemingway is that he claimed to have met and established a romance with Mae Marsh, an actress who had starred in *The Birth of a Nation*, D. W. Griffith's epic about the Civil War. He wrote to his parents on May 14 from the Hotel Earle in Washington Square,

> as soon as I don my officers' uniform I have an engagement with the Mrs. and have already investigated the possibility of the Little Church around the Corner. I've always planned to get married if I could ever get to be an officer, you know.[15]

Dale Wilson, another friend on the *Star* in Kansas City, received a similar letter:

> I have been out to see Mae several times and am out there for dinner tomorrow evening. I have spent every damn cent I have too. Miss Marsh no kidding says she loves me. I suggested the little church around the corner but she opined as how ye war widow appealed not to her. So I sank the 150 plunks Pop gave me in a ring so I am engaged anyway. Also broke. Dead.[16]

Wilson read these comments with skepticism, but Hemingway's parents took them seriously and were flabbergasted. Their son had been involved in no previous romances, and there is some question about whether he had even had a previous date. Dr. Hemingway wrote a frantic letter on May 18 requesting more information. He questioned whether Ernest was telling the truth about getting married and pleaded with him to clarify what really happened. They were taking the matter seriously, and Hemingway's mother was obviously deeply concerned.[17] Another person who took the letter seriously is Peter Griffin, who writes in *Along With Youth* that Ernest met Mae Marsh at a party given by a socialite and that they became engaged. She was, Griffin maintains, "a blue-eyed blonde with a sparkling smile and a wonderful figure." He also adds that "after he left New York, Ernest never saw Mae Marsh again."[18]

The fact is that Hemingway never saw Mae Marsh the first time, as he admitted in a telegram to his parents, for on May 19 Clarence Hemingway wrote to his son again, saying that Ernest's joke had cost his parents five nights of sleep but that they were relieved to have the truth. He ended his letter with the paternal assurance that no one else would ever learn of this episode.[19] But one person who eventually found out was Dale Wilson, who in 1966 was still intrigued by the Mae Marsh story. He phoned her in California:

> "Yes," she said she had been in New York in 1918, in fact had married Lee Armes, still her husband, there in September, that year.
>     "Did you ever meet Ernest Hemingway?"
>     "No," she said, "but I would have liked to."[20]

The incident suggests something of Hemingway's naïve interest in the subject of romance and his willingness to invent where it did not exist.

Hemingway left New York on May 24, 1918, sailing on a French ship launched in 1908 that had been named the *Chicago* in the hopes of attracting American tourists.[21] C. E. Frazer Clark, who had sailed on the same vessel in 1917, recalled that

> she was a coal-burning, twin-screw, steel-hulled steamer with a spar deck stem to stern for ocean watching, and three decks below. For her day, she was fast, 17 knots, middling-large at 10,502 gross tons, wireless equipped, and a tempting prize for the German U-boats.[22]

Clark goes on to explain how the *Chicago* took evasive action attempting to safeguard its cargo of American volunteers going to France. A year later, Hemingway shared quarters on the voyage with Frederick Spiegel, a boy who had graduated from New Trier High School in Winnetka, Illinois, just north of Chicago. Also on board were his friends Ted Brumback, William Horne, and Howell Jenkins. They arrived in Bordeaux on June 1, took a train to Paris almost immediately, and reported to Red Cross Headquarters at 4, Place de la Concorde, as all volunteers were required to do. He stayed at the hotel designated for arriving Red Cross drivers, the Hôtel Alexandria,

29, Boulevard Bourdon.[23] About the time they arrived, the Germans began shelling Paris with Big Bertha, their famous long-range artillery piece. Brumback recalls that he and Ernest raced about the streets in a taxi trying to get close to the action.[24] Quoting from one of Brumback's letters, Carlos Baker relates that "they had just given up and were going back to the hotel when one of the shells 'hit the façade of the Madeleine, chipping off a foot or two of stone.' This was close enough, even for Ernest."[25]

The train left Paris on June 6 from the Gare de Lyon and arrived in Milan at the Garibaldi Station the next day. Following orders, the group reported to American Red Cross Headquarters at 10 Via Manzoni only to be pressed into immediate service helping with the dead and injured from an explosion at a munitions plant. In *Death in the Afternoon*, published in 1932, Hemingway recalled:

> I first saw inversion of the usual sex of the dead after the explosion of a munition factory which had been situated in the countryside near Milan, Italy. We drove to the scene of the disaster in trucks along poplar-shaded roads, bordered with ditches containing much minute animal life, which I could not clearly observe because of the great clouds of dust raised by the trucks. Arriving where the munition plant had been, some of us were put to patrolling about those large stocks of munitions which for some reason had not exploded, while others were put at extinguishing a fire which had gotten into the grass of an adjacent field, which task being concluded, we were ordered to search the immediate vicinity and surrounding fields for bodies. We found and carried to an improvised mortuary a good number of these and, I must admit, frankly, the shock it was to find that these dead were women rather than men.[26]

At the time, Hemingway wrote a postcard to his friends at the *Kansas City Star*: "Having a wonderful time!! Had my first baptism of fire my first day here when an entire munition factory exploded. We carried them in like at the General Hospital, Kansas City."[27] Two days later they took another train for Vicenza, there boarding ambulances for the drive to their base in Schio near the Dolomites. Ernest Hemingway was beginning one of the great adventures of his life.

## THE RED CROSS IN ITALY

To understand that experience, however, it is important to know something of the background of the Red Cross in Italy, its mission and objectives and limitations, and the function of both the units at the front and the hospitals in the major Italian cities, particularly Milan.[28] From the beginning, the ambulance service in World War I had a literary and academic dimension that is at times astonishing. Before the war was over John Dos Passos, E. E. Cummings, Harry Crosby, Louis Bromfield, Dashiell Hammett, and a host of other writers would serve. One of the early supporters of the service was Henry James, who published *The American Volunteer Motor-Ambulance Corps in France* in 1914.[29] James called attention to the work of Richard Norton, the founder of the corps. The son of Charles Eliot Norton, Richard Norton had graduated from Harvard in 1892 and had distinguished himself as an archaeologist, becoming director of the American School of Classical Studies in Rome, a position he held for eight years. When the war broke out he assembled a volunteer corps with the objective of assisting the wounded men in France and freeing the French from such duties. At first the organization was led by the British Red Cross and the St. John Ambulance. It was funded by wealthy Americans living in London, but soon there was support directly from the United States as well, and by October of 1914 there were fifteen vehicles in the unit.[30]

What seems to have pleased Norton a great deal was that his drivers were graduates of the finest colleges in the United States. As Charles A. Fenton has said, "something more than mere snobbery was involved here, since in 1914 the ability to drive an automobile was largely an upper-class talent; the requisite facility with French, as well as the necessary leisure, was equally genteel."[31] Although men from many universities were involved, the corps was dominated by Harvard, with 325 men enrolled by the end of the war; Yale and

Princeton followed with 187 and 181.[32] As a result of this structure, the young men knew one another before and after their enlistment, and the morale in the corps was high.

A year after it started, the service had sixty ambulances and became formally part of the American Red Cross. By April of 1917, when the United States military entered the war, there were over a hundred vehicles, and the entire unit had become known as the "Norton Section." When Norton died in August, Herman Harjes, the official representative of the American Red Cross in France, took command, and the unit assumed the familiar name of "Norton-Harjes."[33] Well over half of the first drivers to serve in Italy were from the Norton-Harjes unit.[34]

The ambulance service in France, and later in Italy, was organized into sections, a strategy that not only established an efficient structure but allowed an intimacy to develop among the men. Each section contained a liaison in the person of a French lieutenant, an American lieutenant who served as *chef*, and a *sous-chef*, a second lieutenant. When a contingent of the ambulance service was sent to Italy, this organization was maintained, complete with French terms of rank.

The American Red Cross officially arrived in Italy on December 20, 1917. For the first few days it was under the supervision of Major Stanton, but Major Guy Lowell took over on January 1, 1918. His explanation of the situation in Italy is contained in his *Report of the Department of Military Affairs: January to July, 1918*.[35] In the spring of 1918 there were 135 ambulance drivers divided into five sections. They had at their disposal 104 ambulances and 25 other vehicles.

> Section 1 is assigned to mountain work in the Monte Grappa region; the 2nd and 3rd sections are working along the Piave, while the 4th Section, which went out in April, is in the mountains near the Asiago Plateau. The 5th Section started to work in June, and is now operating along the Piave near Montello.[36]

Henry Villard was assigned to Section 1, which had fifteen Fords for normal duty and six Fiats for mountain work. Hemingway's Section 4

*The arrival of American Red Cross ambulances in Milan in December of 1917.
The ambulances had been driven to Italy from Paris.*

had six Fords and seventeen Fiats. A Ford ambulance could hold three stretcher cases or five men sitting; the Fiats were larger and could carry four stretchers or fourteen sitting patients. Fifty of the Fords had been donated by the American Poets' Committee,[37] but the Italians did not consider them suitable for mountain duty and preferred that the drivers use the Fiats.[38]

The standard enlistment period for these men was six months, although the Harvard boys had come for the summer and would return to Cambridge in time for the fall semester. Hemingway was in for the standard six months, as he explained in a letter home: "Our six months start from the day we start driving and it will probably carry us pretty well into the winter."[39] The pay for a driver was 500 lire each month, roughly $96, meant to cover all expenses except hospital costs (for which they had insurance) and uniforms, which were provided, although many drivers had their own made.

During the first six months of 1918 the ambulances handled 70,224 cases, 10,533 of them on stretchers, 49,251 of them sitting. The drivers were instructed to provide three kinds of services, the most hazardous of which was taking the wounded from the front lines to distributing stations, called *smistamento* or *sanità*. The second function was to carry the wounded from these stations to the field hospitals behind the lines, and the third was to transport them from the field hospitals to the army transport centers, where they would be sent by trains to the appropriate hospitals.[40]

Major Lowell described the situation:

> The expirations of the enlistments of the original personnel of the first three sections occurred in May. Nineteen of the time-expired men re-enlisted; a majority of the remainder agreed to continue temporarily pending the arrival of new men under Captain Utassy, who had returned to America for a short time, and while there, had enlisted a large number of men. On May 28th Captain Utassy reached Milan with 37 men for this service. Later in the month and during the month of June other new men arrived.[41]

Of the new men, thirty-four were Harvard students who had left school early to spend the summer in the ambulance service, Henry Villard among them. Indeed, when a party was held in Milan for the ambulance drivers, forty-three of the forty-five men who attended were Harvard students.[42] Hemingway, who had never been to a college of any kind, would have been anomalous in this company.

## THE RED CROSS CANTEENS

As further assistance to the Italian military, the American Red Cross had established a network of canteens across the entire front. Each facility was under the direction of a Red Cross lieutenant, an important point for Hemingway scholars, and the principal duties were to dispense coffee, chocolate (a particular favorite), jam, and soup. There was space for the soldiers to rest, and often musical entertainment was provided. A basic station would have guitars and mandolins, sometimes an accordion, and all of them had phonographs and records of popular music. One of them featured a motion picture projector. The volunteers would also carry hot coffee and refreshments to the soldiers on the front line. A variation on the idea was the rolling canteen, a makeshift mobile trailer that could be moved up close to the lines. Hemingway was in charge of such a unit, Canteen No. 14, when he was wounded.[43]

When Hemingway volunteered for this duty he came under the supervision of Captain James Gamble, the Field Inspector of the canteens.[44] Gamble, who had graduated from Yale in 1904, was thirty-six and in a position to command respect from young men of Hemingway's age.[45] Ted Brumback and Bill Horne also volunteered, along with Howell C. Jenkins, who would be a long-term friend. A useful document for understanding the duties of the unit is Major Lowell's *Report of the Department of Military Affairs*, published by the American Red Cross in Italy. His account reveals that the first canteen was established in February of 1918 under the direction of Lt. Edward M. McKey, who was killed near the Piave on June 16. (Hemingway was, therefore, *not* the first American wounded on the Italian front, as many biographers have claimed.) When Ernest arrived in Italy there were seventeen units in operation, and the duty was often hazardous, even in the simple matter of bringing stores to the front. As Major Lowell explained, "to get these supplies to these points it was necessary to travel over roads within the range of Austrian guns and climb slopes covered by numerous machine guns and cannon."[46] At the time he was injured, however, Hemingway's duties were somewhat more mundane. He wrote home to Ruth Morrison on June 22, 1918, that

> what I am supposed to be doing is running a posto di ricovero. That is, I dispense chocolate and cigarettes to the wounded and

*Italian soldiers in the trenches, 1918.*

*Italian soldiers moving camouflaged artillery.*

the soldiers in the front line. Each aft and morning I load up a haversack and take my tin lid and gas mask and beat it up to the trenches. I sure have a good time but miss their [sic] being no Americans.[47]

Hemingway arrived at this new assignment just as the Italians were engaged in a counteroffensive against the Austrian positions, and there was fighting all along the lower Piave.

## HEMINGWAY'S WOUND

In *At the Hemingways: A Family Portrait*, Ernest Hemingway's sister Marcelline describes an experience she had one night in the autumn of 1918:

> Marion Vose, my classmate, and I decided to go to a movie near our school in Chicago. By accident, after the feature, we saw a newsreel about the work of the American Red Cross in Italy. The new Red Cross hospital in Milan was described and shown. Suddenly, in the silent film, Ernest appeared. He was in uniform, sitting in a wheelchair on the hospital porch, being pushed by a pretty nurse. Over his lap was spread a robe of knitted wool squares. He smiled at the camera and waved a crutch for a second. I was hysterical with excitement.[48]

It is a touching moment in Marcelline's account of her family, and the veracity of the event has not been questioned, although no one has been able to find that particular newsreel. Her comment about "the silver plate the Italian surgeons had put in his knee cap," however, would not seem to be true, given the X-rays of Hemingway's knees taken in Milan, and this myth simply contributes to a great deal of misinformation about Hemingway's wound.[49] Some of this confusion may have started with the *New York Sun* article on January 22, 1919, which had him hit not only by a trench mortar burst but by a "storm of machine gun bullets" in the "shoulder and another in the right leg."[50] Mary Harrington repeated the story about the silver kneecap in an article in the *New York Post Week-End Magazine* in 1946.[51]

Since then, there have been many conflicting reports, some of them with alarming implications. Constance Cappel Montgomery, for example, maintains that "besides being shot in the legs . . . he also was shot through the scrotum." She also quotes an unnamed nurse as saying that Dr. Hemingway told her "about the two hundred and thirty-seven pieces of shrapnel (*it was two hundred and twenty-seven*) in his son's groin and of the pain it caused him."[52] The numerical correction here gives the comment a sense of exactitude, and yet her description of the wounds was not accurate.

Hemingway scholars have added to the confusion. Charles A. Fenton, in *The Apprenticeship of Ernest Hemingway*, says that Hemingway was "wounded a moment after he had seized an Italian rifle and began firing toward the Austrian lines," which broadens the issue from the wounds to the events at the time of the wounding.[53] More recent biographers have had their own perspectives. Jeffrey Meyers, working unskeptically from some of Hemingway's letters, elaborates on the "scrotum" theme:

> Apart from the extensive traumata in his legs and knees, Hemingway suffered another significant wound. He claimed he was shot twice through the scrotum and had to rest his testicles—which remained intact—on a pillow.[54]

Kenneth S. Lynn is more indirect, but he too suggests that there was something sexual about the wound. Lynn questions the cause of the wounds, however, concluding that "Hemingway's talk of machine-gun wounds rings false." Lynn's "evidence" about the nature of the wounding is simply a quotation from *A Farewell to Arms*, a practice all too common in Hemingway biography.[55]

Another area of speculation is the issue of "shell shock," a condition Hemingway later gave to his character Nick Adams, to a lesser extent to Frederic Henry, and to a number of other characters. Indeed, the whole matter of the psychic damage done by the war is a major theme in Hemingway's work, and it is perhaps normal for scholars to suspect a biographical basis for this idea. Constance Cappel Montgomery quotes Dr. Guy C. Conkle of Boyne City, Michigan, a physician who treated Hemingway, as saying that "Ernest was badly shell-shocked when he came for treatment in the summer of 1919. . . . Ernest had shrapnel in both of his legs. . . . Ernest was stout and was in good condition, except for his war wounds and their effects."[56] Montgomery also reports that "since he had been injured at night, Ernest was not able to sleep in the dark for a long time."[57] Malcolm Cowley is quoted as having said that Hemingway "found he was shell-shocked, and was guilty in his own eyes of cowardice of some sort."[58] Denis Brian takes the idea further, saying that Hemingway "suffered what was then called shell shock, to the point of mental breakdown."[59]

Agnes von Kurowsky, who treated Hemingway virtually every day, and Henry Villard, who was in the room next to him in August of 1918, and who talked with him at length, saw no sign of shell shock whatever. Indeed, they remember him as being almost incessantly cheerful. Agnes later commented that she "never saw him down in the dumps when he was in the hospital. He was worried about his leg. I remember that he wasn't sure that they were going to save his leg."[60] Nor did Agnes remember that he had a head wound. Hemingway's letters home give no indication of psychic pathology. Michael Reynolds offers wise counsel on this matter. He observes that "in Boyne City, Dr. Conklin[61] had not seen much of the war's aftermath. If he thought Ernest was shell-shocked, it was because Hemingway wanted him to think so."[62] The official records of the American Red Cross Hospital in Milan list no shell-shock victims, nor could Agnes later recall that they ever had such a patient.

There were, of course, numerous shell-shock cases in the Great War. Indeed, the *Red Cross Bulletin* for October 20, 1918, reported that a new ward had been formed back home, "a special psychiatric unit of forty nurses, all specialists in nerve cases and mental depression, to care for victims of shell shock."[63] It would seem likely that Hemingway would have heard about such cases while in Italy and found them an intriguing metaphor for the cultural destruction Western civilization had just experienced. It is also possible that he read about the condition in one of his father's medical journals, since the *American Medical Association Journal*, among others, carried such articles in 1919.[64]

It is difficult in the wake of so much speculation and opinion to attempt to determine what really happened in Hemingway's wounding, and the final "truth" may never be known. The "standard" opinion, if there is any such thing, has been well formulated by Samuel Shaw:

> Hemingway was severely wounded in an Austrian mortar and machine gun attack. He suffered multiple wounds in both legs, the severest damage being done by a machine gun slug in the right knee. Disabled as he was, he managed to carry a wounded Italian soldier to safety. For his courageous act he was awarded the Silver Medal of Valor and the Croce di Guerra and was promoted to first lieutenant in the regular Italian army.[65]

This formulation contains all the central items of dispute: whether Hemingway was "heroic" in the incident, carrying anyone or performing any other extraordinary action; whether he was hit by machine-gun bullets (the shrapnel wounds are not in dispute); what medals he received; and whether he was ever officially in the Italian army in any capacity.

What can be established at the outset is that Hemingway arrived in Schio about June 10, 1918, taking a room on the second floor of a woolen mill next to a stream, in which the men went swimming. Two miles away were the foothills of the Dolomites and the imposing rise of Monte Pasubio. There was little activity at the front. Since the previous October, when the German-Austrian forces had advanced through northern Italy across the Tagliamento to the Piave, they had held their positions, particularly in the area covered by Section 4. The Italian units had fortified their strongholds in the mountains and were prepared to hold the line.[66] Although there was a major Austrian offensive in other areas that June, Hemingway's region was relatively quiet. As a result, after about two weeks of inactivity, Hemingway volunteered for another Red Cross service to the Italian soldiers, the rolling canteen units. It was this duty Hemingway was performing when he was wounded, not driving an ambulance.

The incident took place at Fossalta di Piave on July 8, 1918. Hemingway was in charge of a canteen precisely where Lt. McKey had been killed in June. That region was within the range of Austrian mortars, and attacks were not uncommon. In his letter of August 18, Hemingway recalls that he had been at the front only six days when he was hit. At no point was he a combatant in the war, and Red Cross workers were not issued firearms. Although there is a photograph of Hemingway with a rifle on his bicycle, there is no evidence that he ever fired the weapon. More likely, as was the case with Lt. McKey, he was simply doing his duty, distributing coffee and chocolate and bringing supplies to the front line, when he was hit.

Guy Lowell reported that "during such a trip, E. M. Hemingway was wounded by the explosion of a shell which landed about three feet from him, killing a soldier who stood between him and the point of explosion, and wounding others."[67] On August 5, 1918, Lowell wrote in *The Red Cross Bulletin* that

> volunteer F. M. Hemingway [sic] of Kansas City, an Ambulance Driver of Section No. 4, wounded recently while distributing relief to soldiers in the trenches, is progressing toward complete recovery. He was wounded by a bomb from a trench mortar, receiving 237 separate wounds in the legs. All except ten of these wounds were superficial. He has been commended for the way in which he conducted himself, having carried a wounded Italian some distance to succor after having been wounded himself.[68]

The story ran in the Paris edition of the *Bulletin* on September 14, 1918. On December 7, 1918, the Italian edition of the *Bulletin* printed yet another story on Hemingway:

> Although Lieutenant Ernest M. Hemingway, of Oak Park, Illinois, was wounded in 237 places, he carried a helpless comrade to safety before he collapsed. He is cited to receive the Silver Medal of Valor, the second highest award of the Italian com-

mand. He writes: "The wounds from the trench mortar didn't hurt a bit, and the machine gun bullet just felt like a smack on the leg by an icy snow ball. I got up and got my wounded to the dug-out."[69]

Although there is no way to be absolutely certain of the facts, several points are consistent in the various accounts: that Hemingway was at the front lines when he was struck by a trench mortar explosion; that he had something like 237 wounds (there may well be problems in determining what constitutes a wound when material of different sizes and shapes hits someone in the legs); that he rendered assistance to another wounded man; that he was hit a second time by machine-gun bullets.

Kenneth Lynn is not the only scholar to express doubt about the machine-gun incident, and it does sound like a typically heroic war story. However, the X-rays of Hemingway's legs and the machine-gun bullet in his coin purse would seem to support the account. One X-ray shows a metal object lodged in Hemingway's right knee. The patella, which would be above the object when the knee was bent, is not injured, nor are any of the bones fractured. The foreign object closely matches one view of the bullet. Another X-ray discloses that not only was there a machine-gun bullet in Hemingway's right foot but that it had fractured the bone in his big toe,[70] explaining why he had trouble with his foot during the summer and fall of 1918. Almost twenty years later, nurse Elsie MacDonald wrote to Ernest and recalled this problem:

> Do you remember the Sunday you were going out to a dinner and you insisted in [sic] wearing your boot and how I rugged and tugged to get it on, and how mad you were at me because I told you you should wear your slippers as you simply could not walk with that old boot on your sore foot, and then changed your mind and sneaked back to your room, pulled off the boot, and put your poor sore foot into your comfortable slippers and walked away to your dinner, but you told the nurses not to tell me as we had had a great fight over the boot and slipper.[71]

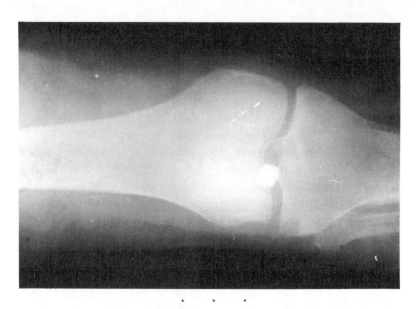

· · ·

*The X-ray of Hemingway's right knee reveals a machine-gun bullet but no damage to the patella, confirming what he said in a letter to his father. Photograph courtesy of Maurice F. Neville.*

· · ·

*The X-ray of Hemingway's right foot reveals that a machine-gun bullet had fractured his toe. Photograph courtesy of Maurice F. Neville.*

· · ·

*A bullet found in Hemingway's coin purse from World War I. It may have been taken from one of his knees.*

This evidence would strongly suggest that Hemingway did not invent the machine-gun story to appear heroic and, indeed, with respect to his foot injury, his wounds were even more severe than he reported. On the other hand, the X-rays discount the story of the silver (sometimes it is aluminum) kneecap.

After he was wounded, Hemingway seems to have been taken to Field Hospital 62 at Villa Toso, Casier, in the province of Treviso.[72] He remained there, he said in a letter, for five days. He would then have been taken by ambulance to a railroad station, probably in Mestre, and from there by train to the American Red Cross Hospital in Milan, arriving early in the morning of July 17. Hemingway went to the Ospedale Maggiore for daily periods of physical therapy after his operation and throughout the autumn of 1918, but he was never a resident patient there.

Henry Villard was under the impression that it was Nurse Anna Scanlon who admitted Ernest to the hospital, and on July 20 Agnes recorded in her diary: "Hemingway—who has the honor of being the 1st Amer. wounded in Italy. [She was wrong about that.] He has shrapnel in his knees, besides a great many flesh wounds." Elsie MacDonald's letters reveal that it was she who took Hemingway to the Misericordia Hospital[73] for X-rays and that Hemingway insisted they speak Italian during the examination.[74]

Ted Brumback saw Hemingway in the hospital in Milan soon after his arrival and wrote to Hemingway's parents to let them know what had happened. His letter, reproduced in Marcelline Hemingway Sanford's *At The Hemingways*, is the kind of optimistic and laudatory comment one would want a friend to write. It suggests that Hemingway would recover "in a couple of weeks," an unrealistic estimate in that Hemingway was still using a cane when he arrived home six months later. Brumback also described the nature of the wounds:

> Although some two hundred pieces of shell were lodged in him, none of them are above the hip joint. Only a few of these pieces were large enough to cut deep, the most serious of these being two in the knee and two in the right foot.

He also recalled how Hemingway had volunteered for canteen duty on the Piave. Not satisfied with the routine, Hemingway suggested that he use his bicycle to bring refreshments to the men. He did so for six days. On the seventh, while handing out chocolate, he was hit. Brumback describes the event:

> The concussion of the explosion knocked him unconscious and buried him in earth. There was an Italian between Ernest and the shell. He was instantly killed, while another standing a few feet away, had both his legs blown off.
> A third Italian was badly wounded and this one Ernest, after he had regained consciousness, picked up on his back and carried to the first aid dugout.

Missing from this account is any mention of machine-gun activity, although the story in other ways is similar to the *Red Cross Bulletin* descriptions. Brumback also mentions minor wounds in Hemingway's fingers, which prevented him from writing. Despite this problem, Hemingway added a postscript: "I am all O.K. and include much love to ye parents. I'm not near so much of a hell roarer as Brummy makes me out."[75]

Hemingway's comments on his wounds and the progress of his recovery in his letters home are significant. His assertion in his letter of July 21 that he is "the first American wounded in Italy" is enigmatic. Since he was serving in the same area where Lt. McKey had been killed, Hemingway would certainly have heard of the incident. Perhaps he felt that being first added significance to his wounds. He also refers to the bullet in his right foot, an injury ignored in Hemingway biography. This letter indicates that there were probably superficial injuries to Hemingway's hands as well as to his left knee, both of which matters are supported by photographs taken in the hospital. Most importantly, it confirms that there was no damage to the patella in his right knee, hence no metal prosthesis of any kind was required.

In his letter of August 7 Hemingway mentions that he will be operated on the "day after tomorrow," although the actual operation was delayed an extra day. Agnes von Kurowsky's diary clearly gives the day of the operation as August 10, a date confirmed in the un-published diary of Henry Villard, in which he recorded:

> Got dressed and took a walk in the afternoon, doing some errands at the same time. It certainly feels good to get about once again. Hemingway was operated on early in the morning.[76]

In 1926 Elsie MacDonald wrote to Hemingway:

> Remember the morning of your operation when you told Dr. Samerelli [sic] that if you did not pull through I was to receive all your back pay, insurance and the Trophy of a bloody boot at the Front. Gee, Kid, the tears came to my eyes that morning & next morning I could not get to the Red Cross Office quick enough to cable your Dad and let him know that you were all right.

Ernest's letter of August 18, a week after the surgery, contains the most extensive description he ever gave about his wounding. His comment about being hit "by a trench mortar and a machine gun bullet while advancing toward the rear" is also of interest, although the singular "bullet" is vexing. He gives the number of wounds as 227, which the Red Cross reports elevate to 237. Ernest's suggestion that even after he was hit by machine-gun bullets he still assisted a wounded soldier, walking 150 yards, cannot be confirmed with certainty. That he was of initial assistance after being hit by the trench mortar is supported by other accounts. This is particularly the case in the assertion that Hemingway asked the stretcher bearers to take some of the other men before carrying him to the ambulance. He also indicates a stay of five days in a field hospital. Of particular interest is the tone of this letter, written more than a month after the wounding and a week after the surgery; it is free of any indication of psychic trauma, mental confusion, or emotional distress.

Hemingway's letter of September 11 makes reference to one his father wrote on August 11 after receiving Elsie MacDonald's cable informing him that Ernest was recovering nicely from his operation.

This letter also gives the name of the surgeon involved, Dr. Sammarelli, and of the progress of the recovery, a matter that is a consistent theme in the rest of Hemingway's letters home.

In the course of his recovery, many of Hemingway's friends came to see him, notably Jim Gamble, Robert Bates (Inspector of Red Cross ambulances), and Meade Detweiler (Milan representative of the American Red Cross).[77] Although there were only four patients in the hospital when Hemingway arrived on July 17, there would soon be more, including Henry Villard and Bill Horne, who spent three weeks in August in the hospital suffering from gastroenteritis.[78]

## THE AMERICAN RED CROSS HOSPITAL

Hemingway was taken to the American Red Cross Hospital in central Milan near the Red Cross Headquarters at 15 Via Manzoni. There has been considerable confusion about the location of the hospital. Carlos Baker gives the address as 10 Via Alessandro Manzoni, which is incorrect.[79] He may have been thinking of the Red Cross Headquarters because nurses at the hospital used stationery from the main office in their correspondence. Reynolds gives the address as 3 Via Bochetto,[80] a slight misspelling of 3 Via Bocchetto, which is printed on some stationery of La Croce Rossa Americana. In his *Instructions and Information for Red Cross Workers in France*, Herbert Clarke gives this address as the location of the Milan office of the American Red Cross in Italy, not of the hospital.[81] Charlotte M. Heilman, one of the nurses, used this address in her letters, and it may have been a convenient place to receive mail.

Agnes, however, gives the address as 4 Via Cesare Cantù in her diary entry for July 15. A letter she received was addressed to this location, the envelope of which survives.[82] This site is confirmed in a letter from Sara E. Shaw on July 11, 1918.[83] It is likely that the director of the hospital would know the correct address. It is also possible, however, that there were several entrances, since the Via Bocchetto runs on one side of the building and Via Cesare Cantù on the other. The Via Manzoni is on the other side of a major street, the

· · ·

*American Red Cross Headquarters in Milan. Photograph from the scrapbook of Agnes von Kurowsky.*

Via Dante, which runs down to the Duomo, a short distance away. The public garden is up Via Manzoni somewhat less than a mile, and the Ospedale Maggiore, where Jeffrey Meyers says Hemingway was housed, is even farther away.[84]

What seems evident is that Hemingway was a patient at the American Red Cross Hospital at 4 Cesare Cantù, but he had physical therapy at the larger facility, the Ospedale Maggiore. Prior to his surgery, Hemingway was taken to the Misericordia Hospital for X-rays.[85] Agnes was assigned to the Red Cross hospital, but when she first arrived in Milan it was not yet open. As a result, on July 8 she reported for duty, treating an American patient, Lt. Rochefort (she spells it "Rochfort"), at the Italian hospital. On July 16 she transferred her personal belongings to the Red Cross building but continued working at the Italian hospital until July 29, when she was able to move her patient. In the meantime, the new Red Cross hospital had officially opened on July 17, the day Hemingway arrived.[86]

It was more than just a hospital, since it also served as an educational center and as a mobilization unit for all the Red Cross nurses in Italy. Major Joseph Collins, the Director of Medical Affairs for the American Red Cross in Italy, described the functions of the new facility:

> Preparation of dressings, demonstration of their use, hospital
> social service work, medical and public health work, and district
> nursing were among some of the fields included in its endeavors.
> In addition, it provided care for our American forces, a small but
> well equipped hospital having been opened in connection therewith.[87]

Sara Shaw was thus in charge of the Red Cross nurses not only in Milan but in all of Italy, which explains how she could send Agnes to several locations on assignment.

Collins goes on to outline the situation in Milan:

> The first American Red Cross Hospital was established at
> Milan in a building previously used as a pension and the rooms
> and furnishings of which were found readily adaptable for hospital use. A certain amount of remodeling and embellishing had to
> be done; the use of plenty of fresh white paint, and brightly
> colored inexpensive cretonne coverings for the furniture, together with a quantity of other dainty furnishings received from
> America served to make the rooms comfortable and, at the same
> time, attractive.
>
> In all there are two floors, the upper being utilized for patients, the lower as a Nurses' Home. The Hospital proper consists of sixteen large airy bed rooms, which open on one side into
> a corridor enclosed by glass doors and windows, making a sun
> parlor, and on the other side upon wide terraces. In addition, the

upper floor contains a small but well equipped operating room with ideal lighting arrangements, an anesthetizing room, a diet kitchen, an office, lavatories and bath rooms. The rooms are all communicating, which facilitates their ready ventilation and makes for convenience in nursing. The arrangement is such that the capacity of the hospital may be readily and comfortably increased in any emergency.[88]

This description omits the fact that the two floors the hospital occupied were the third and fourth floors of the building, not the first two. That all of the rooms were communicating indicates that they were not merely adjacent but, when desired, open so that patients could speak to one another and the breeze could sweep through on a summer day. There was little privacy, in other words, in which to conduct an affair, even among the most willing of participants. An envelope addressed to Hemingway in the hospital reveals that he was in room 106 on the fourth floor; Henry Villard was in the next room.[89]

Collins goes on to describe a few other locations in the hospital. On the nurses' floor, there were ten bedrooms and a large library, along with the utility rooms, an office, a dining room, a kitchen. The library had both a phonograph and a piano to entertain the patients as well as the nurses. The record of admissions and discharges shows that the hospital received seven patients in June of 1918 (they may have been treated by the Red Cross staff at other facilities), seven again in July (Hemingway among them), twenty-two in August, thirteen in September, and twelve in October. The nurses were not overburdened with work, and there was time for them to serve at other locations on temporary assignments, as Agnes did. Of these patients, most had malaria or influenza, since there were epidemics that summer; four are listed as having jaundice (Henry Villard was one of these); three suffered from wounds, including Hemingway; and there was one mental disturbance: Agnes's patient, Lt. Rochefort, who was still recovering from a fractured skull in a streetcar accident and was disoriented, not psychotic. Agnes would later recall that he would greet people twenty times a day, asking them how they were on each occasion.[90] Only two surgical procedures are listed (Hemingway's was one of them) and both were minor operations. There were no cases of shell shock.[91]

It was in this hospital that Ernest, Agnes, and Henry were first united, and their respective documents should be viewed with an understanding of what they were doing in Italy, what motivated them, and the series of events that brought them together. It is fortunate for literary historians and biographers that their letters and diaries have survived, since they provide a contemporaneous record against which to measure Hemingway's fiction about the same locations and events.

### HENRY S. VILLARD: RED CROSS DRIVER IN ITALY

In *Exile's Return*, his memoir of World War I and the expatriate years in Paris, Malcolm Cowley recalls that "during the winter of 1916–17 our professors stopped talking about the international republic of letters and began preaching patriotism."[92] For young Henry Villard, entering Harvard in the autumn of 1917, that idea was already established, and as the academic year proceeded, he became increasingly preoccupied with the possibilities of going abroad and making a contribution to the war effort while there was still time. Since the draft age was twenty years, nine months, Villard had every reason to suspect that it all would be over by the time he was old enough to serve. (Born in New York City on March 30, 1900, to Harold Garrison Villard, a lawyer, and Mariquita Serrano Villard, he would soon be the youngest ambulance driver in Italy.) Unlike Agnes and Ernest, he had been to Europe before and knew Paris well, but the war provided new opportunities for adventure, and he did not want to miss it.

Villard's unpublished diary and letters to his family record the events that led to his service in Italy. In a letter from Harvard on April 24, 1918, he appears to have broached the subject with his parents for the first time:

> I have been doing some rapid thinking since I got back [from New York] and I am going to ask you a question which please

consider carefully. What do you think are the chances of my getting some kind of a government job this summer? . . . I would like to leave college at once and . . . probably return here in the fall. I would only lose one month, or less, of work, and yet receive credit for the year, as I could either take the early exams which they are giving now, or have my year's work mark considered as my final mark. Please let me know as soon as possible what you think of this, and what the chances are.

He went on to discuss two friends entering the Navy and another on Secret Service duty in Denmark. Along with suggesting that he planned to change his major from English to Romance Languages, with a special interest in French and Spanish, he reported that he had been drilling with his R.O.T.C. regiment at the Fresh Pond center. His parents, his next letter suggests, were not very encouraging.[93]

He telephoned them from the Copley Plaza on April 29 and suggested Red Cross ambulance work as a possibility; despite initial encouragement, they refused in a telegram the next day. Since parental consent was a requirement for service, he quickly renewed his appeal in a letter on April 30:

I do not know why you have withheld permission for me to join the Red Cross, but before giving up entirely, I would like to explain the situation to you more fully than was possible over the telephone.

Up to last Saturday, the American Red Cross was only taking older men for work in Italy, but on that day, a War Department order came, which authorized a special unit of fellows under draft age, from 18 yrs to 20 and 4 months. Fifty or one hundred,—I don't know which,—are to be taken from Harvard, and as soon as this was known, applications began pouring in. The news spread like wildfire, and as soon as I heard of it yesterday, I rushed in town and put my name on the waiting list. Now the chance is something extraordinary, and one which will never occur again. What it means is this: we would sail in about 2 weeks, or a little more, go to Southern France probably, and from there be taken to Italy by rail; I don't know what the chances are of going to Northern France and thence to Italy. Once in Italy, we would do transportation work of the wounded, from the dressing stations to the hospitals. In 3 months, or at the very maximum, 6 months, we would be discharged and sent home. This is *absolutely guaranteed*, so there would be no chance of missing college in the fall. The idea of the whole plan is to have volunteers like us go over now until the American army is moved into Italy this summer, and merely keep the Red Cross going temporarily until then. After that, they *refuse to have us* any longer, and we would *not* be allowed to remain in any capacity, as they say "they don't want sight-see-ers." So we would probably be back in August or September, at the very latest October. (Needless to say, we would serve only the time agreed upon, and would NOT be in for the duration of the war.) As for the danger, there is *absolutely none*, seeing that we are not under fire, but merely transporting wounded from one station to another behind the lines.

Writing for a purpose, Villard clearly diminished both the role of the ambulance drivers and the risks involved. The rest of his letter explains the special circumstances at Harvard in the spring of 1918; there would be a set of early examinations for the men leaving for Europe:

A peach of a bunch of fellows are going, all the best fellows in the class (they are all, practically, from 1921), and dozens of whom are my best friends. The man in charge told us last night he wanted only the highest type of Harvard fellows and he is certainly getting it. You can imagine how terribly disappointed I was this morning to get your telegram, when all the fellows are rushing around congratulating each other on getting their parents' consent.

It would be difficult to overstate the enthusiasm for service that Henry displays in this appeal:

I think it is inconceivable that you can let this opportunity pass,—a summer filled with interest, with the knowledge that I

am actually doing something, the guaranty of returning at the
end of the summer, a full year's credit in leaving now, the being
with all my friends, and in no danger whatsoever. It is really
almost unbelievable that such a remarkable opportunity should
be within my grasp.

He goes on at length, with assurances of favorable weather, with
threats of enlistment in the Navy if he is forbidden Red Cross duty,
with additional pledges of his safety in Italy. The response was quick
in coming, for the next morning his parents were at his room at 8
A.M. and spent the day with their son as he underwent his physical
examination and filled out the final papers for the Red Cross. After a
late lunch, he saw them off on the train at 4:00.

But there would be one last obstacle. On April 30, 1918, while
these difficult negotiations were going on within the Villard family,
the faculty of the College of Arts and Sciences at Harvard passed its
own resolution:

> In view of the altered conditions of military service conse-
> quent upon the entrance of the United States into the war, this
> Faculty believes that the best conservation of the resources of the
> country for the prosecution of the war demands that students,
> save in exceptional cases, should persist in the faithful discharge
> of their college duties until they reach the age of twenty years
> and nine months, when they may enter on the regular training
> required for a commission.

President A. Lawrence Lowell sent a copy of this document to Henry's father the following day.[94] Harvard students must have learned of
this maneuver rather quickly, for on May 3 Henry wrote to his parents to say "you may receive a circular from Pres. Lowell about leaving college early, but don't pay any attention to it." He went on to
argue that his education would not be affected by a summer in Italy,
that former President Eliot's grandson was going, and that he had
definitely been accepted into the Red Cross and would sail on May 11.
Henry explained further, "only 40 are being taken now from Harvard,
as they want to make up the quota from the West." (One of the young

men in the western group was Ernest Hemingway.) It is clear that Villard's tactic had worked, and he closed his letter: "I think it's great of you to let me go and can't thank you enough. Much love, from, Harry."

From that time on things developed rapidly. On May 2 Villard had still been uncertain about whether he would be assigned to Italy until fellow student Charles A. Page came by to say they had been accepted and that he was to be Henry's squad leader. The following days were filled with a rush to get ready to depart, with photographs and hurried final examinations, including the one in the R.O.T.C. course in military science. Of particular importance was a driver's license, required in the ambulance service, a provisional version of which he persuaded the Department of Motor Vehicles to grant on the assurance he was learning to drive. There was also time for dating, for a concert by the Boston Pops, and for *Charley's Aunt*, a farce performed by the Henry Jewett Players in Boston.

On May 8 the Harvard students leaving for Italy had a group picture taken, got typhoid shots, and inquired about uniforms. The next day Henry turned in his R.O.T.C. equipment. On Friday, May 10, he took his French 2 final at 2:00 and boarded the 5:00 train for New York. Saturday he spent ordering uniforms and applying all over again for a passport, since the one he had applied for in Cambridge had not come through before he left. On Sunday he got a smallpox vaccination and talked with Charlie Page about what to take to Italy. Monday was devoted to Red Cross details, visas, buying equipment, and saying goodbye to family: "Packed the rest of the evening till 1 A.M.," he wrote in his diary. Finally, three days later than scheduled, Villard and his friends were on board *La Lorraine*, and they sailed out of New York just before noon. Villard recorded in his diary: "I certainly don't seem to realize that this thing started only 2 weeks ago, & that I am actually bound for Europe in uniform."

The trip over was filled with music, with concerts and group singing and periods of sunning on the deck. There were additional vaccinations to be endured, but there were also breakfast in bed, piano and banjo music (with Henry playing a banjo-mandolin), and poker parties among the men in the evenings. In his letter home on

May 19, Henry recorded that "most of the passengers are other Red Cross people, Y.M.C.A. men, or army officers, while the steerage is composed entirely of American soldiers." He laments the quarters and the food of the soldiers below but reports that he has a "good outside cabin" and that "the food we get is delicious, and in great variety, except that there is no butter or sugar." As did Agnes, Henry encountered linguistic difficulties: "I never realized how little French I knew until I struck this boat, as the crew are all Frenchmen of course." He records that they did not find the ships they were to join until May 22: "We picked up our convoy at 5 A.M. this morning,—a very neat French destroyer. The sea is like glass & the sky a heavy lead color. We are zig-zagging every few minutes. Tomorrow we are due in Bordeaux. When this letter arrives, you will know I have landed." He added a postscript on Thursday, May 23: "We arrived early this A.M. & have to spend the whole day at the river's mouth with customs officials. All well." His diary adds details that he did not tell his parents, that there were frequent drills to abandon ship, that the poker games ran on until midnight, that one evening he consumed two glasses of champagne, three cocktails, and two gin fizzes.

After they cleared customs on May 23 they were taken up the river to Bordeaux, arriving early in the evening. Villard and several friends had dinner at the Hôtel de France and caught the 10:00 train to Paris. Red Cross workers were not given sleeping compartments, and the men had to sit up through the night. Villard arrived in Paris at 8 A.M., checked into the Hôtel Palais d'Orsay, and, in accord with regulations, registered at Red Cross Headquarters. That evening Henry and his friends had dinner at the Chinese Umbrella and went to the Follies Bergère: "Not only a poor musical show but the roughest place & the lewdest I've ever seen." The next day they reported to Red Cross Headquarters but were dismissed for the day. They were, however, compelled to change hotels, moving to the cheaper Hôtel Métropolitain to comply with Red Cross expense budgets. On Sunday, May 26, Henry and his friends went to Versailles, toured the palace, and had dinner at the Café Maxim, "where two dames tried their darndest to pick up me. One of them was sitting next to me on one of those long leather-covered benches, & kept loving me up every few seconds. She was quite good on looks, but the situation was embarrassing to say the least." On Monday, back in Paris, the city was being shelled by "Big Bertha" ("it was not very exciting") and the young men secured the necessary visas, rode the baggage truck to the Gare de Lyon, and departed for Italy.

Villard records how the train made its way to Modane, where they changed for Turin, and there caught the 6:30 to Milan, arriving at midnight. Villard and Charlie checked into the Continental Hotel, "quite classy," and reported the next morning to Major Lowell at Red Cross Headquarters. The recruits were divided into sections, most of Henry's friends going to Section 1. That evening there was a dinner for them with songs and speeches. The next morning, May 30, the men boarded an early train, arriving in Vicenza in late afternoon, and riding in a Fiat truck to Bassano: "Our headquarters are an old villa outside the town in a wonderful situation,—at the base of the mountains & on a river. Everything is much finer than I ever imagined." Henry was now an ambulance driver in Italy. The journey he had taken was much like that Ernest and Agnes would soon experience, with virtually identical comments about the uncomfortable train ride from Bordeaux, the charm of Paris, the shelling of Big Bertha. No one has recorded it in such detail as Villard, however, and while his diary gives the facts and names, his memoir expands the story with his feelings at the time and with his retrospective assessment of these youthful events.

Villard's memoir begins in Milan and takes him through his experiences as an ambulance driver to his convalescence from hepatitis in the American Red Cross Hospital from August 1, when he arrived in Milan on the train from Vicenza, to August 23, when he returned to duty at the front. (At this point, of course, Agnes was still dating Capt. Serena, and her relationship with Hemingway was only a friendship.) Villard's letters home during this period say nothing of his illness nor of the hospital, since he was continuing to conceal from his parents anything that might be cause for alarm. His reflections are significant because they provide an intimate record of the experiences of a typical Red Cross volunteer, and they offer sketches of both Agnes and Hemingway at the very time they were falling in love. With a gift for detail, Villard captures what it was like to drive an ambulance on the front lines, to carry mutilated men for emergency treatment, to suffer through the frustrations and the rewards of Red Cross duty in a foreign country. Of particular moment is his memory of the shock of seeing wounded men for the first time: "It deeply affected most Americans as young as we were, and I know it had made a profound impression on Ernie." These scenes in his memoir are dramatic and yet they retain a sense of commonplace reality as well, blending the activity at the front with the workaday matters of mess halls and rooming houses and bathing in the river. That Villard concludes his account with the story of Agnes's life after she returned from Italy, following her to their visit together in Florida in 1976 and her death, at 92, in 1984, gives his story a moving sense of closure.

## AGNES VON KUROWSKY

Agnes sailed for Europe on the steamer *La Lorraine* on June 15, 1918, as part of a contingent of Bellevue nurses who had volunteered for duty in Italy. At the age of twenty-six, Agnes was involved in her first European adventure, one that would record her name not in the annals of nursing but in American literary history.

Virtually nothing was known about the identity of Hemingway's nurse in Milan until Leicester Hemingway published *My Brother, Ernest Hemingway* in 1961.[95] Even then not a great deal of attention was paid to her, although Carlos Baker's *Ernest Hemingway: A Life Story* gave a brief account in 1969. She did not receive extensive attention until Michael S. Reynolds published his landmark study *Hemingway's First War: The Making of A Farewell to Arms* in 1976. Since then there has been little additional scholarship on her. What is known, however, helps to explain what this adventure might have meant to her and why she may have conducted herself as she did, both professionally and romantically.

She was born on January 5, 1892, in Germantown, Pennsylvania. Her father, Paul Moritz Julius von Kurowsky, had come from

Königsberg, Germany, only two years earlier. Inheriting a blend of Polish, Russian, and German ancestry, he quickly became a naturalized citizen of the United States. Agnes was named for her mother, Agnes Theodosia Holabird, daughter of Samuel B. Holabird, Quartermaster General of the U.S. Army during reconstruction.[96] Her parents had met in Washington, D.C., where her father was teaching languages at the Berlitz school. The family moved a great deal, to Alaska and then Vancouver, but Agnes would come to regard Washington as her home, attending Fairmont Seminary and a training program at the public library before becoming a librarian in the cataloging department in 1910. Along the way, she had been tutored in French, although she would later record: "Then I went to Fairmont Seminary. I had had second-year French the year before, so I went into third year even though I couldn't keep up with the others. So I went out and cried."[97]

Contrary to the impression given by Michael Reynolds, Agnes had difficulty with languages,[98] spoke only moderate French, little German, and, as her diary and letters reveal, was never functional in Italian at any time during her stay in Italy. On July 2 she recorded in her diary that "it is surprising how well we can get along without understanding the language." Nearly two months later, on August 26, she wrote: "I felt like a dummy—with a mob of Italian nurses, & I couldn't say boo to them in their own language." Despite daily exposure, and a few lessons, on October 16 she wrote to Hemingway that "everyone speaks Italian with great speed, so I, of course, am forced into silence." In November, however, she seems to have taken satisfaction in writing to Ernest, "I guess I can spell Italian a little better than the Old Master, even if he can speak & understand it better."[99] In his own letters, Hemingway boasts frequently about his developing proficiency in the language.[100]

In 1914 Agnes decided to leave her post at the library and, at age twenty-two, enrolled in the nursing program at the Bellevue Nurses Training School in New York. Upon graduation, on April 24, 1917, she took a position in the School of Nursing, Long Island College Hospital, in Brooklyn, and she became a registered nurse in the state of New York on October 1, 1917. On her application for service with

*Agnes von Kurowsky in Milan, 1918. Photograph from her scrapbook.*

the American Red Cross on January 13, 1918, she gave her age as twenty six, her height as 5'8", her weight as 133, and she described her general physique as "well developed, well nourished." As her photographs indicate, she was physically attractive in every way, and the people who knew her at the time recall that she had a personality to match. She was intelligent and interested, nurturing and supportive, with a sense of humor and a craving for adventure. At the time she applied for Red Cross duty, she was living in an apartment in New York, and she had never been to Europe.

On June 15, 1918, when she sailed out of New York harbor, she left behind a mysterious Dr. S., whom she refers to as "Daddy," under the impression they had a commitment to each other. However, there is no indication in her diary or letters that they were ever formally engaged. On the passage to Bordeaux, Agnes lost no time in flirting with the young officers on board, particularly with a Lt. Collins, a Belgian officer returning from leave. He occupied her thoughts for several days, through the arrival in Bordeaux on June 24 and the trip to Paris that night. On June 27 she arrived in Milan, staying at the Hotel Manin because the Red Cross hospital was not yet open.

The nurses in the hospital came almost exclusively from Bellevue, including Sara Shaw, the director of Red Cross nurses in Italy, and Katherine C. DeLong, who had been the superintendent at the

*Agnes von Kurowsky flirting on her voyage to Europe, 1918. Photograph from her scrapbook.*

New York hospital. Agnes had graduated with two other nurses who were in Milan, Ruth Brooks and Loretta Cavanaugh. Brooks was notorious as a flirt, a reputation Agnes sought to avoid; Cavanaugh became known by Hemingway and Agnes as "Sis Cavie."[101] Elsie Mac-Donald, a Scot who had trained in England, was in charge of the operating room and helped prepare Hemingway for his surgery. Known as "Mac," she apparently struggled to discipline Hemingway during his stay in the hospital but later wrote him affectionate and friendly letters for more than two decades after the Milan experience. Among other nurses involved in the story of Agnes and Hemingway are Ruth Fisher, Caroline Sparrow, Elsie Jessup, and Mabel Fletcher. Agnes was not isolated in a foreign country when she served in Milan; most of the women she was with not only were American but had known one another at Bellevue before their service in Italy.[102]

Upon her arrival in Milan, she was still thinking of Collins, but three days later, during a brief holiday, she met Captain Enrico Serena at a ceremony at Lago Maggiore. The official *Red Cross Bulletin* carried a story about the event, indicating that the purpose of the meeting was to give the Italians an opportunity to thank the American Red Cross for its assistance: "The King's Prefect, Signore Canzio Garibaldi, Captain Serena, Major Hereford and Captain Bywater spoke. The entire district was *en fête* for the occasion."[103] Captain Serena sustained her romantic attentions until he was forced by family obligations to leave Milan some two months later. On his departure she immediately began dating "Kid" Hemingway, just recovering from surgery on his right leg.

Her romance with Hemingway quickly progressed: on August 25, the day before Serena departed, she recorded in her diary that Ernest was in love with her. Less than a week later, on August 31, they went out to dinner together, and on September 11 she gave him a ring, apparently to solidify their relationship. Only a month later, however, Agnes was transferred to Florence to the American Hospital for Italian Wounded to assist with a Mr. Hough, who was suffering from influenza, and the separation created a series of problems. Although she returned from Florence on November 11, after only ten

*Ernest Hemingway in the new uniform he had made in Milan. On his finger is the ring Agnes gave to him on September 11, 1918. Photograph courtesy of the Ernest Hemingway Foundation.*

days she was moved to an army hospital at Treviso. From this time onward, despite frequent comments regarding marriage in her letters, Agnes saw Ernest only once, on December 9, when he came to see her for a single day. After Hemingway sailed for New York on January 4, Agnes was reassigned to a hospital at Torre di Mosta, and sometime after January 10 she began a new romance with a young Italian artillery lieutenant, and this development led to the termination of her relationship with Hemingway in the "Dear John" letter of March 7, 1919.

### THE DIARY OF AGNES VON KUROWSKY

It is fortunate that any diaries were kept at all in Italy in 1918, for Red Cross regulations discouraged them:

> All Workers must thoroughly familiarize themselves with the censorship regulations of the American Expeditionary Forces. It principally prohibits mention in letters, post cards, diaries and all other written matter, the name of any place or locality in connection with any military organization.[104]

The rules regarding letters were similarly restrictive: "All communications to persons connected with the American Expeditionary Force must be endorsed 'official' by the person designated in each department or bureau, and placed in the outgoing mailbasket unsealed."[105] Photographs were also forbidden anywhere near the war zone. Despite all this, both Agnes and Henry Villard kept intimate diaries, Agnes wrote letters to Hemingway several times each week and mailed them outside regulation channels, and scores of photographs, including several from the front, survived in the scrapbooks of both Agnes and Henry. American Red Cross nurses were also forbidden to carry on serious romances, even to be alone with a gentleman caller. As a result, Agnes made every effort to disguise her growing relationship with Hemingway out of fear of being sent home; she even sent postcards suggesting a mere friendship between them.

Such missives were obviously for public consumption. There are no such disguises in the diary.[106]

The diary begins on June 12, 1918, with Agnes, in New York, concerned about the graduation of her *amant*, a young doctor she refers to as "Daddy." It ends October 20 in Florence, with Agnes separated from Hemingway, and exploring a new and enchanting city. Between these two points there is a world of life for her: it is clear that she is just discovering herself, just awakening to the possibilities of romance and adventure, almost giddy at times with the thought that gentlemen find her attractive. A great number of them do, and she, in turn, is ever alert for indications of interest on the part of the young men she meets on her Italian journey.

These ideas dominate her reflections during the months of the diary, but they are not the only things that concern her. She is clearly a dedicated nurse, eager to get to work, ambitious to do a good job. Many of the comments in the diary relate to idealism about her profession, and she would eventually devote more than a decade of her life to Red Cross hospitals in Italy, Romania, and Haiti. Often her accounts are moving despite their brevity, as when she records the death of Lt. Colter, who expires under her care and for whom she weeps without shame. Another theme is the adventure of traveling, encountering new languages, customs, cuisine, shops, and romantic settings. Agnes appears, very early in the diary, to have gotten more than she bargained for.

All these matters, including the romance, relate to what is perhaps the most pervasive underlying theme of the diary, her continuing growth and change, how she relates to the world, what other people make of her, what her possibilities might be, issues remarkable only because she was already twenty-six when she arrived in Italy. It is, perhaps, the thrill of establishing an identity for herself that rests behind the endless parade of names of young men who have flirted openly, or lingered in a glance, or invited her to dine, from Dr. S. in New York and the Belgian officers on her passage to Europe, to the dashing, one-eyed Captain Serena who soon enters her diary, only two weeks after she left New York, as an ardent and sometimes alarming suitor. On July 22 she wrote, "this tempestuous Italian mode of wooing is certainly terrifying. He tells me how much he loves me, & when I say but I don't love you, it squelches him but a moment & then he begins again." A week later she recorded: "Two letters tonight—1 from Daddy & 1 from my Belgian. I'm getting to feel rather confused. Here I've been practically 3 years without the least bit of sentiment or romance, & very little attention & all at once within the last few months, I have had 3 ser. [serious] affairs, and it isn't my fault either." A few days later she reflects, "this has been a fascinating month in some respects. I have gone pretty far in the emotional pathway."

When he left Milan, Serena was immediately replaced by the handsome and charming "Kid" who came to dominate her romantic interests, a young man seriously wounded on the Piave and whose name she records as "Hemingway." The diary ends in the middle of the romance, when she is transferred to Florence, and her letters become her vehicle for recording her experiences.

All his life Hemingway would write about his experiences in Italy, and always with a sense of loss and remorse for the woman who rejected him. Understanding her depth of commitment to the romance, her romantic "development" at the time, her motivation, expectations, and disappointments are central to a grasp of what happened to Hemingway and what it meant. It was a rude beginning to his troubled romantic life, but Agnes seems to have been inspired more by a spirit of adventure and discovery than by any desire to use or hurt anyone. If early on in the diary she is thrilled at having "broken out" into the world of courtship, by the time the diary ends it is apparent that Hemingway is at the center of her attention. She is concerned that he is sometimes jealous or sharp with her, and she often indicates an awareness of his age, but she seems firmly committed to him.

## THE LETTERS OF AGNES VON KUROWSKY

Agnes ended the relationship in her "Dear John" letter of March 7, 1919, one of fifty-two letters she wrote to Ernest. They begin on

September 25, 1918, when Agnes writes from Milan to a vacationing Hemingway in Stresa, and they end on March 7 with the letter of rejection, although there is one final epistle on December 22, 1922, which apparently is an answer to a letter from Hemingway, then married and living in Paris. There is no indication that Hemingway ever responded to that letter, nor did they ever see one another again.

What is remarkable about the letters is that they are so different in tone from the diary. Where the diary is emotionally restricted, the letters are effusive; where it is confused and uncertain, the letters frequently hint at marriage and a life together, with Agnes often signing her letters "Mrs. Kid" or "Mrs. Hemingstein." Part of the reason for this change is that in large measure the letters postdate the diary, although there is an overlap of nine letters from September 25 to October 20. But that is not the entire answer. The diary entries show her weighing romantic options and exploring the new identity she is developing for herself. The letters suggest that Agnes knew what Ernest wanted to hear, and they are filled with expressions of affection. They also contain references to the attentions of other men, problems in terminating previous romances, and speculations about what relationships might be open to her if she were free. Agnes is never subtle about revealing her interest in the possibility of other alliances. Young Hemingway, involved in his first serious courtship, was apparently swept into ever deeper layers of commitment. There is no indication in any of the Italian materials that his love for her ever wavered.

The major themes that invest Agnes's letters are the same as those of the diary: nursing and the situation in her wartime hospitals; exploring Italy (her trips to Florence and Venice and other locations are described at length); her relationship with Hemingway, with protestations of affection and with hints of the problems that would eventually doom their romance. The chronology of events is instructive. Only two weeks after his operation on August 10, Hemingway professed love for Agnes. She says little about him in her diary until Enrico Serena leaves Italy on August 26, at which point her interest in Hemingway appears to develop quickly, moving to their dinner together on August 31 and her gift to him of a ring on September 11. By

September 26, when she wrote her second letter to him, they were involved to such an extent that she says, "if I hadn't been so busy today, I should certainly have cried from loneliness." On October 8 she wrote to him even though they were both in the same building, suggesting a lover's desire for constant communication. The letters then jump to October 15, when Agnes left Milan for Florence, after which she wrote over twenty times in the next three weeks.

These epistles contain not only an account of her adventures but assurances of her affections with an almost adolescent playfulness, as when she says Hemingway is "The Light of My Existence." Agnes, it should be remembered, was twenty-six to Hemingway's nineteen. There are also suggestions of potential problems. The epithets Agnes habitually used for Hemingway are all concerned with age: He is often addressed as "Kid," "Bambino," "my boy," or "Maestro Antico," the inversion of the same concept. As her "Dear John" letter indicates, the seven-year difference in their ages was one of the things that led her to reject him.

She is also aware that he is short-tempered, sometimes sarcastic, and generally outspoken, qualities frequently mentioned. There are also indications, from the beginning, of instability in their relationship: "Don't be afraid I'll get tired of you," she says on October 17. Throughout the letters she speaks of rejecting Dr. S. in New York, although she never gets around to writing a clear dismissal. She did say to Hemingway, only a week after she left Milan, "you have no sympathy for him, but you should." These letters continue through November 7, at which point Hemingway and Agnes are united again in Milan and there is a fortnight hiatus in their correspondence.

The letters resume on November 22, when she was sent to Treviso to work in Field Hospital 331, and she remained there through the end of the year. The two weeks together seem to have deepened the romance, for the letters now speak not only of love but of marriage. The Treviso letters are fascinating in this regard, for they continue the earlier concerns and add such sentiments as the one Agnes expressed on December 1, "I sometimes wish we could marry over here." It is clear in both Agnes's letters to Ernest and in his letters home that he came to Treviso to see her on December 9, a brief interlude that again seems to have solidified their commitment. A few days later, on December 13, she tells him: "I wrote to my mother that I was planning to marry a man younger than I—& it wasn't the Doctor—so I expect she'll give me up in despair as a hopeless flirt. I'd hate to think I was fickle." December 9, 1918, was the last time they ever saw one another. Years later Agnes recalled in an interview: "Hemingway came up to see me there . . . and the men laughed their heads off at him. . . . They thought he was the biggest joke. He came in with his cane, you know, and all his medals and those American doughboys, they just roared."[107]

Even as the relationship deepens there are adumbrations of difficulties, however. Agnes finds it necessary to reassure Hemingway that she is not ashamed of him. Dr. S. and Serena come in for frequent mention, along with a host of other men who, under other circumstances, might have been suitors. On December 16 she rather tactlessly sent Ernest a letter to her from Dr. S., one in which the doctor responds, a little late in the day, to the news that she has been seeing Serena. On December 20 she again suggests a dread possibility: "What if our hearts should change? Both, I mean, & we should lose this beautiful world of us." Given subsequent events, her heart may already have been changing. At this point, with Hemingway off on holiday in Sicily, their letters again cease for ten days.

They resume on December 31. Since the mail generally took ten days between Milan and Treviso, this letter was calculated to reach Hemingway in Oak Park. He sailed on January 4 for New York. Now, and for the rest of their correspondence over the next three months, there are increasing indications of the end of the relationship. On December 31 she says that "Capt. Moore was teasing me today about my fondness for Italian officers." If that comment did not raise an eyebrow on the ardent Hemingway, the next remark should have caught his attention: "You are to me a wonderful boy, & when you add on a few years & some dignity & calm, you'll be very much worth while." Young ladies do not marry young gentlemen who are not yet worth while.

In January Agnes made yet another transition when she moved to the hospital at Torre di Mosta to care for Italian children. Loretta

*Agnes von Kurowsky with Domenico Caracciolo, for whom she rejected Ernest Hemingway.*

Cavanaugh, "Cavie," was in charge of the new facility. On the way Agnes returned briefly to Milan, where she saw President Woodrow Wilson, touring a victorious Italy after the war, although in the crowd she was able to see only "his ear & Mrs. W.'s hat."[108] When she arrives in Torre di Mosta on January 10 her letters begin to change. It is here that she meets Domenico Caracciolo, an artillery officer in the Arditi. On January 21 she mentions she has a new admirer, Domenico, but she describes him as being only fourteen. Although she hints about becoming "Mrs. Hemingstein," she is clearly becoming confused, as she openly expresses on February 3: "The little tenente I spoke of before, is giving me a desperate rush— now don't get excited." Hemingway must have noticed that she had not written for two weeks, a matter even more crucial when she adds, "the future is a puzzle to me." When she writes on February 15 she dwells on nursing, an understandable concern for her, but probably not what Hemingway was most longing to hear. Then, on March 1, she suggests that she has changed in his absence: she has learned to smoke and gamble: "I know one thing—I'm not at all the perfect being you think I am." That she signs her letter "Afft" should also have indicated some adjustment of her commitment.

Despite these indications of trouble in their relationship, all the biographical evidence suggests that Hemingway was unprepared for the letter of March 7. From the salutation to the close, it must have been devastating for him to read. It begins, "Ernie, dear boy," and it is filled with reminders of his youth and their age differences. Agnes says to him, "I know that I am still very fond of you, but, it is more as a mother than as a sweetheart"; she follows with the observation that "I am now & always will be too old, & that's the truth, & I can't get away from the fact that you're just a boy—a kid." Two other remarks carry a particular sting. There is both condescension and insult in her comment that "I somehow feel that some day I'll have reason to be proud of you, but, dear boy, I can't wait for that day, & it is wrong to hurry a career." It is easy to understand why Hemingway never showed this letter to anyone and led even his closest friends to believe that it had been destroyed. But the real impact would have come in the final paragraph: "Then—& believe me when I say this is sudden for me, too—I expect to be married soon." Contrary to speculation about the letter, there is no mention of the name of the man she intends to marry nor of her motivation or circumstances or plans for the future, but external evidence makes it clear that the man was Domenico Caracciolo, the heir to an Italian dukedom, and that Agnes expected to marry to royalty and live out her life in Italy. Many decades later she remembered that "I was at Torre di Mosto, I think. . . . That's where I met Caracciolo. He was very gentle, a gentle, nice soul, much more interesting to me than a nineteen-year-old Hemingway. . . . I was very fickle in those days anyhow."[109]

One of the ironies in all of this is that Hemingway eventually married Hadley Richardson, who was even older than Agnes, a fact she did not know when she wrote her letter of December 22, 1922. Her reference to how everything had worked out for the best and that he should "think of what an antique I am at the present writing" would have had special irony. Her sharing of memories of the period after the "Dear John" letter is also interesting, particularly the observation that she came back from Italy a "sadder but a wiser girl" after her own rejection[110] and that she then had another meeting with "the poor Doc," or Daddy, still apparently on the string through three of Agnes's interim relationships. In due course, as she discloses, she rejected him too. These sentiments, and the observations about travel, and what good friends the two of them had been in the old days, seem not to have elicited any response from Hemingway, and this letter, so far as is currently known, marks the end of their correspondence and their relationship. As Agnes reflected years later, "I was surprised to hear from him, but I wrote saying I was pleased to have an old friend back, and how proud I'd be one day to say I once knew him well. I never heard from him again."[111]

What is important about Agnes's diary and letters is that they provide the details of these experiences, not simply dates and places, although even those are of value, but the expressions of intimate feelings and hopes and fears. The diary reveals a great deal about her character, her development into the new, more adventurous person she was becoming. Far from a worldly sophisticate, she was still growing and changing, almost adolescent in her interest in men, still concerned about what her mother might think about her romances. Her letters establish the personality she chose to show to Hemingway, and they suggest that she had all the exuberance and vacillation of the coquette.

The diary and the letters disclose, though indirectly, a good deal about Ernest as well, his forceful and exuberant personality, the ways in which other people responded to him (not always with admiration), his infectious humor and good spirits. He was perceived by the people who saw him in the hospital every day as almost incessantly cheerful, a view that compromises the widespread belief that he had suffered shell shock in the war and spent a lifetime attempting to assuage the depression and neurosis it left behind. Those assumptions can now be said to be without factual basis. That such pathologies exist in the fiction Hemingway wrote about World War I is another matter altogether. Such information fills Agnes's diary and letters, giving them a significance far beyond the events and conversations they record. What makes all of this especially important, of course, is what it suggests about the imagination of a young man who would become recognized as a writer of stunning power and craftsmanship, one who would use his Italian experience to create one of the most remarkable novels in the English language.

## HEMINGWAY'S LETTERS

The fourteen letters from Ernest Hemingway to his family in Oak Park are important in a number of ways. Since only four of them have previously been published, this group of letters is a valuable new source of information about Hemingway's behavior, attitudes, mood, and communication with his family during this crucial period in his life. The correspondence needs to be read with skepticism, however, for it obviously conceals as much as it expresses. There is little here of fear and apprehension, of pain, of resentment. The letters convey only what Hemingway wanted his family to know (he says almost nothing about his romance with Agnes, for example, and never mentions her name), how he wanted them to regard his attitude toward his experience, and the kinds of idealistic views of war and sacrifice and duty that would become suspect in his fiction a decade later. They reveal an innocent and idealistic young man, wounded very shortly after he arrived in Italy, who matured quickly during his six months in the hospital in Milan.

The letters begin on July 21, roughly two weeks after Hemingway was wounded. After initial treatment at a field hospital, he was moved to the new hospital for Red Cross volunteers in Milan. Agnes mentions Hemingway for the first time in her diary on July 20, so they had certainly met by the time this letter was written, although she did not begin regular duty there until July 29. His two letters in July deal briefly with his wounds and pending surgery, and they convey an affection for family not characteristic of Hemingway in later years. He is matter-of-fact about his wounds and seeks the counsel of his physician father. The letters also suggest that he enjoys the role of the man of the world commenting on the cities of Europe (at this point, apart from his hospitalization, he had been only briefly in Paris and Milan), Atlantic crossings (he had crossed once), and a knowledge of foreign languages (he was picking up Italian, which he would never speak fluently).[112] It is clear that, despite his wounds, this was the adventure of his young life, and he was excited about it.

The letter of August 18 is of central concern: for the first time, he tells his parents the details of his wounds, that he had been only six days at the front, that he was "advancing toward the rear" when he was hit, that he was wounded both by shrapnel and machine-gun fire, that he assisted, perhaps carried, another wounded man and then refused assistance himself until the other men had been cared for. It is also significant that he mentions that Jim Gamble was there when he was wounded, for Gamble would have filed the official Red Cross record of the incident. This letter, by far the most important in the series, was written eight days after the operation on Hemingway's right knee and foot. As Agnes records, until the operation he was unsure whether his leg could be saved. He would have been certain of recovery when he wrote this letter.

Given the Mae Marsh incident in New York before he left, it is understandable that he is reticent about describing his new relationship, although on August 29 he wrote home to say he was in love again. He gives few details, other than a disclaimer about the seriousness of the relationship, clearly information for family consumption. The next day he left the hospital on crutches, and the day after that he took Agnes to dinner, although he does not include these events in any of his letters.

The correspondence traces his recovery in September and his pleasure at the medals he is being awarded and at his promotion to first lieutenant. The letters encompass his holiday trip to Stresa with John Miller, where he met not only Count Emanuele Greppi (transformed into Count Greffi in *A Farewell to Arms*) but the Bellia family, who would continue to befriend him throughout the rest of his stay in Italy. Agnes's diary indicates that Hemingway left Milan on September 24 and returned not on October 5, as Peter Griffin suggests,[113] but September 30, apparently cutting short the ten-day leave he had been granted. There would later be rumors about a romance in Stresa between Hemingway and Count Bellia's daughter Bianca. Considering that Hemingway was wearing the ring Agnes had given him and had only recently professed a love he would carry for many months, if not years, such a flirtation seems unlikely, although it is interesting that two weeks after Ernest's return Agnes wrote from Florence to say, "I haven't even discovered any Bellia's to help me pass the time," suggesting at least a hint of jealousy.[114]

Back in Milan, Hemingway wrote on October 18 to defend the value of Red Cross work in Italy and to express his commitment to remaining in Europe for the duration of the war. More clearly than anywhere else, he reiterates that he does not, and cannot, serve in the regular army. His observations on the dangers of Red Cross work, on the simplicity of dying, on how one offers one's body as a sacrifice, and on how a mother should be proud to lose a son in combat all reflect the romantic idealism of youth. There is little here of war fatigue, cynicism, or the "separate peace" motifs that pervade Hemingway's mature fiction, nor is there any sign at any point in the letters of shell shock or psychic trauma.

Indeed, Hemingway's despair in mid-October would have been of a different order, for on October 15 Agnes had been sent to Florence, separating them at a crucial moment in their romance. Hemingway returned briefly to the front on October 24, still limping badly and using a cane, as he would for many months. He was in time to observe the offensive on Mount Grappa but quickly returned to Milan, ill with hepatitis, the subject of his letter of November 1. When he wrote next, on November 11, the war was over, and the subject of his letters changes to "the war to make the world safe for Ernie Hemingway." Now he is concerned with his medals and honors, plans for travel in Italy, and of the future. Absent from the correspondence is his commitment to Agnes, their plans for marriage, his need for a job to support a wife and family. Instead, he speaks of his friends returning home ahead of him because he is still receiving physical therapy in the hospital. His last letter home, on December 11, contains news not only of the date of his passage but that he had been to Treviso to see "the girl." Their relationship was in full flower at that point, as her papers reveal: on December 1 she wrote to him of marriage; on December 9 he made his visit; on December 13 she informed him that she had written her mother that she was to be married to a younger man. Hemingway had every reason to feel that there was a commitment between them, that his plans should include a future with her, and yet he was never to see her again.

## HEMINGWAY AND THE ITALIAN ARMY

In a review of *Men Without Women* in 1927, a staff writer for *Time* stated that "author Hemingway was a football star and a boxer at school. In the War he was severely wounded, serving with the Italian Arditi, of whom he was almost the youngest member."[115] No part of this assertion would seem to be the case. Hemingway was a somewhat awkward athlete all his life and did not make the varsity football team, nor is there any record of his being on a boxing team. But many of the biographers, Samuel Shaw among them, report that Hemingway was "promoted to first lieutenant in the regular Italian army."[116] The idea that Hemingway served for a time in the Italian army has been so widely disseminated that it has become accepted as fact. Charles A. Fenton stated in *The Apprenticeship of Ernest Hemingway* in 1954 that "a few weeks after his convalescent leave ended in the early fall, Hemingway managed to get himself assigned to the Italian infantry. He served with them during October and until the Armistice in November."[117] This notion appears in authoritative places, on the dust jackets of Hemingway's novels and in the comments of some of the finest scholars, among them Malcolm Cowley, Philip Young, and Robert Penn Warren.[118]

Those reports are simply inaccurate, as Bill Horne was to write to Hemingway's older sister some years later. Horne said that Hemingway was not an officer in the Italian army and that "that is one of those myths that grow up about colorful and famous people." He goes on to say that

> when we arrived at Section IV (at Schio, Provinzia Veneto, at the rail-head north of Vicenza and at the mouth of the passes that come down from Mt. Pasubio), we were told that *all of us*

ambulance drivers *rated as honorary second lieutenants in the Italian Army.* How true that was I don't know—but it makes good sense. That would allow us to mess (eat) at the officers' mess when we were "on post" at the line with Italian troops. We always did. It helped give our ambulances priority on the roads, which we had. It got us preferred treatment at the Army gasoline dumps. Certainly we always were welcome at the same restaurants, saloons and other pleasure spots where the *Italian officers went* and the *Italian soldiers did not go.*[119]

The key word is "honorary." Eager to have American involvement in the war effort, the Italians extended every courtesy to the volunteers driving ambulances and serving at canteen posts.

Hemingway was in the Red Cross at all times, never in any army or combative position. Nor would he have been encouraged to transfer to fighting duties had he been physically able. On August 20, 1918, while Hemingway was in the hospital recovering from his operation, the *Red Cross Bulletin* carried a request from President Woodrow Wilson that Red Cross workers stay with their current positions "until specifically called to other and clearly more important duty."[120] Hemingway's letter home of October 18 indicates his acceptance of this idea:

All of us Red X men here were ordered not to register. It would be foolish for us to come home because the Red X is a necessary organization and they would just have to get more men from the states to keep it going. Besides we never came over here until we were all disqualified for military service you know. . . . I was disqualified before I left the states because of my eye. I now have a bum leg and foot and there isn't any army in the world that would take me.

That letter alone should put to rest the widespread myth that Hemingway was in the Italian army.[121]

Further, the chronology of his experience in Italy leaves no time for a transfer to army duties. He served two weeks at Schio as an ambulance driver, then with a canteen unit on the Piave, where he was wounded. After he was released from the hospital in October, he went back to the front, limping and using a cane, for only one day, at which point he contracted hepatitis and returned to the hospital in Milan. He was in the hospital when the armistice was declared on November 3 and never had an opportunity to return to the front lines. Nor would his physical condition have permitted it: as his letter of November 14 indicates, he continued receiving physical therapy after the armistice. His official discharge papers, signed by Robert Perkins in Rome on December 31, 1918, clearly indicate purely Red Cross duty:

> I hereby certify that Lieut. E. M. Hemingway, has completed his term of service with the Italian Commission of the American Red Cross. Lieut. Hemingway has served in the capacity of ambulance driver in a faithful and efficient manner, and is hereby given an honorable discharge from the service of the American Red Cross.[122]

The photographs of him back home in Oak Park indicate that he was using a cane through the first several months of 1919. Indeed, a photograph of him taken in 1920 as he was about to leave for Toronto shows him with a cane. Many years later Agnes von Kurowsky was to comment that "they think because he came home with an Italian cloak that he was in the Italian army, but he never was. He never was."[123]

### HEMINGWAY'S MEDALS

Edwin Wells, in his account of Hemingway's speech to Oak Park High School in March of 1919, suggests that Hemingway was "awarded the highest decoration given by the Italian Government" and that the medal was given to him "personally by the King of Italy."[124] Leicester Hemingway, in his biography of his brother, reports that Ernest won a "silver medal and a bronze one. . . . The silver one had been presented to him by the Italian King." Later in his book Leicester contradicts himself and says that the "Silver Medal of

Summum Magisterium
aestimat Te

# Ernest Hemingway

pro meritis dignum qui adscribaris in Equitum Militiam Militaris Capitularis Ordinis Gladii Aurei Cypri Anno Domini Willesimo Centesimo Nonagesimo Quinto, ex disciplina Sancti Basilii praeceptis, constituti a Principe Guidone de Lusiniana Gente pro-gnato, Burgundionibus Regibus edito, Cypriorum Rege, Chiennae et Pictonum Agrorum et aliarum Francorum terrarum Domino, contra nominis Christiani hostes, Equitum Gladii vel Silentii ope et auxilio Fidei tuendae causa
et his temporibus novam in lucem relati atque pristinam in dignitatem restituti ,iisdem animo ac studio ex quibus tunc institutus est, miserorum inopiae ad opitulandum et doctrinas disciplinasque ad augendas quae hominum misericordiae et caritati adiumento sint, Tibi confert dignitatem quae inscribitur

## Cavaliere di Gran Croce al Merito

et tuis pro meritis laudabilis concedit ut hunc Titulum geras, ex Legibus Praescriptis et eiusdem honoris Insignibus aptis exor-nerie moribus huius Ordinis Liberi ac Soluti ex cuius Equitibus es iam nunc.
Proinde hoc Breve habeas Summi Magisterii pro iure Sigillo obsignatum et Subscriptionibus omnium Ordinis Dignitatum, quae Tibi Salutem dicunt.

*Some of Hemingway's decorations, awarded for his service at Fossalta di Piave.*

*Hemingway with his decoration from the King of Italy.*

*Hemingway, center, home in Oak Park, February 16, 1919. The guests at the party were from the Italian consulate. Dr. and Mrs. Hemingway are back row, center. Photograph courtesy of the Ernest Hemingway Foundation.*

Military Valor" was presented to Ernest in Chicago by General Diaz, who commanded the Italian forces to victory.[125] In a more recent biography, Jeffrey Meyers echoes Leicester's account, saying that "Hemingway was formally presented with the Italian Medaglia d'Argento al Valore by General Armando Diaz at a banquet in Chicago."[126] Hemingway did finally get his medal in the mail in Oak Park, but neither the King nor General Diaz was in attendance.[127]

Hemingway's comments in his letters home are of interest in this matter. On September 11 he wrote that he would soon receive the "silver medaglia valore" and perhaps a "war cross," and both predictions came true. (The medals themselves, along with the citations that came with them, are in the John F. Kennedy Library.) By November 11 Hemingway had received ribbons for his medals but not the medals themselves, which would not come for some years. Hemingway mentioned the matter again in a letter three days later: "When my Doctor heard about my latest medal, the Croix D'guerre, he kissed me tonsolitis and all."

The official record supports Hemingway's comments. One document dated November 10, 1918, indicates that Hemingway was awarded "la Croce al Merito di Guerra," the War Cross of Merit. It is accompanied by a formal proclamation dated December 18, 1918, giving the award to "Hemingnay M. Ernest" (sic). The silver medal would take longer. One document indicates that the King of Italy issued a decree on January 4, 1920, awarding the "silver medal for military valor" to Hemingway. It carries an explanation:

> Officer of the American Red Cross, charged with taking articles of comfort to Italian troops engaged in combat, he gave proof of courage and self-abnegation. Seriously wounded by numerous enemy shell splinters, with an admirable spirit of brotherhood, before letting himself be cared for he gave generous assistance to Italian soldiers more seriously wounded than he by the same explosion, and did not permit himself to be carried elsewhere until the latter had been removed."

This document also contains the notation "Fossalta (Piave), July 8, 1918." Despite the date of the decree, the document was not issued until March 15, 1921, and not mailed to Hemingway until April 4, 1922.[128]

These two medals were not at all unusual for Red Cross volunteers on the Italian front. Hemingway's suggestion that he would get the war cross "because of general foolish conduct in the trenches" is somewhat misleading. As Robert Lewis has established, the silver medal was given to virtually all the wounded men; the cross of war "was awarded to all who were engaged in action in the war (like U.S. Army campaign ribbons)."[129] Indeed, the *Red Cross Bulletin* carried a story on July 20, 1918, that everyone in Section 3 of the ambulance corps had received the cross of war for service in the Austrian offensive in June.[130]

On August 5, 1918, the *Red Cross Bulletin* reported that on July 28 the King of Italy had decorated a number of Americans in Section 2 of the ambulance corps, among them J. P. Gillespie, A. R. Collinson, F. J. Agate, R. C. Cory, and Hemingway's friend John W. Miller. All of them received the Silver Medal of Valor.[131] Hemingway would have known that Lt. McKey had been awarded the silver medal posthumously, since the *Red Cross Bulletin* reported it on August 20 while Ernest was still in the hospital.[132] In his *Report of the Department of Military Affairs*, Guy Lowell listed fifty Red Cross volunteers who had been decorated, several of whom were in the hospital in Milan at the same time Hemingway was there, among them M. D. Detweiler, Edward E. Allen, and John Miller (with whom Hemingway went on holiday to Stresa).[133]

CONCLUSION

When Hemingway returned home to Oak Park the stories he told about the war were often enlarged and romanticized, inflated the way Krebs fabricates his adventures in "Soldier's Home." He told his hometown newspaper, the *Oak Parker*, that he had been hit by thirty-two 45–caliber slugs and that twenty-eight of them had been removed without aid of anesthesia. In response to a questionnaire sent to returning veterans, he indicated that he had been a first lieutenant in the Italian Army, serving with the 69oth Infantry Brigatta Anacona

*Ernest Hemingway in Oak Park, 1919, wearing an Italian officer's cape. He is still using a cane.*

and fighting in the Piave Offensive, on Monte Grappa, and at Vittorio Veneto. In a lecture in Oak Park he explained that the Red Cross workers had thrown away their revolvers to diminish the temptation of suicide. Michael Reynolds observes that "Red Cross men, delivering chocolate, were not issued revolvers, but it gave an authentic note to the story."[134] The conclusion is inescapable that not only is Hemingway's fiction an unreliable guide to the truth but also that his pronouncements in public forums, letters, and personal comments are suspect.

This is true about his military exploits as well as his personal life. One example is Ernest's trip from Milan to visit Jim Gamble in Sicily in December of 1918. His official travel papers show that he was authorized to leave Milan on December 15; they were good for sixteen days. Jim Gamble had written to him on December 11 with an invitation, explaining that he had rented the home of an English artist for a few months. Gamble had been in charge of the canteen service when Hemingway was wounded and had befriended the younger man, seeing him often in the hospital. Hemingway accepted, went to Taormina on holiday, and returned to Milan in time to prepare for the voyage home. Every indication is that it was a simple trip, a visit between friends, a quiet vacation in southern Italy.

But that is apparently not the story he told when he returned to Milan. His friend Chink Dorman-Smith, later known as Edward Eric Dorman-O'Gowan, recalled that Hemingway had said that he had been wounded leading the Arditi in an assault on Monte Grappa and that when he went to Sicily he had seen nothing "'except from a bedroom window because his hostess in the first small hotel he stopped in had hidden his clothes and kept him to herself for a week. The food she brought him was excellent and she was affectionate; Hem had no complaints except that he saw very little of the country'" and never saw Jim Gamble.[135] But Gamble's letters to Hemingway clearly show that he arrived on schedule and that they enjoyed the holiday together. Gamble observed in a letter on April 16, 1919, that "after you left I saw practically nothing of the English speaking population."[136]

Hemingway had invented the romance with Mae Marsh in New York, the licentious episode in Sicily with an innkeeper, and, in all probability, a sexual affair with Agnes. The issue of whether Ernest and Agnes ever consummated their relationship is of significance beyond prurient gossip, for it relates to the creative process of his work. That Hemingway's fiction of World War I shows fully developed romances has led a number of biographers to assume the literal transcription of life into art. Hemingway's comments in the years that followed also suggest a mature sexual relationship. Chink Dorman-Smith wrote to Carlos Baker in 1961 to say that Hemingway had so indicated to him: "She was a gay, charming person of whom Hem said that it takes a trained nurse to make love to a man with one leg in a splint."[137] Apparently Bill Horne received some letters from Hemingway with similar suggestions, as Peter Griffin asserts: "Those letters clearly show that Ernest was profoundly in love with Kurowsky, that they were sleeping together, and that Hemingway was devastated when she rejected him and after that rejection he began writing like Hemingway for the first time."[138] A more careful formulation would be that Hemingway's letters *said* they were sleeping together, a rather different matter. Griffin also assumes that Hemingway had been sexually active as a teenager with the Indian girls at Lake Walloon and, taking *The Torrents of Spring* as fact, that he had experienced a particularly ribald evening in Paris.[139]

In *Along With Youth* Griffin interprets Agnes's letters as clear indication of an "affair" between them.[140] He particularly uses the letter of October 16, in which Agnes says "when I saw that couple on the train yesterday I kept wishing I had you alongside of me, so I could put my head on that nice place—you know—the hollow place for my face—& go to sleep with your arm around me."[141] There is more than a little conjecture in using that comment as evidence of sexual consummation. Kenneth Lynn takes the matter even further, and he thinks he knows the frequency of their ardor and what positions the lovers most enjoyed in their trysts:

> For weeks their lovemaking routine was largely unvaried. As night fell, he would lie on his back in bed or recline in a chair on the balcony outside his room with his foot propped up on another chair. When he and Agnes embraced, the immobility of his leg presumably required that he stay beneath her. In years to come, there would be indications that he liked this posture—for reasons that would only gradually become clear.[142]

What is evident immediately is that Lynn has no conclusive evidence for his assertions; rather, he speculates from rumor and from the fiction, formulates a psychological thesis, and comes to regard his assumptions as fact. Agnes's diary, Villard's memoir, the recollections of his friends, and the social circumstances of the time suggest a rather different interpretation: that Ernest and Agnes were sexual innocents and their romance did not advance beyond the petting stage. Hemingway's high school friend Lewis Clarahan recalled that Ernest "did no dating in high school at all. He just didn't. He had four sisters, so he was used to girls, but he just didn't care to date."[143] Young men who do not date have few sexual conquests.

Agnes's diary gives strong indications that she was not a sexual adventuress. On September 19, a week after she had given Hemingway her ring, she recorded: "I was so disgusted last night. When I got on duty I found Fisher having a high old time with Lewis in a chaise longue on the balcony. . . . Hem. was furious—, & it was so common. I couldn't get over them." This is hardly the response of a woman in the midst of an affair. Indeed, although her diary betrays a profound interest in men and dating and romantic dreams, there is nothing to indicate any adult sexual experience.

Rather, the entry for June 12, covering the farewell dinner with Daddy in New York, suggests only that he may have been a bit fresh, for she records a "bad impression" of him. There is certainly no indication that she had a sexual involvement with her doctor. The flirtation on ship with Adjutant Collins has the clear tone of adolescent infatuation: "I am too disappointed for words. No more M. Collins, & must leave these girls I have grown to like so much," she writes on June 25. In Milan Agnes is fascinated by the activities of Nurse Brooks but comments, "of course she has much more romance to tell than I have, as she always was inclined to draw romance to her, and I have only lately broken out." The closest thing to an affair recorded in the diary is the relationship with Enrico Serena, but her entries do not indicate active sexuality: on July 13 she writes "it's so funny, he tries to kiss my hand, & I get furious & go into my patient's room, & then my patient kisses my hand. It must be the air of Italy." Hand kissing is not the immediate precursor of coitus. She seems conscious of propriety at all times: "Today, in the little dressing room where I sit when Mr. Rochfort sleeps—Capitano [Serena] did not frighten me, but he might have if I had been far away from assistance," she says on July 23. Even this wooing seems too much for her, and on August 26, when Serena leaves Milan, she records that "the old affair is over, thanks be!"

The entries about other men suggest a similar prudery. On August 12 she writes that "Mr. Seeley—our oldest patient (not in yrs.) is inclined to be spoony, I fear. He was looking for shooting stars this evening—so I had to quietly but firmly leave. Enough said!" She describes the flirtations of Mr. Michels on August 21 in a manner that reflects schoolgirl fascination rather than the condescension of the experienced lover. That she would bother to document a goodbye kiss with him on August 30 with the observation that she was not ashamed indicates a similar naïveté.

There is absolutely nothing in her diary about the romance with Hemingway that supports an interpretation of sexual activity, and the diary covers the entire period of Ernest's recovery from surgery, the very period of Lynn's inventive speculations. The diary takes the romance from Hemingway's having a "case" on her on August 25 through their dinner together and the gift of the ring. The most suggestive remark concerns the hairpin that MacDonald discovered under Hemingway's pillow on September 7, but the very fact that she is aghast at the revelation suggests there was little to hide. Her letters also convey a tone of innocence, although when she says on October 21, "I think every day how nice it would be to feel your arms around me again," there is reason to suspect ardent embracing. In the last years of her life Agnes said that "I think both Hemingway and I were very innocent at that time, very innocent, both of us. He was too in those days. We were all pretty innocent."[144] Henry Villard's embarrassment at the attentions of the young ladies in France certainly supports the view of a more puritanical age, as does the observation of Agnes's husband, William Stanfield, Jr., who said that "Agnes had no serious sex intentions with either Hemingway or the Italian officer. I don't think she was very serious with any man until she was around thirty, thirty-two. And that happened in New York, long after this European thing was all over."[145]

As was the case with his sexual adventures, Hemingway enlarged on his military adventures, his wounds, the battles he had witnessed, the trauma he had observed. Why he did so is known only to him, but enlargement was unnecessary, for the true story is in many respects more moving and more dramatic. He had volunteered for hazardous duty, been severely wounded, and had spent months recovering in a Milan hospital. There, for the first time, he had fallen in love, had contemplated marriage to Agnes, and had returned home to find a job. Instead of a wedding in the summer of 1919, he had received a letter of rejection in March, and it had hurt him severely, so deeply that he wrote about it all his life. As he confessed to his friend Bill Horne after receiving the letter: "Oh, Bill, I can't kid about it, and I can't be bitter because I'm just smashed by it." Perhaps to save face, he gave a sexual edge to the relationship, saying that "you make love to a girl and then you go away. She needs somebody to make love to her. If the right person turns up, you're out of luck."[146] Years later, after he had received Agnes's letter in 1922, Ernest told Lincoln Steffens in Paris that "if the nurse from Italy were to come back into his life he would give up everything for her."[147]

In *Green Hills of Africa*, published in 1935, Hemingway commented,

> what a great advantage an experience of war was to a writer. It was one of the major subjects and certainly one of the hardest to write truly of and those writers who had not seen it were always very jealous and tried to make it seem unimportant, or abnormal, or a disease as a subject, while, really, it was just something quite irreplaceable that they had missed.[148]

But Hemingway had little personal exposure to the front, was not a combatant, and spent most of his time in Italy in the hospital. So, too, with his fiction. Most of the activity in *A Farewell to Arms* is away from the front, and the war gradually gives way to the romance as the novel progresses. In *Across the River and Into the Trees* Colonel Cantwell visits Italy after World War II, thinks back on the first war, and visits the place where he was wounded. Most of the stories focus on the hospital in Milan, disillusioned soldiers returning to the front, the psychological effects of having been wounded, and the loss of a woman. Although he invented much and read newspapers and books for some of his material, Hemingway concentrated on those aspects of war he knew firsthand.

Early in his career he wrote a poem entitled "Killed Piave—July 8—1918" using the location and date of his own wounding. At the time of his death in 1961 he was working on A *Moveable Feast*, and in that memoir he recalls how Gertrude Stein had commented to him about the fate of the Lost Generation:

> But that night walking home I thought about the boy in the garage and if he had ever been hauled in one of those vehicles when they were converted to ambulances. I remembered how they used to burn out their brakes going down the mountain roads with a full load of wounded and braking in low and finally using the reverse, and how the last ones were driven over the mountainside empty, so they could be replaced by big Fiats with a good H-shift and metal to metal brakes.[149]

There is no doubt that from the beginning of his career to the last, his Italian journey was a source of material for him, and he used nearly every aspect of it.

That is particularly true of his romance with Agnes, her rejection of him, and his sense of pain and loss. These ideas show up very early in his work, even in a humorous article for the *Toronto Star* in 1920, in which he described the old pencil stubs and trolley tickets in a reporter's pocket. He also put into that pocket "a collection of letters from his best girl who hasn't yet realized that she is going to marry somebody else."[150] His fictional use of the ideas came a few years later in "A Very Short Story," which portrays a soldier in a hospital in Padua who is cared for by a nurse named Luz. She is on night duty, and they fall in love and want to get married. When he returns to the front,

> Luz wrote him many letters that he never got until after the armistice. Fifteen came in a bunch to the front and he sorted them by the dates and read them all straight through. They were all about the hospital, and how much she loved him and how it

was impossible to get along without him and how terrible it was missing him at night.[151]

When the war ends he returns home to get a job so they can be married. Instead, she falls in love with an Arditi major and sends the protagonist a letter of rejection, saying

> that theirs had been only a boy and girl affair. She was sorry, and she knew he would probably not be able to understand, but might some day forgive her, and be grateful to her, and she expected, absolutely unexpectedly, to be married in the spring [p. 108].

There is no doubt about the biographical basis for the story: the name of the nurse when it was first published as Chapter 10 of *In Our Time* was "Ag." In a letter to Maxwell Perkins on July 12, 1938, Hemingway explained why he made the alteration: "It should stay as Luz in the book. Ag is libelous. Short for Agnes."[152] Years later, in "The Snows of Kilimanjaro," his protagonist recalls how

> he had written her, the first one, the one who left him, a letter telling her how he had never been able to kill it. . . . How when he thought he saw her outside the Regence one time it made him go all faint and sick inside, and that he would follow a woman who looked like her in some way, along the Boulevard, afraid to see it was not she, afraid to lose the feeling it gave him [p. 48].

The year of the letter was 1922.

Another story in which he used material from Italy is "A Way You'll Never Be," one of his finest. The story recounts how Nick Adams is returning to the front after recovering from being wounded at Fossalta while serving on the lower Piave. Nick is in the canteen service, providing cigarettes and postcards and chocolate for the soldiers. He is wearing a new uniform made for him by a tailor named Spagnolini (who made Hemingway's uniform), and he has the ribbons and papers for medals but not the medals themselves. What Hemingway changed in this story from his own experience is that Nick suffers from shell shock and is on the verge of insanity (pp. 312–13). His mind begins "working" beyond his control, and the conflict is psychological, revealing the emotional effects of the violence of war.

A related story is "Now I Lay Me" (the title derives, ironically, from a bedtime prayer—the issue of the story is insomnia). As Hemingway had been, Nick is in Schio, but he is there after he has been wounded. His mind runs out of control, and in the night he finds solace in his sleeplessness by thinking about fishing the trout streams of his youth. He has been a journalist and plans to return to a paper after the war. The conflict he discusses with his friend John is whether he should get married. The conclusion of this retrospective story reveals that he did not:

> He came to the hospital in Milan to see me several months after and was very disappointed that I had not yet married, and I know he would feel very badly if he knew that, so far, I have never married. He was going back to America and he was very certain about marriage and knew it would fix up everything [p. 282].

A similar theme is at the center of "In Another Country," in which an unnamed protagonist tells about his physical therapy in a hospital in Milan. The story is filled with the details of the city, the walk from his hospital to the old Italian one for treatments, passing by the Café Cova next to the Scala, concern for his medals and ribbons, and his problems with Italian grammar. Again the issue is marriage, and it comes up in his conversation with an Italian major:

> "What will you do when the war is over if it is over?" he asked me. "Speak grammatically!"
> "I will go to the States."
> "Are you married?"
> "No, but I hope to be."
> "The more of a fool you are," he said. He seemed very angry.
> "A man must not marry" [p. 209].

As the conversation continues the major discloses that his wife has just died, and he weeps openly. Characteristically, the war and its effects are linked to romance and a sense of loss, the dominant themes of Hemingway's Italian fiction.

The most important work to derive from Hemingway's experience in Italy is *A Farewell to Arms.* Here are the familiar biographical elements of an ambulance driver who is wounded and taken to a hospital in Milan, falls in love with the nurse, returns to the front, and eventually loses her when she dies in childbirth in Switzerland.[153] What is fascinating about this novel, however, is not the extent to which it follows Hemingway's experience but how it differs in important respects.

Hemingway arrived in Italy in 1918, served only two weeks as an ambulance driver during a period of relative inactivity in the war, was wounded after only six days of serving refreshments to the Italian soldiers, and went on to an innocent affair with Agnes. All these elements are transformed in the novel. For one thing, Frederic Henry is a good deal older than Hemingway was at the time, and he is in Italy from 1915 onward. Consequently, he is in the Italian Army, since the American Red Cross did not arrive until December of 1917. Moving the time back allowed Hemingway to portray the disastrous retreat from Caporetto in the autumn of 1917, a disorganized flight from the front that resulted in Italian soldiers' shooting their own men as they attempted to cross the bridges. That fact not only provided a justification for Frederic's desertion but allowed the novel to end at a moment of complete despair: Frederic has lost Catherine at a time when the war is going badly for Italy. The progression is thus toward total defeat. Hemingway, on the other hand, left Italy after the victorious conclusion of the war with the expectation of a life with Agnes.[154] A coordinate pattern traces Frederic from intense involvement in the army and fellowship with the other officers to a nearly exclusive relationship with Catherine, to her death, and to his walk home alone in the rain. The inexorable movement toward loss and isolation invests the novel with much of its emotional power.

Of biographical interest is the fact that Hemingway chose to have his protagonist tell the novel himself in retrospect. The internal evidence, plus the early drafts of the manuscript, suggest that Hemingway, writing in 1928 and thinking about the events of World War I, placed Frederic Henry the same distance from the experience. Hemingway could thus draw not only on the Milan events and his memory of losing Agnes but on more recent events as well, including the suicide of his father; his divorce from Hadley and the simultaneous loss of a son, Bumby; and the near death of Pauline and their son Patrick in childbirth. It was rich emotional material, and it invests this novel with unique power.[155] The implications of the retrospective narration for Frederic are that he has been a decade in mourning for Catherine, that he has not replaced her in his life, and that he is still coming to terms with the loss he has suffered. The novel thus dwells not so much on physical realism as on Frederic's psychological states. The narrative assumptions require that Catherine appear only in the memory of Frederic, and it is clear that he has idealized her. At the same time he is unsparing about his own weakness, about how he attempted to use her sexually when he first met her, about how strong and giving she was, about how badly he acted. The language he uses is restrained and controlled, suggesting that the emotion generated in telling the story is almost too much for him to bear. A *Farewell to Arms* is related, in effect, by a man who feels he has nothing left in the world, nothing but the memories of the most painful and meaningful episode of his life.[156]

Hemingway's only recapturing of the past was to be in his art. It was no good returning to the old places, he wrote after he had taken Hadley to Italy in 1922: "It is like going into the empty gloom of a theater where the charwomen are scrubbing. I know because I have just been back to my own front."[157] They went up to the area of the "Schio Country Club," where Hemingway had been an ambulance driver, motored across to Mestre, where he had been put on a train to Milan after being wounded, and finally reached Fossalta, where he had been wounded. But it was no good, everything had been changed:

> I climbed the grassy slope and above the sunken road where the
> dugouts had been to look at the Piave and looked down an even

slope to the blue river. . . . Across the river were two new houses where the two rubble heaps had been just inside the Austrian lines.

The rubble of the village had had a dignity for him, he remembered, "as though it had died for something. It had died for something and something better was to come. It was all part of the great sacrifice. Now there is just the new, ugly futility of it all." There was no going back, he discovered, but there would ultimately be no need to do so, for he would capture much of it in his fiction, restoring the dignity it had lost through the integrity of his craft and the depth of his feelings, and preserving the memory of Schio and Fossalta and Milan and Agnes von Kurowsky for all time.

# NOTES

· · ·

## CHAPTER ONE

1. This essay, somewhat revised, derives from "Red Cross Driver in Italy: A Memoir of the First World War," which Henry Villard wrote for private distribution. See, especially, pp. 107–41.

2. The interview was originally published in the *Oak Parker*. Quoted from Carlos Baker, *Ernest Hemingway: A Life Story* (New York: Scribners, 1969), p. 57.

3. Henry Villard was born on March 30, 1900.

4. Ernest Hemingway, *A Farewell to Arms* (New York: Scribners, 1957), p. 111.

5. Ernest Hemingway, "Al Receives Another Letter," *Ciao* (June 1918), p. 2.

6. See Charlotte M. Heilman, letter to Mr. Durfee, November 11, 1952. This letter is in the Hemingway Collection of the John F. Kennedy Library in Boston.

7. "Pure water, fresh wine
   beautiful figs, hard prick."
"Fica" has ribald suggestions of the female vagina, hence the pun.

8. Haiti was under U.S. military occupation, which is why an American was a financial advisor.

9. Commander K. C. Melhorn, Medical Corps, United States Navy.

10. The passport picture and the photographs appear in this volume.

## CHAPTER TWO

1. Henry Villard found the following Bellevue poem among Agnes's papers. He comments that "no doubt it expressed her sentiments toward what she made her life's work and perhaps helped form her character as well."

### Bellevue Speaks

I stand by the side of a river
That's salt with the tang of the sea,
There's never a port of any sort
But sends her sons to me.
To me, from the ships on the river
They come to be eased of their pain,
But when they at length regain their strength
They're off to the ships again.
I stand by the side of a current
That's deeper far than the sea,
And storm-beaten craft of every draught
Come in to be healed by me.
But some have more sin than fever,
And some have more grief than pain,
God help me make whole both body and soul
Before they go out again.

Hyla S. Watters, M.D.

2. The text of Agnes's diary is transcribed directly with changes only as noted. Her misspellings and irregular grammar have been retained along with cavalier punctuation. However, periods have been supplied at the ends of sentences, a practice Agnes regularly avoided. Agnes used "c" to mean "with" and "s" to mean "without" throughout the diary, and the words have been substituted for ease in reading. Agnes also gives the time in various ways; it is given in this volume consistently in her most common method: 9.30, for example. It should also be noted that Agnes sometimes wrote so much on a given day that it covers the space for two entries. Caution should be used, therefore, in determining the date for a given event. In the space for August 27, for example, she notes that she has not written in her diary for a week, and yet the space for all the entries is filled.

3. "Daddy" was a physician at Bellevue Hospital in New York, where Agnes had taken her training in nursing. She does not mention his name in the diary, although she refers to him once as Dr. S. A search of the files at Bellevue (a teaching hospital with a staff made up of physicians, residents, and interns from a number of universities in New York) did not reveal an identity for Daddy. Significantly, Agnes did not break with him at any point

in her relationship with Hemingway nor in the subsequent romance with Domenico Caracciolo.

4. Henry Villard comments that "the ship on which Agnes sailed, *La Lorraine*, happened to be the same one on which I had departed for Italy a month earlier. Armed with seventy-five-mm guns and elaborately camouflaged against the U-boats then prowling the Atlantic, this fast mail steamer had a single funnel that emitted thick clouds of coal smoke. At the gangplank passengers were handed a very important notice: 'It is well known that, in cases of disaster at sea, the means of saving life on board have not been utilized to their fullest extent. Had passengers kept cool and obeyed the orders of the ship's officers, the loss of life would have been considerably reduced.' Passengers, therefore, were urged to 'acquaint themselves with the general rules in the event of the steamer having to be abandoned.' As the vessel slipped down the Hudson and headed out to sea Agnes must have wondered, like all Red Cross personnel bound for the war zone, when she would see the Statue of Liberty again. On arrival in France each passenger was entitled to send a postcard reading 'the vessel on which I was traveling has arrived safely.'"

5. The trouble with the passport may have resulted from the German name "Agnes von Kurowsky," a matter that would come up again in her life.

6. Henry Villard recalls that "sitting up all night on the train was one of the horrors of war experienced by everyone who made the journey to Italy via Bordeaux and Paris. Second class tickets did not provide for the luxury of a *wagon-lit*; compartments were invariably crowded, small persons having been known to bed down in the luggage rack overhead."

7. The first patient was not Hemingway.

8. Several Hemingway biographers have had the notion that Agnes spoke fluent Italian. As her diary indicates, that was not the case. She had a few Italian lessons on the journey over, but she is, throughout her stay in Italy, much more comfortable in French.

9. Enrico Serena was a captain in the Alpini corps of the Italian Army. Until he was forced to leave Milan to attend to an ailing mother, he occupied much of Agnes's attention, as her diary reveals. Hemingway's romance with Agnes did not begin until Serena had departed. In 1971 Agnes was to remember: "Captain Serena was a fascinating person. He spoke English. I didn't have to worry about my Italian. He was very witty and good company." See Michael Reynolds, *Hemingway's First War: The Making of "A Farewell to Arms"* (Princeton: Princeton Univ. Press, 1976), p. 197.

10. Henry Villard recalls that "the Hotel du Nord was one of a group of unpretentious Italian hotels located near the central railway station. Its *trattoria* [restaurant] was reputed to be better than the rest."

11. Henry Villard says that "the covered Gallerìa Vittorio Emanuele, connecting the Piazza del Duomo with the Piazza della Scala, was the favorite meeting place as well as a center of attraction for nurses, ambulatory patients, as well as their friends. Built in the form of a Latin cross, with an octagon in the center over which rose a lofty glass cupola, it was probably the most spacious and handsome structure of its kind in Europe. Its fine shops, restaurants, and cafés all flourished in wartime Italy."

12. This address is important in trying to determine the precise location of the American Red Cross Hospital.

13. July 20 is the first mention of Hemingway in the diary, probably because Agnes was still assigned to the Ospedale Maggiore. She had a room in the American Red Cross Hospital, however, so she undoubtedly had met the few patients there.

14. Agnes, of course, was wrong on this point, since Lt. McKey had been killed on canteen duty on June 16.

15. Hemingway was born July 21, 1899.

16. Coles van B. Seeley, from Newark, N.J., had suffered injuries when he tried to take a mortar shell for a souvenir.

17. Until she left Milan, Agnes was now assigned to the American Red Cross Hospital, where she would see Hemingway virtually every day.

18. Henry Villard recalls that airplanes and a silvery, aluminum-colored dirigible flew frequent patrols over the city, to the entertainment of both patients and nurses.

19. Henry Villard remembers that the Pirelli family was one of the most distinguished in Milan. They owned the company that still manufactures rubber tires.

20. Agnes almost continuously used epithets of youth to describe Hemingway, a matter of humor at first that would eventually contribute to the termination of their romance.

21. Herbert S. Darling, Jr., was with Henry Villard in Section 1. From Brookline, Mass., he was called "June" for Junior. Villard remembers that he, too, was being treated for hepatitis.

22. Agnes's reference to "Mr. Hemingway" strongly suggests there was no romantic relationship between them prior to August 10, the day of Hemingway's surgery.

23. William D. Horne, Jr., graduated from Princeton in 1913. Originally in Section 4 with Hemingway, he had also volunteered for canteen duty. He would later room with Hemingway in Chicago. Henry Villard remembers that "he arrived at the hospital with a mysterious internal ailment diagnosed as 'sub-acute enteritis,' a form of dysentery that was common at the front."

24. Henry Villard has commented, "I had no idea I had given Agnes

the impression of being sarcastic, but I think she changed her mind about this as we got to know each other better."

25. Henry Villard comments that "Edward E. Allen was a fellow member of the class of 1921 at Harvard and part of the so-called 'Harvard unit,' composed of under-draft-age students who sought to enlist in the ambulance service. Apparently Allen got off on the wrong foot in the hospital because of this incident and never recovered in Agnes's estimation."

26. John W. Miller, Jr., from Minnesota, had also been wounded on the Piave. He and Hemingway were to become friends and go on holiday together in Stresa later in September.

27. The normal hour for "lights-out" in the hospital was 10:00.

28. Henry Villard doubts that the hairpin incident suggests a sexual affair between Hemingway and Agnes: "While there can be no doubt that demonstrations of affection took place between Ernie and Agnes, in the circumscribed limits of the hospital things could not have gone very far. That a nurse's hairpin should find its way into a patient's bed does not mean that any part of her anatomy must follow."

29. Henry Villard recalls that the "pronounciation of the name 'Seeley' identified its bearer with an area north of Venice know as Caposile, prominent in the war communiqués; the similarity between Seeley and the Italian *sile* led to the nickname 'Capo.'"

30. The ring shows clearly in the photograph of Hemingway in his new uniform. Certainly the gift of a ring would indicate an advance in their relationship.

31. Henry Villard recalls that "it was not unusual for a bat to stray into one of the bedrooms, the windows of which were unscreened. Bats were almost as numerous as pigeons around Milan's famous Duomo nearby." Hemingway used the bat incident in *A Farewell to Arms*.

32. Henry Villard remembers that "a principal amusement for hospital inmates was the consumption of ices, *gelati*, at such popular bistros as Campari's in the Gallerìa. Much frequented, too, were Biffi's, also in the Gallerìa, and the Cova restaurant with its garden, close to the Scala on Via San Giuseppe, which was noted for its sherry flips and *café* or *chocolate latte frappé*, the next best drink to a milkshake."

33. Henry Villard recalls that "there was no prohibition against wine in the nurses' quarters downstairs, and plenty of drinking must have occurred when outsiders were introduced as guests. The aviators were a high-flying lot."

34. As Henry Villard remembers the hospital, the elevator was one of the few places where two people could exchange an embrace without being observed.

35. The Red Cross had another station in Taormina, so the nurses were sometimes rotated to Sicily.

36. Unfortunately, Hemingway's letters to Agnes have not been discovered, if they still exist.

37. "Today we adm. 3 aviators" is written at the end of the entry for September 29. However, since Agnes began that entry "Today was most strenuous," it is unlikely she would use the "today" formulation twice in describing the events of one day, especially since the rest of the sentence continues under September 30.

38. No Lt. Colter is listed on the rosters of ambulance drivers for the Red Cross in 1918, so he was in some other branch of service. There was an epidemic of influenza in 1918, which may have been the cause of his death. Agnes later refers to it as the "Spanish Fever."

39. Agnes misspells "Viva la Pace," long live the peace. Her Italian was never precise, nor was that of Hemingway.

40. Elsie Jessup was a British nurse who had earlier served in Serbia. She is important in that many of the details of her life correspond to the background of Catherine Barkley in A *Farewell to Arms*.

41. Sultry southeast wind.

42. Although the word "really" falls under the entry for October 20, Agnes may have intended it to be the final thought about Miss Jessup in the previous comment. It is not always clear when the entries adhere to the space alloted for them.

CHAPTER THREE

1. See Reynolds, *Hemingway's First War*, p. 209.

2. Hemingway had left on holiday to Stresa the day before, September 24, to return on September 30. These letters are particularly useful in revealing the state of their romance at this stage in their relationship, before Agnes was transferred to Florence.

3. Envelope addressed to Lieut. Ernesto M. Hemingway, Hotel Stresa, Stresa, Lago Maggiori, Italia. There is no date on the letter, but the envelope is stamped September 25. Agnes may have written it a day or two before.

4. Parts of this letter have been obscured by water and ink stains.

5. The date is given in another hand.

6. Envelope addressed to Tenente E. M. Hemingway, Hotel Stresa, Stresa, Lago Maggiore, Italy.

7. Agnes's letters are here presented as written with only a few exceptions. Agnes is not consistent in her use of punctuation to end sentences. She sometimes uses the dash, or a hyphen, as an all-purpose punctuation.

Her dashes are retained except when they clearly end a sentence, in which case, for clarity, a period has been used consistently. Agnes is also not consistent in the manner in which she gives the time, which in all instances is given in her most frequent form, as in 9.30. All other alterations of text are given either in brackets or in the notes to the text.

8. Elsie MacDonald.

9. Miller, of course, was in Stresa with Hemingway.

10. There is no date on this letter, but the mention of the "demonstration last night" would seem to be a reference to the false armistice rumor, which caused an uproar on October 7. Given the return address in Milan, the letter was certainly written before Agnes left for Florence on October 15. Written on American Red Cross stationery.

11. Hemingway had been befriended by the Bellia family, which included three daughters roughly Hemingway's age, when he vacationed in Stresa, September 24–30. There may have been rumors about Hemingway and Bianca Bellia, since they surfaced many years after the events.

12. Date not in Agnes's hand.

13. Agnes writes on letterhead from Ospedale Territoriale No. 10, the American Hospital for Italian Wounded, Via di Camerata, 6, Florence.

14. Envelope addressed to Hemingway at the British-American Officers' Club, Milan.

15. Henry Villard recalls that "the ubiquitous Caproni twin-engined bomber biplane, produced at the company's factory near Milan, was Italy's chief contribution to aerial warfare."

16. Mailed to Lieutenant E. M. Hemingway, c/o American Red Cross, 10 via Manzoni, Milan, Italy. Postmarked October 18, 1918, Firenze.

17. Addressed to Hemingway at the British-American Officers' Club, Milan.

18. Agnes's diary ends on October 20, so the letters continue her story from that point onward.

19. Addressed to Hemingway at the British-American Officers' Club, Milan.

20. Paper was in short supply in Italy during the war, and the *Red Cross Bulletin* ran appeals to use paper sparingly, especially in personal correspondence.

21. Henry Villard suggests that "Agnes's tender regard for the absent Ernie was increased by the boredom of her solitary night duty."

22. Sent to Lieut. E. M. Hemingway, c/o American Red Cross, 10 Via Manzoni, Milano.

23. Agnes went to the usual tourist places, in this instance the Ponte Vecchio, a medieval bridge over the Arno River that is crowded with small shops.

24. Agnes, of course, would have been in the market for a ring, since she had given hers to Hemingway on September 11, as her diary indicates.

25. Henry Villard recalls that "the interest Agnes displayed in learning about Florence was in keeping with her zest for adventure; as she made known in conversation on more than one occasion, she was always attracted by new places, especially if they were in foreign parts."

26. Postcard mailed from Florence on October 22, 1918, addressed to Hemingway, c/o American Red Cross, 10 Via Manzoni, Milano. The photograph on the reverse side depicts "Firenze—Uffizi e Palazzo Vecchio."

27. William Tandy, from Seattle, was in Section 5 of the ambulance corps.

28. Addressed to Lieut. E. M. Hemingway, c/o American Red Cross, Milan, Italy. The envelope contains the notation that it was forwarded to Section Four. Hemingway had been released from the hospital and had returned to the front.

29. To Hemingway at 10 Via Manzoni, Milan.

30. Katherine DeLong.

31. To Tenente Ernesto M. Hemingway, c/o Crose Rossa Americano, 10 Via Manzoni, Milano.

32. Note the similarity in circumstances of Miss Jessup and Catherine Barkley in *A Farewell to Arms*, who also is British and has lost a lover.

33. Mailed to Hemingway, c/o American Red Cross, Milan.

34. The French *froufrou* means rustle or swish, a sound her writing paper perhaps makes.

35. Sent to Lieut. Ernest M. Hemingway, c/o American Red Cross, 10 Via Manzoni, Milan. Written on the envelope is "Section 4 Auto Ambulanza Amer."

36. Agnes was wrong about the duration of her stay in Florence. She did not return to Milan until November 11, the day a general armistice was declared in Europe.

37. This letter was most likely mailed in the same envelope as the letter of October 26.

38. Envelope addressed to Mr. Ernest M. Hemingway, Section 4 Auto-Ambulance, c/o American Red Cross, 10 Via Manzoni, Milano.

39. This comment is further evidence that Hemingway did, in fact, return to the front after leaving the hospital in Milan. He was there only briefly, however, and he was certainly limping and using a cane the entire time, since he did so afterward. Indeed, he continued to have physical therapy on his knee for another two months.

40. Although the identity of Dr. S. has not been determined, it is known that he graduated in June of 1918 and, from Agnes's letter to Hemingway of December 22, 1922, that he married a few years later.

41. Addressed to Hemingway at 10 Via Manzoni, Milan.

42. As Henry Villard remembers, "Section 4 of the ambulance service was on the high Asiago Plateau at the small village of Schio. Section 1, at the foot of Monte Grappa, was the keystone of the Italian defense line; Section 2 was at Roncade on the winding Piave River; Section 3 was at Casale Sul Sile, also on the Piave. A fifth section was later established at Fanzolo near the strategically important Montello, a seven-mile-long hog's back of woods and farms where the Piave left the region of the Alps and entered the plain."

43. Addressed to Hemingway at 10 Via Manzoni.

44. Hemingway was back in the hospital with hepatitis.

45. Agnes by this date had sent sixteen letters plus one postcard since she left Milan.

46. To Hemingway, c/o American Red Cross, Milan.

47. Agnes would be referring to the news of peace, since the armistice was declared the following day, Nov. 3, 1918.

48. To Hemingway, c/o American Red Cross, 10 Via Manzoni, Milan.

49. In Italian "frotta" means a crowd. Agnes probably intends "frutta," fruit juice.

50. Hemingway had contracted infectious hepatitis and would have been yellow, a symptom known as jaundice. The men in Milan often referred to the disease itself as jaundice.

51. Ironically, given Agnes's praise of her own Italian in the next sentence, her spelling and grammar here are garbled. The general sense of her comment is "Then, my darling, when I see you, I am happy because I have forgotten nothing. Understand?"

52. Agnes was in Milan November 11–21, hence the break in letters. Her journey on Nov. 21 apparently took her from Milan to Padua to Treviso and back to Padua.

53. Addressed to Lieut. Ernest Hemingway, c/o Amer. Red Cross, Via Manzoni 10, Milano.

54. Sara Shaw, in charge of the hospital.

55. Agnes has finally made it to her assignment in Treviso.

56. According to Henry Villard, "the hospital was located at Dosson, on the main road between Treviso and Mestre. Designated as Field Hospital 331 of the American Expeditionary Force, it occupied a splendid building known as the Villa Reali. It commenced to function at the beginning of October 1918 when the first cases of influenza broke out. Two other American hospitals were in the area: Base Hospital 102 at Vicenza and a hospital at Padua for critical cases and infectuous diseases."

57. Agnes now writes on Y.M.C.A. stationery.

58. To Hemingway at 10 Via Manzoni.

59. The return address reads, "From, A.V. Kurowsky, F. H. [Field

Hospital] 331, U.S. Army." Envelope addressed to Lieut. E. M. Hemingway, c/o Amer. Red Cross, 10 Via Manzoni, Milano.

60. Written on Army & Navy Y.M.C.A. stationery; sent to Hemingway at Via Manzoni 10.

61. Actually, Agnes stayed in Treviso until about January 5, 1919, when she went briefly to Milan and Padua for four days before being assigned to Torre di Mosta on January 10.

62. Della C. DeGraw, who had been in charge of the hospital in Genoa, had moved to Rome, then Padua, and finally Treviso, to assist during the influenza epidemic.

63. Written on Y.M.C.A. stationery and sent to Hemingway, c/o American Red Cross, Milan.

64. In fact Hemingway was there the following day, December 9, as he explains in his letter of December 11.

65. To Hemingway, c/o American Red Cross, Milan. On top of the first page Agnes wrote, "Are you still figuring it out. I'll expect to hear soon your deduction."

66. Hemingway had been in Treviso the day before, December 9.

67. Marguerite Hummel served with Agnes in the hospital in Treviso. She returned to the U.S. in January.

68. To Hemingway, c/o Croce Rossa Americano, Milano.

69. Charlotte Anne Miller Heilman was a widow who specialized in tuberculosis cases.

70. To Hemingway, c/o American Red Cross, Milan.

71. Gertrude Smith had been at the hospital for refugees in Rimini but had transferred in November to Treviso.

72. To Hemingway, c/o American Red Cross, Milan.

73. The letter is evidently from Dr. S., responding to one from Agnes in which she confessed to dating Enrico Serena.

74. Written on Y.M.C.A. stationery to Lieut. E. M. Hemingway, c/o Croce Rossa Americano, Milan.

75. Henry Villard recalls that "one of the most popular and risqué pulp magazines of those comparatively innocent days was *Snappy Stories*. It would be considered pretty tame by present standards."

76. The references here are to Elsie MacDonald, Ruth Fisher (who had been transferred from Milan to Rome), and Caroline Sparrow (who was in charge of the hospital in Rome).

77. Written on Y.M.C.A. stationery.

78. Agnes was often concerned about the volume of Hemingway's drinking, which must have been considerable for it to worry her.

79. Written on Y.M.C.A. stationery and sent to Tenente E. M. Hemingway, c/o Croce Rossa Americano, Via Manzoni 10, Milan. Hemingway had

apparently left by the time the letter arrived; it was forwarded to 600 North Kenilworth, Oak Park, Ill.
80. In Torre di Mosta. Agnes went there on January 10.
81. Addressed to Lieut. E. M. Hemingway, 600 N. Kenilworth Ave., Oak Park, Illinois, U.S.A. All Agnes's subsequent letters to Hemingway are addressed to him in Oak Park.
82. Agnes had an opportunity to see President Woodrow Wilson while she was in Milan, before going to Padua.
83. Anne Larkin had been in charge of a home for refugee children in Sicily but moved to Milan at the beginning of January.
84. Hemingway had gone to Sicily with Jim Gamble in December.
85. From A. V. Kurowsky, c/o Amer. Red Cross, Padova, Italy.
86. From A. V. Kurowsky, c/o Amer. Red Cross, Rome, Italy.
87. Some time after this letter, Agnes sent an intriguing postcard to Hemingway in Oak Park. The card reads: "I thought this might interest you. These were given me by an Ital. Artillery officer to send to America. Agnes."
88. Agnes was planning to marry Domenico Caracciolo, the heir to an Italian dukedom. His family objected, and the romance ended.
89. Hemingway continued to correspond with Elsie MacDonald into the 1930s.
90. Hemingway and Hadley Richardson were married on September 3, 1921.
91. Domenico Caracciolo was from Naples.

CHAPTER FOUR

1. Theodore Brumback, with whom Hemingway had joined the ambulance corps.
2. Robert W. Bates, from Boston, was director of Field Service for the Ambulance Corps.
3. Hemingway was the first wounded only if the death of Edward McKey on June 16 is discounted. Hemingway was wounded on the Piave front where McKey had been killed.
4. Dr. M. Sammarelli.
5. Hemingway here deleted the word "is."
6. "Without" deleted.
7. The Hemingway family enjoyed nicknames, a habit that Ernest continued throughout his life. His name for Marcelline was "Ivory."
8. Hemingway would hardly have been an authority on European cities at this point. He had landed at Bordeaux, spent a brief period in Paris, and,

apart from the front, had been only in Milan. He is clearly enjoying his new status as an informed and widely traveled man of the world.

9. The name "Robert" is not clear.

10. Edward J. Welch, Jr.

11. The surgery took place on August 10.

12. Howell G. Jenkins

13. Deletion illegible here.

14. Hemingway's hometown newspaper, from Oak Park, Illinois.

15. Captain James Gamble, head of the canteen units.

16. Hemingway here draws a shape about an inch long.

17. Hemingway here makes a square of about 3/4 inch.

18. Arthur C. Newburn was also from Oak Park.

19. Hemingway had first written "left." He was wounded in both legs, but it was his right that was operated on and was in a cast.

20. Hemingway crossed out "possibility" and inserted "vocabulary."

21. Hemingway might have stressed this point because his parents were upset that he chose not to attend college.

22. Hemingway had first written "steel" and then crossed it out to insert "copper." The bullet found in his coin purse appears to be steel.

23. The letterhead indicates that Hemingway wrote from the "Grand Hotel et des Iles Borromées, Stresa." He had gone to Stresa with John Miller on holiday.

24. This letter was also written on letterhead of the Grand Hotel in Stresa.

25. Sentence originally "As he." Hemingway deleted "As."

26. Published in the *Oak Parker* (November 16, 1918), pp. 6−7.

27. This letter is the first Hemingway typed while in the hospital. In typing he habitually leaves a space between the last letter of a sentence and the period and sometimes between the last letter of a word and the comma that follows. For the convenience of reading, those spaces have been eliminated in the transcription of the letter.

28. In 1916 Hemingway had a flirtation with Frances Coates, a classmate in Oak Park.

29. Probably Nick Neroni.

30. At this point in his life, Hemingway had no experience with the Atlantic in winter.

31. "Medal a" deleted after "The."

32. "Almost" deleted.

33. "Case" deleted.

34. Hemingway went to the Ospedale Maggiore for his treatments.

35. Nick Neroni.

CHAPTER FIVE

1. See "Has 227 Wounds, but Is Looking for Job," *Conversations with Ernest Hemingway*, ed. Matthew J. Bruccoli (Jackson: University Press of Mississippi, 1986), pp. 1–2. This volume hereafter cited as *Conversations*. Reprinted from *New York Sun* (Jan. 22, 1919), p. 8.

2. See Reynolds, *Hemingway's First War*; Baker, *Ernest Hemingway: A Life Story*; Peter Griffin, *Along With Youth: Hemingway, The Early Years* (New York: Oxford, 1985); Kenneth S. Lynn, *Hemingway* (New York: Simon and Schuster, 1987); and Jeffrey Meyers, *Hemingway: A Biography* (New York: Harper & Row, 1985).

3. *Conversations*, pp. 3–4. Reprinted from the Oak Park High School *Trapeze* (March 21, 1919), pp. 1, 3. The song to Hemingway is in *Conversations*, p. 5.

4. See Michael Reynolds, *The Young Hemingway* (New York: Basil Blackwell, 1986), p. 45. Reynolds's account of Hemingway's life in Oak Park is the best record of this period.

5. Quoted in Reynolds, *The Young Hemingway*, p. 23.

6. See Griffin, p. 37. Griffin's book is useful on many points, but he treats the fiction as biographical fact and thus often cannot be trusted.

7. See Griffin, p. 41.

8. See Dale Wilson, "Hemingway in Kansas City," *Fitzgerald/Hemingway Annual* (1976), pp. 211–16. Wilson was a fellow reporter on the newspaper.

9. See the comments of William Horne in "Young Hemingway: A Panel," *Fitzgerald/Hemingway Annual* (1972), p. 120. The remarks were made at a meeting of the Modern Language Association in Chicago in December of 1971.

10. See Griffin, p. 51, and Lynn, p. 73.

11. For information about Hemingway's service in the Home Guard I am indebted to Michael Culver, "The 'Short-Stop Run': Hemingway in Kansas City," *Hemingway Review*, 2, No. 1 (1982), 79. Griffin, in *Along With Youth*, gives November 5, 1917, as the date of Hemingway's enlistment (p. 51). Reynolds, in *The Young Hemingway*, says he was not accepted into the Home Guard until January of 1918 (p. 45). As is clear from an unpublished letter Hemingway wrote to his parents on Dec. 6, 1917, he had just received his uniform and was, presumably, already a member of the unit. Hemingway's letter is in the manuscript collection of the Lilly Library of Indiana University.

12. Marjorie Bump was a girl Hemingway had met during his summers at Walloon Lake. Her sister's nickname was "Pudge."

13. Carl Edgar was a friend of Hemingway's from the Walloon Lake area in Michigan who was now working in Kansas City.

14. See Ernest Hemingway to "Dear Dad and Mother," December 6, 1917, in the manuscript collection of the Lilly Library at Indiana University.

15. See Hemingway's letter in *Ernest Hemingway: Selected Letters 1917–1961*, ed. Carlos Baker (New York: Scribners, 1981), p. 7. This volume hereafter cited as *Letters*.

16. See *Letters*, p. 8.

17. Clarence Hemingway to Ernest Hemingway, May 18, 1918, in the manuscript collection of the Lilly Library, Indiana University.

18. Griffin, p. 57.

19. Clarence Hemingway to Ernest Hemingway, May 19, 1918, in the manuscript collection of the Lilly Library, Indiana University. Clarence wrote to his son in care of Leo Skelly, Red Cross Superintendent, 222 Fourth Avenue, New York.

20. Wilson, "Hemingway in Kansas City," p. 216.

21. Frederick Spiegel, who roomed with Hemingway on the voyage to Bordeaux, sets the date of departure as May 24. See "Young Hemingway: A Panel," p. 114. Griffin puts it on May 21 in *Along With Youth*, p. 62. Hemingway's sister says he sailed on May 28. See Marcelline Hemingway Sanford, *At The Hemingways: A Family Portrait* (Boston: Little, Brown, 1962), p. 159. There are other conflicting accounts of the precise date.

22. Col. C. E. Frazer Clark, "This is the Way It Was on the *Chicago* and At the Front: 1917 War Letters," *Fitzgerald/Hemingway Annual* (1970), p. 153.

23. See Herbert Clarke, *Instructions and Information for Red Cross Workers in France* (Paris: American Red Cross in France, 1918), pp. 4, 10, 25. This edition of the regulations was issued April 1, 1918.

24. For an account of this experience, see Baker, *A Life Story*, p. 40.

25. Baker, *A Life Story*, p. 40.

26. Ernest Hemingway, *Death in the Afternoon* (New York: Scribners, 1955), pp. 135–36.

27. Quoted in Baker, *A Life Story*, p. 40.

28. For an excellent discussion of these matters, see Charles A. Fenton, "Ambulance Drivers in France and Italy: 1914–1918," *American Quarterly*, 3 (1951), 326–43.

29. Henry James, *The American Volunteer Motor-Ambulance Corps in France* (London: Macmillan, 1914). I am indebted here to Fenton, "Ambulance Drivers," pp. 327–31.

30. My account here is based closely on Fenton, "Ambulance Drivers," p. 328.

31. Fenton, "Ambulance Drivers," p. 328.

32. See Fenton, "Ambulance Drivers," pp. 337–38.

33. Another ambulance unit, the American Ambulance Field Service, was organized by A. Piatt Andrew. He had been Professor of Economics at Harvard and had come to France late in 1914 to drive an ambulance. See Fenton, "Ambulance Drivers," pp. 329–31, for a history of this unit.

34. See Reynolds, *Hemingway's First War*, pp. 161–62.

35. See Guy Lowell, *Report of the Department of Military Affairs: January to July, 1918* (Rome: American Red Cross, 1918), p. 3. My account of the situation in Italy is based heavily on this document.

36. Lowell, *Report*, p. 6.

37. Lowell, *Report*, p. 11.

38. See John Howard Lawson, "No Man's Land," *Lost Generation Journal*, 5, No. 2 (1977–78), 12–13, 20.

39. *Letters*, p. 10.

40. See Lowell, *Report*, pp. 7–9.

41. Lowell, *Report*, p. 10.

42. See Guy Lowell, "Military Affairs," *Red Cross Bulletin* (June 20, 1918), p. 1; (September 5, 1918), p. 5.

43. My account of the canteen service is based on the official statements by Lowell, *Report*, pp. 11–16. This document lists Hemingway as having been in charge of Canteen No. 14; thus he would have been eligible for promotion to the rank of first lieutenant in the American Red Cross.

44. See C. E. Frazer Clark, Jr., "American Red Cross Reports on the Wounding of Lieutenant Ernest M. Hemingway—1918," *Fitzgerald/Hemingway Annual* (1974), p. 132.

45. See Griffin, p. 76.

46. Lowell, *Report*, p. 19.

47. *Letters*, p. 11.

48. Sanford, p. 171.

49. See Sanford, pp. 170–71.

50. Quoted in *Conversations*, p. 1.

51. See Mary Harrington, "They Call Him Papa," *New York Post Week-End Magazine* (December 28, 1946), p. 3.

52. Constance Cappel Montgomery, *Hemingway in Michigan* (Waitsfield: Vermont Crossroads Press, 1977), p. 117.

53. Charles A. Fenton, *The Apprenticeship of Ernest Hemingway: The Early Years* (New York: Viking, 1958), p. 66.

54. See Meyers, *Hemingway*, p. 33.

55. See Lynn, pp. 79, 83, 328.

56. See Montgomery, p. 118.

57. Montgomery, pp. 16–17

58. Malcolm Cowley is quoted in Denis Brian, *The True Gen: An Inti-*

*mate Portrait of Ernest Hemingway by Those Who Knew Him* (New York: Grove Press, 1988), p. 297.

59. Brian, p. 317.

60. Agnes is quoted in Michael S. Reynolds, "The Agnes Tapes: A Farewell to Catherine Barkley," *Fitzgerald/Hemingway Annual* (1979), pp. 269, 271. Hereafter cited as "The Agnes Tapes."

61. Montgomery gives the name as Dr. Guy C. Conkle; Reynolds refers to Dr. Guy Conklin. Since both are in Boyne City, they must be the same man.

62. Reynolds, *The Young Hemingway*, p. 69.

63. See the *Red Cross Bulletin* (October 20, 1918), p. 6.

64. I am indebted here to Reynolds, *The Young Hemingway*, p. 47.

65. Samuel Shaw, *Ernest Hemingway* (New York: Ungar, 1973), p. 19.

66. See Fenton, *The Apprenticeship of Ernest Hemingway*, p. 61.

67. Lowell, *Report*, p. 14.

68. Guy Lowell, "Department of Military Affairs," *Red Cross Bulletin*, 1, No. 4 (Aug. 5, 1918), 6.

69. See the *Red Cross Bulletin* (December 7, 1918), p. 3. This issue also ran a photograph of Hemingway in the sidecar of a motorcycle.

70. For the interpretation of these X-rays I am indebted to Carl C. Spector, M.D., an orthopedic surgeon at the Newton-Wellesley Hospital, Newton, Massachusetts.

71. Elsie MacDonald to Ernest Hemingway, May 23, 1937. The letter is in the Hemingway Collection at the John F. Kennedy Library, Boston. All other letters from her to Hemingway cited in this essay are part of this collection.

72. I am indebted here to the research of Giovanni Cecchin, who conveyed this informatiion to me in a letter.

73. There are differences in the various documents about the spelling of the name of this hospital. Elsie MacDonald spells it "Mercicordia."

74. See Elsie MacDonald to Ernest Hemingway, January 20, 1928.

75. See Sanford, pp. 161–62.

76. See the unpublished diary of Henry Villard, at the Boston University Library, entry for August 10, 1918.

77. See Baker, *A Life Story*, p. 48.

78. Also of value on Hemingway's wounding is Robert W. Lewis, "Hemingway in Italy: Making It Up," *Journal of Modern Literature*, 9 (1982), 209–36. I am grateful to Lewis for numerous conversations about the evidence for Hemingway's wounding.

79. See Baker, *A Life Story*, p. 46. There were at least two sets of stationery for American Red Cross Headquarters in Milan, one giving 10 Via

Manzoni and another 15 Via Manzoni as the address. The two locations may have been for different departments of the Red Cross.

80. See Reynolds, *Hemingway's First War*, p. 173.

81. Clarke, p. 26.

82. It is in the Agnes von Kurowsky papers at the Kennedy Library.

83. See Sara E. Shaw to Miss Noyes, July 11, 1918, in the Hemingway Collection at the Kennedy Library.

84. See Meyers, *Hemingway*, p. 36.

85. See Elsie MacDonald to Ernest Hemingway, January 20, 1928.

86. See Agnes's diary entries for July 8 and July 16.

87. Joseph Collins, *Report of the Department of Medical Affairs* (Rome: American Red Cross, 1918), p. 39.

88. Collins, p. 42.

89. I am indebted here to Waring Jones, who shared with me his collection of Agnes von Kurowsky papers. The envelope was mixed in with her materials. No one has previously identified the specific room Hemingway occupied.

90. "The Agnes Tapes," p. 272. Agnes mistakenly misremembers the accident here as one involving a truck. Her contemporaneous record in her diary would seem to be the more accurate.

91. See Collins, pp. 38–45.

92. Malcolm Cowley, *Exile's Return: A Literary Odyssey of the 1920s* (New York: Viking, 1951), p. 36.

93. For these and other details of the experience of Henry Villard, I am indebted to his unpublished diary and letters. These documents are on deposit at the Boston University Library. Since they are not paginated, references will be to date.

94. The letter was addressed to Harold G. Villard, Esquire, 205 West 57th Street, New York City.

95. See Leicester Hemingway, *My Brother, Ernest Hemingway* (Cleveland: World Publishing Co., 1961).

96. See Baker, *A Life Story*, p. 572.

97. "The Agnes Tapes," p. 256. For basic information on Agnes's life, I am also indebted to Reynolds, *Hemingway's First War*, pp. 183–89.

98. Reynolds portrays Agnes as an "accomplished linguist" who quickly picked up Italian. See *Hemingway's First War*, p. 180.

99. In this connection it is interesting to note that Bill Horne wrote a letter in Italian to Hemingway on February 23, 1919.

100. See Hemingway's letters of July 29, August 7, August 29, and September 29.

101. Carlos Baker discusses the nurses in Milan in *A Life Story*, pp. 46–47.

102. Reynolds discusses the nurses in Milan, with a somewhat different emphasis, in *Hemingway's First War*, p. 179.

103. See the *Red Cross Bulletin*, 1 (July 5, 1918), 2.

104. See Clarke, p. 20. There would not have been time for a separate set of regulations to have been published in Italy, and no such documents have been found.

105. Clarke, p. 21.

106. The diary is in a black book labeled, "Agenda 1918." The inside title, printed by the publisher, reads "Memoriale di Gabinetto per 1918." Agnes added, "Beginning June 12."

107. Agnes's comments are in "The Agnes Tapes," p. 261.

108. The *Red Cross Bulletin* for January 15, 1919, records that President Wilson arrived in Rome on January 3 and rode with King Victor Emanuel III in a carriage through the streets of Rome (p. 1). The next stop on the tour for the president was apparently Milan.

109. "The Agnes Tapes," p. 263.

110. According to Bernice Kert, Agnes arrived home July 9, 1919, on the S.S. *Re d' Italia*. See *The Hemingway Women* (New York: Norton, 1983), p. 68.

111. Agnes is quoted in Brian, p. 35.

112. Gianfranco Ivancich told me at the Villa Micheli in June of 1986 that Hemingway throughout his life knew only a few phrases of Italian.

113. See Griffin, p. 89.

114. See Agnes's letter of October 17.

115. See the review of *Men Without Women*, *Time* (October 24, 1927), p. 38.

116. Shaw, p. 19.

117. Fenton, *Apprenticeship of Ernest Hemingway*, p. 69.

118. See Lynn, p. 86.

119. Bill Horne's letter is quoted in Sanford, p. 180.

120. *Red Cross Bulletin* (August 20, 1918), p. 3.

121. Jeffrey Meyers is particularly good in recording Hemingway's misleading statements about his service in the Arditi. See his *Hemingway*, p. 39.

122. This document is in the Hemingway Collection at the Kennedy Library.

123. See "The Agnes Tapes," p. 267.

124. See Edwin Wells, "Hemingway Speaks to High School," in *Conversations*, p. 4. Reprinted from the Oak Park High School *Trapeze* (March 21, 1919), pp. 1, 3.

125. See Leicester Hemingway, *My Brother, Ernest Hemingway*, pp. 57, 75.

126. Meyers, *Hemingway*, p. 61.
127. See Reynolds, *The Young Hemingway*, p. 257.
128. All these documents are in the Hemingway Collection at the Kennedy Library.
129. See Lewis, "Hemingway in Italy: Making It Up," p. 224. I am indebted to Lewis for his excellent discussion of Hemingway's medals.
130. See the *Red Cross Bulletin* (July 20, 1918), p. 7.
131. See the *Red Cross Bulletin* (August 5, 1918), p. 6.
132. See the *Red Cross Bulletin* (August 20, 1918), p. 5.
133. Lowell, *Report*, pp. 29–30.
134. See Reynolds, *The Young Hemingway*, p. 57. I am indebted to Reynolds, pp. 55–57, for the comments on Hemingway's depiction of his service when he returned home.
135. See Baker, *A Life Story*, pp. 55–56. Baker is skeptical of the authenticity of Hemingway's story. Meyers gives a similar account in *Hemingway*, pp. 42–43. Meyers suspects a homosexual attraction between Hemingway and Gamble.
136. See James Gamble to Ernest Hemingway, April 16, 1919, in the Hemingway Collection at the Kennedy Library.
137. Quoted in Reynolds, *Hemingway's First War*, p. 181.
138. Quoted in Brian, p. 31.
139. See Griffin, pp. 32, 65.
140. Griffin, p. 239.
141. See Griffin, p. 93.
142. Lynn, p. 88.
143. Clarahan is quoted in "Young Hemingway: A Panel," p. 140.
144. See "The Agnes Tapes," p. 265.
145. See Brian, p. 31.
146. Griffin quotes Bill Horne's letter in *Along With Youth*, p. 113.
147. Quoted in Kert, p. 154.
148. Ernest Hemingway, *Green Hills of Africa* (New York: Scribners, 1935), p. 70.
149. Ernest Hemingway, *A Moveable Feast* (New York: Scribners, 1964), p. 30.
150. See Ernest Hemingway, "Newspaperman's Pockets," in *Dateline: Toronto. The Complete "Toronto Star" Dispatches, 1920–1924*, ed. William White (New York: Scribners, 1985), p. 61.
151. Ernest Hemingway, "A Very Short Story," in *The Complete Short Stories of Ernest Hemingway* (New York: Scribners, 1987), p. 107. All quotations from Hemingway's short stories refer to this edition.
152. See *Letters*, p. 469.

NOTES TO PAGES 267–268

153. Ernest Hemingway, *A Farewell to Arms* (New York: Scribners, 1957). All references are to this edition. The novel was first published in 1929.

154. I am deeply indebted here to Reynolds, *Hemingway's First War*, for my discussion of these matters; see especially p. 46. Reynolds gives an excellent comparison of Hemingway's life and the novel in this study, which has influenced me a great deal. Also valuable is Bernard Oldsey, *Hemingway's Hidden Craft: The Writing of "A Farewell to Arms"* (University Park: Pennsylvania State University Press, 1979), pp. 37–54.

155. The best discussion of the relationship of Hemingway's life in 1928 to the novel is Millicent Bell, "*A Farewell to Arms*: Pseudoautobiography and Personal Metaphor," in *Ernest Hemingway: The Writer in Context*, ed. James Nagel (Madison: University of Wisconsin Press, 1984), pp. 107–28.

156. For a more complete development of these ideas, see James Nagel, "Catherine Barkley and Retrospective Narration in *A Farewell to Arms*," in *Ernest Hemingway: Six Decades of Criticism*, ed. Linda W. Wagner (East Lansing: Michigan State University Press, 1987), pp. 171–85.

157. Ernest Hemingway, "A Veteran Visits the Old Front," in *Dateline: Toronto*, pp. 176–80. Hemingway's article originally appeared on July 22, 1922.

# WORKS CONSULTED

· · ·

Baker, Carlos. *Ernest Hemingway: A Life Story.* New York: Scribner's, 1969.
——, ed. *Ernest Hemingway: Selected Letters.* New York: Scribners, 1981.
Bakewell, Charles M. *The Story of the American Red Cross in Italy.* New York: MacMillan, 1920.
Bell, Millicent. "A Farewell to Arms: Pseudoautobiography and Personal Metaphor." In *Ernest Hemingway: The Writer in Context,* ed. James Nagel. Madison: Univ. of Wisconsin Press, 1984.
Benson, Jackson J. "Ernest Hemingway as Short Story Writer." In *The Short Stories of Ernest Hemingway: Critical Views,* ed. Jackson J. Benson. Durham: Duke Univ. Press, 1975, pp. 272–311.
——. "Patterns of Connection and Their Development in Hemingway's *In Our Time.*" *Rendevous,* 5 (Winter, 1970), 37–52.
Brenner, Gerry. *Concealments in Hemingway's Works.* Columbus: Ohio State Univ. Press, 1983.
Brian, Denis. *The True Gen: An Intimate Portrait of Ernest Hemingway by Those Who Knew Him.* New York: Grove Press, 1988.
Bruccoli, Matthew J., ed. *Conversations with Ernest Hemingway.* Jackson: Univ. Press of Mississippi, 1986.
Cecchin, Giovanni. *Hemingway, G. M. Trevelyan e il Friuli: Alle Origini di Addio Alle Armi.* Lignano: Comme di Lignano Sabbiadoro, 1986.
Clark, Col. C. E. Frazer. "This is the Way It Was on the *Chicago* and At the Front: 1917 War Letters." *Fitzgerald/Hemingway Annual* (1970), pp. 153–68.
Clark, C. E. Frazer, Jr. "American Red Cross Reports on the Wounding of Lieutenant Ernest M. Hemingway—1918." *Fitzgerald/Hemingway Annual* (1974), pp. 131–36.

Clarke, Herbert. *Instructions and Information for Red Cross Workers in France.* Paris: American Red Cross in France, 1918. Edition of April 1, 1918.

Collins, Joseph. *Report of the Department of Medical Affairs.* Rome: American Red Cross, 1918.

Cowley, Malcolm. *Exile's Return: A Literary Odyssey of the 1920s.* New York: Viking, 1951.

Culver, Michael. "The 'Short-Stop Run': Hemingway in Kansas City." *Hemingway Review*, 2, No. 1 (1982), 77–80.

Davidson, Arnold E. "The Dantean Perspective in Hemingway's A *Farewell to Arms.*" *Journal of Narrative Technique*, 3 (1973), 121–30.

DeMarr, Mary Jean. "Hemingway's Narrative Methods." *Indiana English Journal*, 4 (1970), 31–36.

Doctorow, E. L. "Braver Than We Thought." *The New York Times Book Review* (May 18, 1986), pp. 1, 44–45.

Donaldson, Scott. *By Force of Will: The Life and Art of Ernest Hemingway.* New York: Viking, 1977.

———. "Frederic Henry's Escape and the Pose of Passivity." In *Hemingway: A Revaluation*, ed. Donald R. Noble. Troy: Whitston, 1983, pp. 165–85.

Dos Passos, John. *One Man's Initiation: 1917.* Ithaca: Cornell Univ. Press, 1969.

Edmonds, Dale. "*When* Does Frederic Henry Narrate A *Farewell to Arms?*" *Notes on Modern American Literature*, 4 (1980), Item 14.

Fenton, Charles A. "Ambulance Drivers in France and Italy: 1914–1918." *American Quarterly*, 3 (1951), 326–43.

———. *The Apprenticeship of Ernest Hemingway: The Early Years.* New York: Mentor, 1961.

Ficken, Carl. "Point of View in the Nick Adams Stories." *The Short Stories of Ernest Hemingway: Critical Views*, ed. Jackson J. Benson. Durham: Duke Univ. Press, 1975, pp. 93–112. Reprinted from *Fitzgerald/Hemingway Annual* (1971), pp. 212–35.

Grebstein, Sheldon Norman. *Hemingway's Craft.* Carbondale: Southern Illinois Univ. Press, 1973.

Green, James L. "Symbolic Sentences in 'Big Two-Hearted River.'" *Modern Fiction Studies*, 14 (1968), 307–12.

Griffin, Peter. *Along With Youth: Hemingway, The Early Years.* New York: Oxford, 1985.

Harrington, Mary. "They Call Him Papa." *New York Post Week-End Magazine* (December 28, 1946), p. 3.

Hemingway, Ernest. "Al Receives Another Letter." *Ciao* (June, 1918), p. 2.

———. *The Complete Short Stories of Ernest Hemingway*. New York: Scribners, 1987.

———. *Dateline: Toronto. The Complete "Toronto Star" Dispatches, 1920–1924*, ed. William White. New York: Scribners, 1985.

———. *Death in the Afternoon*. New York: Scribners, 1955.

———. *A Farewell to Arms*. New York: Scribners, 1957.

———. *Green Hills of Africa*. New York: Scribners, 1935.

———. "Introduction," *Men At War*. New York: Bramhall House, 1979.

———. *A Moveable Feast*. New York: Scribners, 1964.

———. *The Torrents of Spring*. New York: Scribners, 1972.

Hemingway, Leicester. *My Brother, Ernest Hemingway*. Cleveland: World Publishing Co., 1961.

Hemingway, Lorian. "Ernest Hemingway's Farewell to Art." *Rolling Stone* (June 5, 1986), pp. 41–42, 72.

Hemingway, Mary Welsh. *How It Was*. New York: Knopf, 1976.

James, Henry. *The American Volunteer Motor-Ambulance Corps in France*. London: Macmillan, 1914.

Kert, Bernice. *The Hemingway Women*. New York: Norton, 1983.

Koenig, Rhoda. "Adam and Eve on a Raft." *New York*, 19 (May 12, 1986), 134, 137.

Lawson, John Howard. "No Man's Land." *Lost Generation Journal*, 5, No. 2 (1977–78), 12–13, 20.

Levin, Harry. "Observations on the Style of Ernest Hemingway." *Kenyon Review*, 13 (1951), 581–609.

Lewis, Robert W. "Hemingway in Italy: Making It Up." *Journal of Modern Literature*, 9 (1982), 209–36.

———. *Hemingway on Love*. Austin: Univ. of Texas Press, 1965.

Lowell, Guy. "Department of Military Affairs." *Red Cross Bulletin* (Aug. 15, 1918), p. 7.

———. "Department of Military Affairs." *Red Cross Bulletin*, 1, No. 4 (Aug. 5, 1918), 6.

———. "Military Affairs." *Red Cross Bulletin* (June 20, 1918), p. 1.

———. "Military Affairs." *Red Cross Bulletin* (September 5, 1918), p. 5.

———. *Report of the Department of Military Affairs: January to July, 1918*. Rome: American Red Cross, 1918.

———. *Report of the Department of Military Affairs*. Rome: American Red Cross, 1919.

Lynn, Kenneth S. *Hemingway*. New York: Simon and Schuster, 1987.

Meyers, Jeffrey. *Hemingway: A Biography*. New York: Harper & Row, 1985.

———. "Tonsorial." *National Review*, 38 (May 23, 1986), 44–46.

Miller, Madelaine Hemingway. *Ernie: Hemingway's Sister 'Sunny' Remembers.* New York: Crown, 1975.

Montgomery, Constance Cappel. *Hemingway in Michigan.* Waitsfield: Vermont Crossroads Press, 1977.

Nagel, James. "Catherine Barkley and Retrospective Narration in *A Farewell to Arms.*" In *Ernest Hemingway: Six Decades of Criticism,* ed. Linda W. Wagner. East Lansing: Michigan State University Press, 1987, pp. 171–85.

———, ed. *Ernest Hemingway: The Writer in Context.* Madison: University of Wisconsin Press, 1984.

Oldsey, Bernard. *Hemingway's Hidden Craft: The Writing of "A Farewell to Arms."* University Park: Pennsylvania State Univ. Press, 1979.

Plimpton, George. "An Interview with Ernest Hemingway." In *Ernest Hemingway: Five Decades of Criticism,* ed. Linda Welshimer Wagner. East Lansing: Michigan State Univ. Press, 1974, pp. 21–38. Reprinted from *The Paris Review,* 18 (Spring 1958), 60–89.

*Red Cross Bulletin.* Rome: American Red Cross. Issued in 1918–1919.

Review of *Fiesta. Times Literary Supplement* (June 30, 1927), p. 454.

Review of *Men Without Women. Time* (October 24, 1927), p. 38.

Review of *Three Stories and Ten Poems* and *in our time. Kansas City Star* (Dec. 20, 1924), p. 6.

Reynolds, Michael S. "The Agnes Tapes: A Farewell to Catherine Barkley." *Fitzgerald/Hemingway Annual* (1979), pp. 251–78.

———. *Hemingway's First War: The Making of "A Farewell to Arms."* Princeton: Princeton Univ. Press, 1976.

———. *Hemingway's Reading 1910–1940: An Inventory.* Princeton: Princeton Univ. Press, 1981.

———. *The Young Hemingway.* New York: Basil Blackwell, 1986.

Rosenfeld, Paul. "Tough Earth." *New Republic,* 45 (November 25, 1925), 22–23.

Sanford, Marcelline Hemingway. *At the Hemingways: A Family Portrait.* Boston: Little, Brown, 1962.

Shaw, Samuel. *Ernest Hemingway.* New York: Ungar, 1973.

Stobie, Margaret. "Ernest Hemingway, Craftsman." *Canadian Forum,* 33 (Nov. 1953), 179, 181–82.

Wagner, Linda Welshimer. *Hemingway and Faulkner: inventors/masters.* Metuchen: Scarecrow, 1975.

Waldhorn, Arthur. *A Reader's Guide to Ernest Hemingway.* New York: Farrar, Straus & Giroux, 1972.

Wexler, Joyce. "E.R.A. for Hemingway: A Feminist Defense of A Farewell to Arms." *Georgia Review,* 35 (1981), 111–23.

## Works Consulted

Whitlow, Roger. *Cassandra's Daughters: The Women in Hemingway.* Westport: Greenwood Press, 1984.

Williams, Wirt. *The Tragic Art of Ernest Hemingway.* Baton Rouge: Louisiana State Univ. Press, 1981.

Wilson, Dale. "Hemingway in Kansas City." *Fitzgerald/Hemingway Annual* (1976), pp. 211–16.

Wilson, Edmund. "Letter to the Russians about Hemingway." *New Republic* (Dec. 11, 1935), pp. 135–36.

"Young Hemingway: A Panel." *Fitzgerald/Hemingway Annual* (1972), pp. 113–44.

# INDEX

. . .